**THE
GAME**

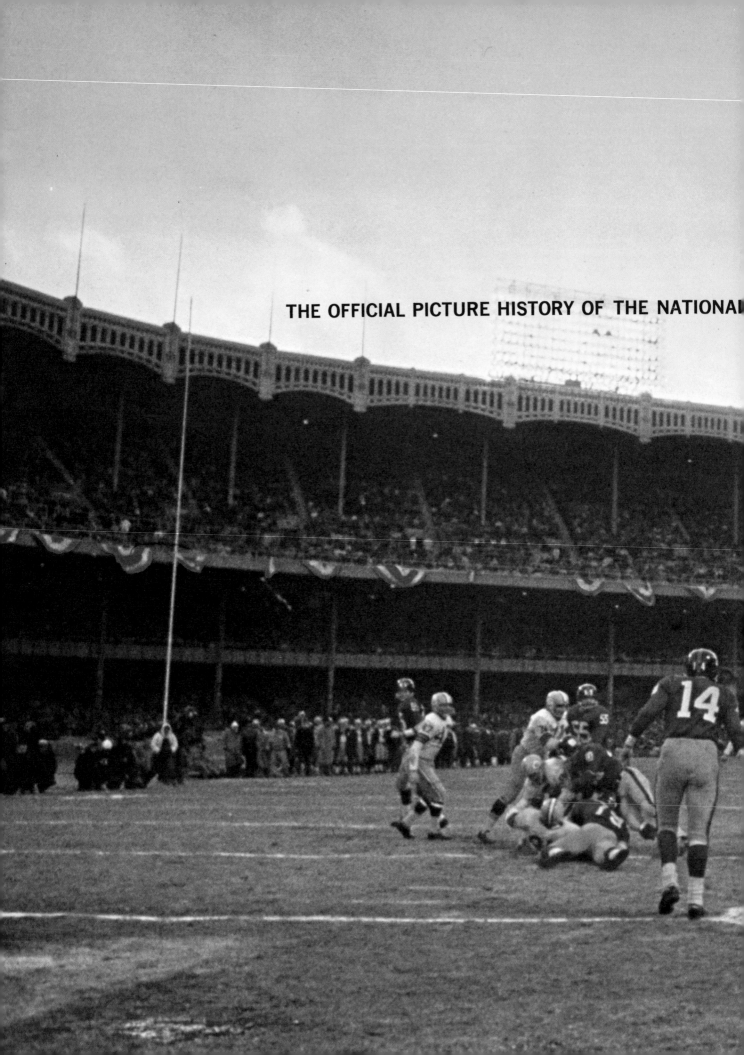

THE OFFICIAL PICTURE HISTORY OF THE NATIONAL

FOOTBALL LEAGUE

# THE GAME

by
## Tex Maule

FOREWORD BY PETE ROZELLE, COMMISSIONER, NATIONAL FOOTBALL LEAGUE

RANDOM HOUSE  NEW YORK

Library of Congress catalog card number: 63-16852

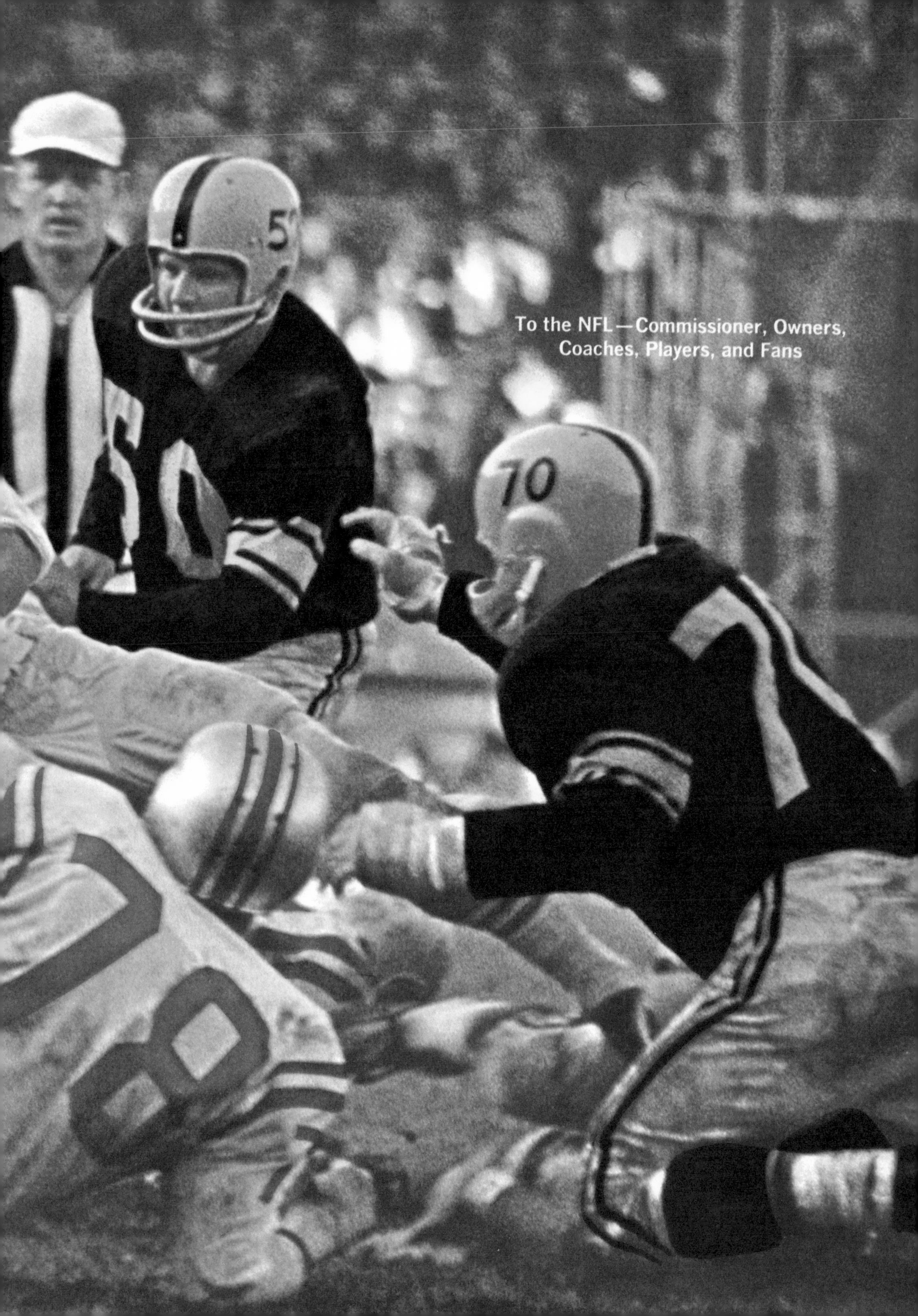

To the NFL—Commissioner, Owners, Coaches, Players, and Fans

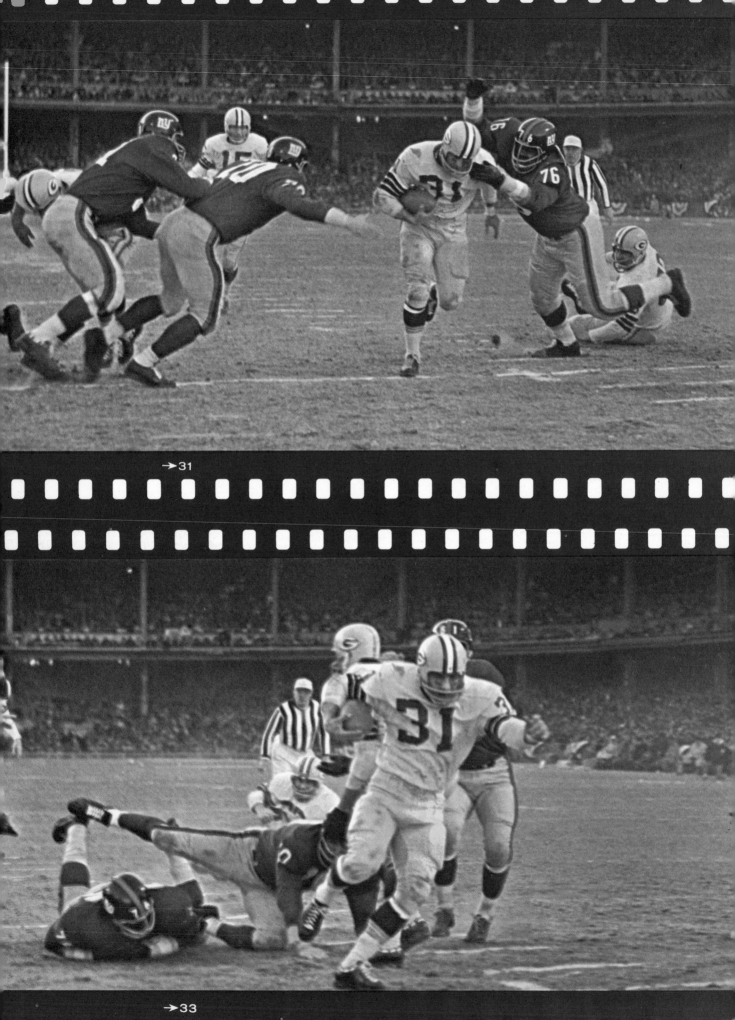

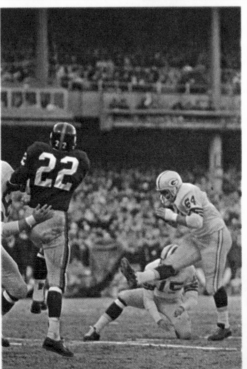

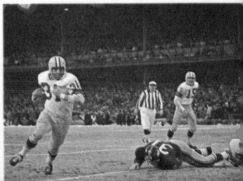

# CONTENTS

# FOREWORD

THE GAME is much more than that.

It is the fans — as Tex Maule so vividly describes them in the chapter on the Baltimore Colts. It is a science — as the sections on Philadelphia and Cleveland detail the changes and adaptations that men like Greasy Neale and Paul Brown contributed. It is a living story of pioneers like George Marshall and George Halas.

"The Game," as played in the National Football League, is eleven starters on offense, eleven on defense. It is six weeks of training camp each year and hundreds of hours of skull sessions. Sometimes you see it all in the last two minutes of a thrilling contest. Sometimes you hear it talked for hour after hour at a family gathering in March.

In short, it is far more than something that is played in a stadium ninety-eight times a season, sixty minutes at a time. It is a national organization. It is top-rated television. It is many, many young executives and professional men who play football five months a year, build lasting careers during the other seven.

*The Game,* as published by Random House, is much more than the over 200 pictures and 288 pages. It doesn't list all the scores and it doesn't name all the players, nor does it attempt to.

But in *The Game*, Tex Maule has told the story of "The Game" through careful selection of words and pictures. It is as simple as that.

My close personal association with the National Football League goes back only a little more than a decade. When I read the manuscript of this book, I quickly made up for much of the three decades I had missed.

Frankly, reading *The Game* is an education in professional football. For me, it was like a postgraduate course in the intrinsic meaning of the sport. But just as a diploma does not result merely from an education in facts and figures, this deep insight into the National Football League does not come from scores and standings, but rather from anecdotes, interviews, personalities and pennant wavers.

Just as more than four million fans showed their appreciation by attending our games last season, I think you, too, will appreciate *The Game.*

PETE ROZELLE

*Commissioner, The National Football League*

Pete Rozelle, commissioner of the National Football league since 1960, is regarded as best in all pro sports.

# THE
# LEAGUE

THE six men in the small conference room of a Los Angeles hotel were quiet and tense. On the table before one of them lay two sealed envelopes, containing bids for the purchase of the Los Angeles Rams professional football franchise.

Pete Rozelle, the young commissioner of the National Football League, picked up the envelopes, held them a moment, then opened one of them carefully.

"Mr. Reeves bids $7,100,000. Mr. Pauley, Mr. Levy and Mr. Seley bid $6,100,000. Gentlemen, you have thirty minutes in which to decide if you want to better Mr. Reeves' bid by twenty per cent."

Ed Pauley, Fred Levy and Hal Seley left the room to confer with their attorneys. Their bid would now have to be $8,520,000. It was twenty-six minutes before they returned.

"Our congratulations to Mr. Reeves," Pauley said drily.

In 1941, when Dan Reeves and Fred Levy bought the Ram franchise (then in Cleveland), the price was $100,000; in twenty-two years the value of the club had increased by some seven million dollars.

This was a rather dramatic but roughly accurate example of the growth of professional football in the last two decades. Over four million paying customers watched the National Football League teams in action during the regular season of 1962.

Of the four top-rated sports programs on television, two were pro football games— the championship game between the New York Giants and the Green Bay Packers on December 30 and the Thanksgiving Day game between the Packers and the Detroit Lions in Detroit. Millions of viewers watched each of the seven NFL games televised every Sunday. In the last five years professional football, as it is played in the National League, has come to be recognized, almost without dissent, as the new national sport of the United States.

Oddly enough, much of the burgeoning success of the pros came about almost by accident. The game was born in poverty, raised in confusion and survived to so healthy a maturity only with the help of a series of almost haphazard inventions mothered, as usual, by necessity.

It is doubtful, for instance, that pro football could have reached its present stature if its teams competed on Saturday afternoon, in competition with the colleges. But the clubs were forced, willy-nilly, to play on Sunday. In the old days, most of their players were not available on Saturday; they were playing under their real names for their college teams.

The great University of Michigan halfback, Willie Heston, had much to do with the development of the player contract and foreshadowed the draft when he tried to auction himself off to the highest bidder among three teams in 1905. The teams agreed that none would bid for him. The precipitous flight of Red Grange from the Illinois campus to the Chicago Bears' bench raised a storm of protest from the colleges in the mid-twenties and led the league to adopt its present firm policy against signing college athletes to play before their class has been graduated.

Possibly all of these developments would have come about through the slow process of evolution, but the organism must survive to evolve. The survival of pro football would have been doubtful indeed had the teams competed directly with the colleges for talent and for Saturday's spectators and had the clubs competed, no holds barred, with one another for players.

Red Grange, shown here in his role as the Wheaton Ice Man, stirred nation-wide interest in the pros when he joined the Chicago Bears in 1925. Although he never reached his college peak as a pro, he was box office magic.

In the early days of pro football, there were no contracts and the players jumped from club to club with the alacrity of fleas. In 1915, for instance, the Columbus Panhandles played against Knute Rockne six times and each time Rockne was with a different team. Greasy Neale, the former coach of the Philadelphia Eagles, played with a variety of pro clubs while he coached at West Virginia Wesleyan just after World War I. He and Pete Calac, an Indian back who played for him at Wesleyan, would leave after a Saturday game to play with whichever pro club made them the best offer for the week.

Possibly the first professional football player in the history of the game and almost certainly one of the first ringers was, surprisingly, the fabled Pudge Heffelfinger. In the archives of the Professional Football Hall of Fame there is a yellowed financial statement for a game played in Pittsburgh in 1892 between two Pittsburgh athletic clubs. Listed under expenses is "Pudge Heffelfinger, $500 (for playing)." The Yale All-American brought three more players with him from Chicago, each of whom received "twice railroad fare" for his services.

Heffelfinger, incidentally, turned out to be worth the $500. His team won the game, 6-0, when Pudge smashed through the opponents' line, shook the ball loose from a back and then lumbered off with it for a touchdown.

Heffelfinger and his companions were probably the only mercenaries in that game. The first game between teams composed entirely of professionals occurred in Latrobe, Pa., in 1895 between Latrobe (sponsored by the local YMCA) and Jeanette. The players received $10 each and Latrobe won the game, 12-0.

For the next twenty-five years, the pattern of professional football was to remain much the same, although the players were paid a little more. Teams flourished for a while and died in Rhode Island, New York, Pennsylvania and Ohio. There were the Providence Steamrollers, the Duquesne Country and Athletic Club, the Homestead Library and Athletic Club, the Massillon Tigers, the Canton Bulldogs, the Columbus Panhandles, the Watertown Red and Blacks and the Philadelphia Athletics, among many others.

The first night game was played in 1902 with impromptu lights set along the sidelines in Elmira, N. Y. The Philadelphia Athletics, coached, more or less, by Connie Mack, won the game and Rube Waddell played in it briefly. He was a considerably less effective member of the football Athletics than of the baseball Athletics.

An indoor football tournament was played in Madison Square Garden in December of 1903, matching teams from Franklin, Pa., Philadelphia, Watertown, N. Y. and Orange, N. J. Franklin won the round robin easily. The tournament was notable more for the costumes of the officials than for the effect it would have on pro football. The officials wore full dress, including top hats. No more indoor football was played until 1932, when the Chicago Bears, forced indoors by a blizzard, beat the Portsmouth Spartans, 9-0, in Chicago Stadium for the league championship.

Most of the rash of what would now be called semi-professional football teams sprang up in the coal and steel belts of New York, Pennsylvania and Ohio, for good reason. Many clubs were subsidized in whole or in part by steel companies; Sunday pro football was the kind of entertainment which appealed to the hard-bitten miners and steel workers. And in an era when hours were long, pay small and work exhausting, it provided a concrete example of a job even tougher than the mines or the mills. The steel-mill owners found that professional football provided a healthy release for their employees, whether they watched or played.

These are the Canton Bulldogs, world professional football champions in 1922-23. From left to right: Lyman, Chamberlain,

A possibly apocryphal story about the Philadelphia Athletics illustrates this close relationship between steel and football. Connie Mack claimed the national championship for his 1902 Athletic football team. Under the circumstances, this was a somewhat tenuous claim and it was challenged by a Pittsburgh club.

Mack had been guaranteed $3000 for the game, but when he arrived in Pittsburgh, the money was not forthcoming.

Mack, even then a crusty, austere man, was loading his team into hansom cabs to take them back to the train when a prosperous-looking fan stopped him.

"What's the matter?" he asked.

"I haven't got my guarantee," Mack said. "We're not playing."

"How much is it?"

"Three thousand," said Mack, sourly.

"I'll give you a check," the fan said.

The check was signed "William Corey" and it was good. Corey was the president of Carnegie Steel.

Smythe, Williams, Griggs, Jones, Henry, Conover, Robb, Speck, Comstock, Elliott, Osborne, Hendrian, Carroll, Roberts.

In the next few years, the small tide of interest in professional football moved west, but not far. The pattern of steel and football continued. The Columbus Panhandles in effect represented the Panhandle shops of the Pennsylvania Railroad and for years most of the team was made up of a family of boilermakers—the seven Nesser brothers and, in later years, the son of one of the brothers.

An attorney in Canton, Ohio, Bill Day, formed the Canton Bulldogs. Eight miles away, in Massillon, the city editor of the Massillon Independent bought up the leftover stock of football jerseys from the local sporting goods store and named his team the Tigers because the jerseys happened to be striped.

The violent rivalry between Massillon and Canton led to the first and only known case of fixing in pro football history and halted the development of pro football in the area for some ten years.

In 1906, three years after the neighboring cities had begun their series, Blondy Wallace was the coach and manager of the Canton team. The year before, Canton had lost to Massillon in Massillon when the Tigers, given the privilege of providing the football as the home team, came up with a ten-ounce high school ball instead of the regulation sixteen-ounce ball used by the pros. In retaliation, Wallace hired away the Massillon backfield for the 1906 season. He also hired an end named Eddie Wood who was to make history in the fall of 1906 by catching the first forward pass ever thrown in a pro game. The forward pass was made legal that year.

The first game between Canton and Massillon was played in Canton and the Bulldogs won, 10-5. Canton was favored to win the second game, two weeks later in Massillon, but the Bulldogs lost, 12-6.

The first (and only substantiated) football scandal broke in the Massillon *Independent* the day after the game. The paper printed a story accusing Wallace of first having tried to tamper with some of the players on the Massillon team; failing to bribe them, Wallace turned to his own team and instructed one of his players to throw the game, which he did. The player was run out of town by the irate citizens. Wallace sued the *Independent* for libel but withdrew the suit when confronted with proof of his dishonesty.

The scandal almost killed pro football in Ohio. Not until the advent of one of the two most important players in pro football history ten years later — Jim Thorpe — did the game again begin to move forward. The second player was Red Grange.

Thorpe was a Sac and Fox Indian, raised in a small town in Oklahoma. He was not a big man, as modern pro backs are judged. He stood about six-one, weighed from 185 to 190 at playing weight. By the time he joined the Canton Bulldogs for the 1915 season, he had won the decathlon and pentathlon championships in the 1912 Olympics and had his gold medals taken away because it was found that he had played semi-professional baseball one summer. He had led the Carlisle Indian Institute team, under Glenn (Pop) Warner, to what would now have been recognized as a national football championship.

He was, in everything but competitive sports, a childish man. When the Indians went on the road, Warner roomed with Thorpe to make sure he did not sneak out to the nearest bar and miss the game entirely. At home, the Indians were confined to the grounds at Carlisle, although the athletes were not as closely supervised as the other students. Thorpe managed occasionally to slip away to town for a drink even then.

As a football player, though, he could do everything anyone has ever done. He was a prodigious punter and drop-kicked field goals from the fifty-yard line. He was a combination of Jim Taylor and Lennie Moore as a runner.

Pete Calac, a Mission Indian who played with Thorpe during Thorpe's senior year at Carlisle and played professional football with him as well, was probably Thorpe's closest friend over the years.

"He had a way of running I never saw before," Calac said. "We didn't wear helmets much in those days. Jim would shift his hip toward the guy about to tackle him, then swing it away and then, when the player moved in to hit him, he'd swing his hip back, hard, against the tackler's head and leave him laying there."

Calac was a small halfback on the Canton team with Jim.

"He talked a lot during a game," Pete said. "I mean, he'd say to a tackle on the other side, 'I'm coming right over,' then, like as not, he would. He liked practical jokes too. I guess I'm getting old, I don't remember any specific ones he pulled on us at Carlisle but I remember he liked to joke."

Thorpe brought the forerunner of modern pro football offense with him to Canton. The Bulldogs, like the Carlisle Indians, ran out of a double-wing formation. The forward pass had been legalized in 1906 and Thorpe, trained by Pop Warner, used it lavishly on the Canton team.

The 1915 Canton Bulldogs were organized and operated by a Texan, Jack Cusack. It was Cusack who designed and had made Thorpe's special shoulder pads. They were not, as has often been written, made of galvanized iron, although they must have felt like that to Thorpe's opponents. They were of sole leather, made to Cusack's specifications by a Canton shoemaker. Thorpe wore them until he joined the New York Giants late in his career and found that the pads had been made illegal.

"They hit like iron," says George Halas, the owner of the Chicago Bears, who played against Thorpe for several years. "He blocked with his shoulder and it felt like he had hit you with a four-by-four. He was a great defensive player, too, you know. His tackling was as unusual as his running style — he never tackled with his arms and shoulders. He'd leg-whip the ball carrier. If he hit you from behind, he'd throw that big body across your back and damn near break you in two."

Thorpe's drawing power animated pro football from the time he joined the Bulldogs in 1915 until 1925, when a new star arrived to project the game onto another plateau of public acceptance. There were, of course, many other fine players during the decade of Thorpe, but his was the impetus which carried the game over into the era of organization.

Thorpe, of course, was no Galahad. He had no fear, but by modern standards, he was surely not beyond reproach. He did not always feel in the mood to play well; during his career with Canton, the Bulldogs won when Thorpe went well, lost when he did not.

Like most players of that era, Thorpe bet on himself and on his team. He left Canton in a dudgeon after a game in which he was accused, not of shaving points, but of setting up a situation in which he could profit enormously.

In 1916, Thorpe was injured in the first Canton-Massillon game, which ended in a scoreless tie. Canton won the second game, 23-0, with Thorpe scoring all the points in one of the strongest performances of his career. But Thorpe, the story has it, had bet $2500 on Canton to win after first circulating a rumor that his injuries in the first game were so serious that he would not be able to suit up for the second.

He returned to the Bulldogs not long after and he was a member of the Canton team when, for the first time, professional football made at least a formal bow to organization.

Canton's Wilbur (Fats) Henry, who is in pro football's Hall of Fame as a tackle, is shown here in rare picture carrying the ball on a tackle around play against the Massillon Tigers. Note helmetless Massillon pursuer.

This was in September, 1920, at the Ralph E. Hay Motor Co., 122-134 McKinley Avenue North, in Canton. The Hay Motor Co. sold Jordans and Marmons. Today, the United States Post Office occupies the same site in Canton.

On that warm September evening, the showroom held eight automobiles. Sitting on the running boards were representatives from Canton, Cleveland, Dayton, Akron and Massillon, Ohio; Rochester, N. Y.; Rock Island, Decatur and Chicago, Ill., and Hammond and Muncie, Ind. Thorpe, who had played baseball that afternoon for Akron and hit twice in four times at bat, represented Canton. George Halas represented a starch company in Decatur, Ill. That evening the American Professional Football Association was formed and Thorpe, probably the least qualified man in the showroom, was chosen as the first president. A franchise cost $100. No schedule was drawn up. Indeed, no definite schedules would be drawn up for over ten years. In the first year of the American Professional Football Association, three teams — Canton, Akron and Buffalo — all claimed the national championship, leading Massillon to give up football in disgust.

The league was reorganized in 1921, in a meeting in the Cortland Hotel in Canton, and Thorpe's brief tenure as league president came to an end. Elected in his place was Joe Carr, a newspaperman who had been general managr of the Columbus Panhandles. The league was renamed the National Football League in 1922 by George Halas.

The 1921 season is the first listed in the National Football League handbook as producing a recognized champion and season standings. George Halas' Decatur Staleys won ten, lost one and tied one and took the championship. Green Bay, in its first season in the

This is Jim Thorpe in 1908. When this picture was taken, Thorpe was playing for Pop Warner on the famous Carlisle Indian Institute team. Thorpe was fresh from Oklahoma, with Olympic and football glory ahead.

league, finished fourth with a 6-2-2 record. Although these were official standings, the teams still did not play a regular schedule; games were arranged from week to week for the most part and this haphazard scheduling was to bring about at least two controversies over who had indeed won the championship.

Buffalo, which finished second to the Bears in 1921, has claimed for a long time that it should have finished first since some of the games included in the Bears' record were not played in league competition. Unfortunately, it is impossible to determine the validity of the Buffalo claim since most of the Bear records for that year were destroyed in a fire a few years ago.

In 1925, the Chicago Cardinals won the league championship, with eleven victories, two losses and a tie. In second place was Pottsville, 10-2-0. It was no accident that the Cardinals played 14 games that year to Pottsville's 12. Pottsville had beaten the Cardinals in the final game of the season and considered itself league champions, but Chris O'brien, at that time the owner of the Chicago team, hurriedly scheduled two more games. One was with Milwaukee, a team which played four high school players during the game and was fined and its owner given ninety days to dispose of the franchise as a consequence. The Cardinals won, 59-0. The second game was against Hammond, Ind., and the Cardinals won that one easily, too. O'Brien added the two victories to the Cardinals' legitimate 9-2-1 record and claimed the championship.

Pottsville, in the meantime, scheduled a post-season game in Philadelphia against the Notre Dame All-Stars, a team which included the Four Horsemen — Elmer Layden, Harry

Jim Thorpe, nearing the end of his fabulous career, makes an uncharacteristic arm tackle in this 1926 game for the Canton Bulldogs. Thorpe's more usual style of tackling was to throw his body at the unfortunate runner.

OFFICIAL PHOTO
POTTSVILLE MAROON FOOTBALL TEAM - 1925
NATIONAL LEAGUE CHAMPIONS - 1925. DEFEATED THE CHICAGO CARDINALS, AT CHICAGO DECEMBER 6, 1925 - 21 to 7.
WORLD CHAMPIONS - 1925. DEFEATED THE "FOUR HORSEMEN AND SEVEN MULES" OF NOTRE DAME, AT SHIBE PARK, PHILADELPHIA, PA.
DECEMBER 12, 1925 - 9 to 7. THE FIRST "ALL STAR" GAME PLAYED IN THIS COUNTRY.
OFFICIAL OUTFITTERS: ZACKO'S SPORTING GOODS, POTTSVILLE, PA.

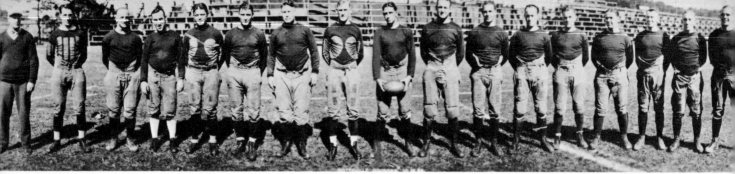

*Eddie Gillespie*     *F. Bucher*     *"Hoot" Flanagan*     *"Russ" Stein*     *"Denny" Hughes*     *Dick Rauch*
*Trainer*    *"Tony" Latone*     *Frankie Racis*     *Charlie Berry*     *"Fungy" Lebengood*   *"Eddie" Doyle*    *Coach*
*Jack Ernst*     *Duke Osborne*     *Russ Hathaway*     *"Herb" Stein*     *"Barney" Wentz*    *Walter French*

Although the Pottsville Maroons list themselves as National League champions, this team was later to be deprived of its title when the Chicago Cardinals won two more games to finish with a better record than Pottsville.

Stuhldreher, Jim Crowley and Don Miller. The Maroons won, 9-7, but provided O'Brien with another reason for claiming the championship. O'Brien charged that Pottsville had violated the territorial rights of the Frankford Yellow Jackets by playing in Philadelphia, and the league ruled that Pottsville must forfeit its championship.

At the 1963 National Football League meeting in Miami, Pottsville, long out of the league, presented a belated claim for the 1925 title. Armed with the size nine shoe Charlie Berry used to kick a 30-yard field goal to beat the Notre Dame All-Stars, Joe Zacko, a Pottsville sporting goods dealers, offered the league, in effect, a trade of the shoe for the 1925 championship. The Professional Football Hall of Fame wanted the shoe, but the Cardinals succeeded in having the Pottsville proposal tabled.

In 1926, Carr drew up the first league constitution and by-laws in a thin, three-by-five-inch pamphlet. The rules under which the pros operated were rather sketchy. An applicant for a franchise in the National Football League must have organized, or contemplated the organization of, a team to play professional or semi-professional football. No player could use an assumed name and "no player on a Saturday team in one city is eligible to play on a Sunday team in another city."

However, one team could lend another a player or two in an emergency. Since the player limit was set at fifteen, emergencies happened occasionally. The salary limit was set at $1200 per game, including players, coach and manager (if the coach or manager played).

The championship team was to be given eighteen engraved gold footballs (not to cost more than $10 apiece) and a suitable pennant, not to cost more than $37.50.

But the most important section of the new constitution was an unequivocal recognition of the rights of the colleges.

"The National Football League places itself on record as unalterably opposed to any encroachment upon college football and hereby pledges its hearty support to college authorities in maintaining and advancing interest in college football and in preserving the amateur standing of all college athletes," the resolution read. ". . . it is the unanimous decision of this meeting that every member of the National Football League be positively prohibited from inducing or attempting to induce any college player to engage in professional football until his class at college shall have graduated, and any member violating this rule shall be fined not less than one thousand dollars or loss of its franchise, or both."

This resolution was brought about by the advent of Red Grange into pro football in 1925. Never before or since has a football player so thoroughly captured the imagination of the American public. His decision to join the Chicago Bears immediately after his last game for the University of Illinois started a storm of protest from the colleges. In a few weeks, professional football was given more publicity than it had had in the entire twenty-five years before Grange.

Grange was managed by a mercurial promoter named C. C. (Cash and Carry) Pyle. The contract that Pyle extracted from George Halas for Grange's first season as a pro reduced the Bears, in effect, to the role of supporting cast for Grange. But the heavy price paid for Grange proved eventually to be the biggest bargain in pro football history.

Grange played his first professional football game for the Chicago Bears against the Cardinals in Wrigley Field on Thanksgiving Day, 1925. The 36,000 people who crammed themselves into the park to watch the Galloping Ghost got little for their money. Paddy Driscoll, the punter for the Cardinals, studiously avoided kicking the ball anywhere near Grange and the game ended in a 0-0 tie. Grange and Pyle split almost $25,000 as their share of the gate and the Bears also did much better than usual for this game.

Three days later, Grange did more to earn his pay as the Bears beat the Columbus Tigers, 14-13, before 28,000 spectators, again at Wrigley Field. Red gained nearly 150 yards in the three quarters he played in this game and again he and Pyle and the Bears split a healthy gate.

In the next twelve days, the Bears played eight games in what was to be, literally, a bone-breaking schedule devised to milk as much money as possible out of the presence of Grange. They played in St. Louis, drew 35,000 in Philadelphia, then played the next day before more than 65,000 in the Polo Grounds in New York, where no accurate gate count could be made because several thousand fans stormed the gates and forced their way into the park after the ticket sale had ended.

From New York, the tired, bruised Bears went to Washington, Boston, Pittsburgh (where Grange was kicked in the arm and hurt so badly that he missed the next game), Detroit and finally back to Chicago. Grange, who could hardly lift his battered arm, played against the Giants in Chicago so that Halas would not have to refund any money to disappointed spectators.

Grange and Pyle pocketed $50,000 apiece on this tour. On a subsequent sweep through the South and Far West, they made another $50,000 each. This record of $100,000 in three months made Grange the highest-paid player in the history of pro football, but of more importance to the league was the fact that, for the first time, pro football monopolized sports pages all over the nation. This was the first big impact the sport had on the American public and the interest created by Grange was never to die down again.

For the 1926 season, Pyle demanded one-third of the Bear ball club for Grange's services and Halas wisely refused. Pyle then organized his own league and put a team in Yankee Stadium but the league was not successful and Pyle went on to other projects, such as running the Brooklyn team in the NFL and promoting a transcontinental footrace called "The Bunion Derby."

Grange's first year proved to be Jim Thorpe's last. Thorpe played part of the 1925 season with the Giants; he was paid on the basis of how long he could last each game and the time grew shorter and shorter. He left the Giants after a brawl with another Indian one night in Harlem and never again returned to pro football.

In 1926, there were twenty-two teams in the National Football League, many of which

Ed Sternaman, left, and George Halas, right, pose for publicity picture with the most expensive rookie in National Football League history: Red Grange. Grange joined the Bears in 1925, before end of school year.

played only skeleton schedules. Hammond, Ind., and Louisville, Ky., played only four games each in that season and both teams lost all four. The Frankford Yellow jackets, fore-runners of the Philadelphia Eagles, won the championship and played sixteen games.

The league was a weird mixture of amateur, semi-professional and professional foot-ball teams, playing fluid, confused schedules. In July of 1927, ten of the twenty-two clubs dropped out of the league, leaving a hard core of twelve teams, which was reduced to ten the following year. Of the ten teams that competed in 1928, only six remained in 1963 — the Chicago Bears, the Chicago (now St. Louis) Cardinals, the Detroit Lions, the Green Bay Packers, the New York Giants and the Philadelphia Eagles, nee the Frankford Yellow Jackets.

In the next few years, the small town teams slowly died out as the fiscal demands of professional football outstripped the ability of cities the size of Duluth and Pottsville and Providence and Dayton to support the game. Providence won the championship in 1928 but the depression hit the town soon after and the club went out of existence in 1932. By that season, only eight teams were left in the league and the explosion set off by Grange appeared ready to peter out.

But in 1932 a new figure appeared in the league — George Preston Marshall, who was granted a franchise in Boston on July 9. In the next few years, Marshall, an energetic, flamboyant and far-seeing man, instituted changes in the league which gave it the impetus to survive through World War II and enter an era of unparalleled popularity.

Marshall's first proposal, made almost a year to the day after he was granted a fran-chise, was that the league should be separated into two divisions and that the divisional champions should play off for the world title. Marshall insisted, too, that the schedule be standardized so that each team played a like number of games against common opposition. He and Halas led the move to legalize passing from anywhere behind the line of scrimmage

14

and to put the goal posts back on the goal line, changes which quickly made professional football a far more exciting, high-scoring game than the college variety.

Marshall introduced team songs, the half-time extravaganza and a team band, as well. He had always been interested in show business; he brought that interest to pro football.

The 1933 season began the modern era of professional football. In 1934, the first College All-Star game was played in Chicago, with the All-Stars holding the Chicago Bears to a scoreless tie. In 1935, Bert Bell, who had joined the league in 1933 as part-owner of the Philadelphia Eagles, proposed what proved to be the most important single rule in pro football.

This was the player selection system which, over the years, has insured that no pro football team can ever dominate the National Football League as the New York Yankees dominate the American League in baseball.

Bell, a short, fat, gravel-voiced man, had discovered in two years as an owner of the Philadelphia Eagles that he had almost no chance of luring college players from the Bears, Giants or Packers. Not only were the established pro clubs better able financially to secure the services of the top college graduates, but the collegians themselves felt it an honor to be approached by any one of the big three. They couldn't care less about playing for the Philadelphia Eagles.

The draft system changed the picture radically. Now the have-nots were given first pick of the college crop; the last-place team drafted first, followed by the rest of the league in reverse order of their standing at the end of the season. The first player selected in the first draft in 1936 was Chicago's Jay Berwanger. The man who picked him, naturally, was Bert Bell, whose Eagles had, as usual, managed to compile the worst record in the league in 1935, with two victories against nine losses. Berwanger, incidentally, decided against playing professional football.

The full impact of the draft was not felt for several years, or until the big three finally used up the accumulated player wealth of the non-draft years and were forced to replenish their rosters with draftees. Since that time, it has been rare that any team has managed to stay at the top for more than three years at a time.

Here Grange carries the ball for the Bears against the All-Star Collegians during barnstorming tour set up by Halas to capitalize on Grange name after the end of the 1925 season. Tour made a healthy profit for everyone.

Paul Brown, the brilliant coach of the Cleveland Browns, paid unconscious tribute to Bell's invention when asked how a winning team is built in pro football. "You finish last for several years," Brown said. "Then you get a Vince Lombardi to tie all those first-draft choices together for you."

By 1940, the cost of a pro-football franchise had been placed at $50,000; the only small town left in the league was Green Bay, where the game was a religion and not a sport. Marshall had moved the Redskins from Boston to Washington. Joe Carr, who had been president of the league from 1921, died in 1939; his death seemed to underscore the end of the old catch-as-catch-can era. Carl L. Storck, who had been secretary of the league since 1921, succeeded Carr; he was followed in 1941 by Elmer Layden, who was the first commissioner.

World War II was a period of marking time. The Cleveland Rams suspended operation for a year; Philadelphia and Pittsburgh operated as the Phil-Pitt "Steagles" one year, then Pittsburgh and the Chicago Cardinals merged for a year as Card-Pitt.

In 1944, Arch Ward, the sports editor of the *Chicago Tribune,* proposed that a second pro football league be organized. It proved to be an ideal time for the formation of another league; many of the stars of the National Football League were in service and many of the college seniors who would normally have gone directly to an NFL club went instead into service.

This created a reservoir of players for the new teams in the All-American Conference to draw upon. Paul Brown, who was coaching at Great Lakes, took over at Cleveland and

This publicity man's nightmare shows the Four Horsemen of Notre Dame before the game with Pottsville. They are, left to right: Don Miller, Elmer Layden, Jim Crowley and Harry Stuhldreher. Pottsville won, 9-7.

started league play in 1946 with the nucleus of what was to be one of the finest teams of all time. Dan Topping, who had operated the Brooklyn franchise in the old league, gave that up to organize the New York Yankees in the new conference. The new league placed franchises in Los Angeles, San Francisco, Buffalo, Baltimore, Chicago, New York, Cleveland and Miami and began a bitter three-year war with the National Football League which was, eventually, to cost its owners some eleven million dollars.

The Browns, the San Francisco Forty-Niners and the Buffalo Bills were almost immediately successful. The Chicago Rockets learned a bitter lesson quickly: you cannot compete with the Bears in Chicago. Nor did the New York Yankees have much better luck competing with the New York Giants. New York pro football fans had been raised on the Giants and they showed no enthusiasm for the Yankees.

In 1946, as the battle was joined, the National Football League elected Bert Bell commissioner. Elmer Layden, unfortunately, had greeted the formation of the new league with disdain.

"Let them," said Layden, "get a football."

During the next four years, the All-America Conference teams not only acquired a large supply of footballs, some of them also acquired a large supply of good football players. In the areas where they did not compete directly with the National Football League, the AAC teams did reasonably well. Miami soon proved to be a poor site for pro football, even without NFL competition. Cleveland, conditioned by the Cleveland Rams, took to the Cleveland Browns with the enthusiasm bred of winning.

San Francisco reacted with surprising warmth to the advent of the Forty-Niners, and in Los Angeles the crucial battles of the pro football war were fought. The Cleveland Rams had won the National Football League championship in 1945 and Dan Reeves, the youngest owner in the league, had promptly asked to move his team to Los Angeles. He managed to force this through the league meeting after considerable difficulty. When he reached Los Angeles, he faced the strong competition of the Los Angeles Dons, a team backed by Ben Lindheimer, the richest owner in the All-America Conference.

The struggle between the Rams and the Dons was a Homeric one. Both teams shed fiscal blood by the bucket. In the early competition, it seemed that the Dons might have the edge, but in 1949, the Rams produced one of the most spectacular teams in history. The quarterbacks were Bob Waterfield and Norman Van Brocklin, throwing to ends Elroy Hirsch and Tom Fears. The halfbacks might successfully have competed in an Olympic sprint relay: they were Army's great All-American, Glenn Davis; Vitamin Smith, a 9.6-second 100-yard dash man from Abilene Christian College; Tommy Kalmanir, another sprinter from Nevada; and Jerry Williams, the fastest back on the Pacific Coast the year before.

This team won the Western Conference championship and, in doing so, wrote the finish of the Dons.

The end of the Dons was the end of the All-America Conference. Both leagues drafted college players after the 1949 season. Shortly thereafter, the two drafts were thrown out when the National Football League announced that it had "merged" with the All-America Conference.

This was more of a surrender than a merger. The National Football League had won the war hands down. In the brief meetings between the two leagues which preceded the death of the AAC, the only point of contention was which clubs of the new league would be allowed to survive.

The choice was a good one. The Cleveland Browns, the San Francisco Forty-Niners and the Baltimore Colts were accepted in the National Football League. A long wrangle developed over the distribution of talent from the deceased clubs in the All-America Conference. It was settled arbitrarily by Bert Bell, who was beginning to demonstrate the strength of character that made him one of the finest commissioners in any sport.

In his first year in the job, the second scandal to affect football until that time broke over Bell's head. Two players on the New York Giants were approached with bribe offers before the 1946 championship game; they did not accept the offers, but they did not report the bribe attempts, either.

Bell's action was quick and conclusive. He suspended Merl Hapes and Frank Filchock and began a campaign for federal legislation against bribing athletes which was later to bear fruit with the passage of a toothed law. The quick, forthright crackdown kept pro football clear of any suspicion of bribing or point-shaving from then on.

With the help of some of the far-sighted owners in the league, Bell also solved the problem of television. Major league baseball failed signally to evaluate the impact of television. The free-wheeling baseball program eventually killed off most of the minor leagues in the sport and cut deeply into home attendance for major league clubs as the teams grabbed at maximum income from the new medium.

The Los Angeles Rams experimented with television of home games. A contract with

Typical of the growth of professional football is the new stadium in which the Washington Redskins now play. Here the

a television manufacturer guaranteed, in effect, that the team would break even on home attendance, with the sponsor making up the difference between actual attendance and the attendance necessary for the club to avoid going into the red. The contract lasted one year. With the choice of attending the game or staying home to watch it on television, the Los Angeles fans stayed home in overwhelming numbers.

Since then, the league has televised away games and blacked out home games. The policy has paid off in enormous gains in home attendance. Fans whose appetites were whetted by television of the road games poured out in ever-increasing numbers to swell the gates for the home games.

The first Pro Bowl game was played in Los Angeles in 1951 between All-Star teams from the East and West and was an immediate success. Beginning in 1952, the league broke its attendance record every year for eight years, moving from a total attendance of 2,052,126 in 1952 to 3,140,409 in 1959. Three years later, in 1962, despite the competition of the American Football League, the NFL total attendance crept over the four-million mark.

The decade of the fifties was not one of unalloyed success, however. In 1952, a new franchise was born in Dallas. The Dallas Texans started with high hopes and foundered, before the season was finished, on the rocks of woeful mismanagement, a team which won only one game (and that after the club had gone bankrupt and become a road team), and

famous Redskin Marching Band performs during the half; even if the 'Skins falter, the half-time show is always tops.

an enthusiastic apathy demonstrated by Dallas football fans. The franchise was turned over to Baltimore the folowing year. Within five years, the Baltimore franchise became one of the most successful in football — and one of the most valuable.

But the overall picture was one of stupendous growth. In Los Angeles and San Francisco and Detroit and Chicago, in Baltimore and New York, it became impossible to get good seats to a pro game unless you inherited good season tickets. Season tickets became bones of contention in divorce cases. And, again, success bred competition.

Bert Bell, who had guided the league surely through the shoal water of the All-America battle and the television question, died in 1959 and at first it seemed too much to hope that the National Football League could replace him with as competent a commissioner.

At the winter league meeting in Miami in 1960, the league split as cleanly as a ripe watermelon over the selection of a new commissioner. The old heads wanted Austin Gunsel, a capable man who had served as league treasurer under Bell and who had directed the network of sixteen ex-FBI agents whose responsibility was checking on rumors of possible misbehavior by players.

The younger owners wanted a San Francisco attorney, Marshall Leahy. Through some twenty-eight ballots, the issue remained unresolved. Leahy wanted to move the league office to San Francisco, where he had five girls in school; the old-timers preferred to keep it in Philadelphia, where it had always been. They knew Gunsel and trusted him.

The entire axis of power in the league shifted on this decision. The compromise candidate, eventually, was Pete Rozelle, the young, competent manager of the Los Angeles Rams.

Rozelle began his stewardship under much the same circumstances which had greeted Bell. Like Bell, he took office as a new, competitive league was being formed. For Bell, it had been the All-America Conference; for Rozelle, it was the American Football League.

Like Bell, Rozelle had to solve a television problem. In 1961, Judge Allan K. Grim, in Philadelphia, voided a single-network television contract for the NFL which would have increased revenue of individual ball clubs, although a similar contract for the American Football League was not challenged. A bill by Representative Emanuel Celler, legalizing single-network television, was passed by Congress in September of 1960, too late for that season, but early enough to make the single network (CBS) operative in 1961.

During Rozelle's administration, two clubs were added. The Dallas Cowboys, owned by a group of Texans headed by multi-millionaire Clint Murchison, Jr., fought desperately for three years against the Dallas Texans of the American Football League, a fight capped by the announcement in 1963 that the Texans planned to move to Kansas City.

In Minneapolis-St. Paul, the most spectacularly successful new venture in pro football, the Minnesota Vikings, earned a profit in each of their first two years, despite losing seasons.

Under Rozelle, too, the National Football League fought and won a $10,000,000 anti-trust suit brought against it by the American Football League. The original action was tried before Judge Roszel Thomson in Baltimore and resulted in a sweeping, conclusive victory by the National Football League.

As the league passed its forty-fourth milestone, ahead lay such unopened packages of money as pay television, which could overnight multiply the value of a franchise by two or three. Back in 1920, on a September evening in an automobile agency, a franchise sold for $100. The latest price was $7,167,633. Oddly enough, the latest price is the best buy.

George Preston Marshall, owner of the Washington Redskins, has contributed as much as any man to the explosive growth of pro football. Showman and innovator, Marshall added glamor to the spectacle of football.

# THE GAME

**W**HILE the fiscal organizational growth of the National Football League was fitful, dictated as often by good luck as by good judgment, the development of the game itself followed a steady trend from the conservative to the spectacular.

There were, of course, sudden shifts in direction; the Chicago Bears' massacre of the Washington Redskins in 1940 produced the most wholesale change in football strategy in the history of the game. But it only accentuated something that had been developing slowly from the time the forward pass was legalized in 1906.

Basically, the evolution of pro football has led steadily to increasing the width and depth of the area of attack. Before the pass became legal, the only target area available to the offense was at the line of scrimmage; this was one-dimensional trench warfare. Victory went almost invariably to the team with the heavier troops, and the use of strategy, tactics and deception was confined to the ten or twelve yards between the two offensive ends, along the line of scrimmage.

By contrast, today's area of attack stretches from sideline to sideline and extends some forty yards behind the defensive line. Before the development of the modern attack and the forward pass, the eleven men on defense had about ninety square feet of territory to protect; if you accept forty yards behind the defensive line as the deepest point of attack today, the same number of men must patrol 19,200 square feet of football field.

Oddly enough, the forward pass was added to football not as a device to make the game more exciting, but as a safety measure. The most exciting play of the antediluvian era of football was the flying wedge, used most often and most successfully on the kickoff. It was precisely what the name denotes. Suitcase handles were sewed to the seats of the pants of the players; the receiver dropped into the pocket of a vee of ten players, each of whom held on to the handle on the rump of the player in front of him, like so many elephants. It was an effective blocking formation, but the defenders who tried to break through to the ball carrier were, as often as not, left for dead.

When President Theodore Roosevelt threatened to abolish football entirely in 1905 because of the mounting mortality rate, the wedge was outlawed and the pass made legal so that the game would be opened up and the likelihood of injury lessened.

Probably the first coach to understand and use the pass effectively was Pop Warner, who devised the double-wing formation for the Carlisle Indians. Since Warner had Jim Thorpe, Joe Guyon, Pete Calac and many other fine Indian backs to implement his offense, it worked very well. Thorpe, of course, was the very model of even a modern major league tailback, who could run, throw and kick superbly. It was Thorpe, when he left Carlisle to enter professional football, who introduced both the formation and the appreciation of the

The man whose genius had the most far-reaching effect on the game of professional football was Clark Shaughnessy. As an assistant to George Halas, Shaughnessy revitalized the T formation by installing variations off the man in motion, and it was Shaughnessy who brought the wide-open aerial game of the pros to its present state of near perfection.

forward pass to pro football.

Since Thorpe's career as a pro began in Pine Village, Indiana, in 1913 and included seasons in Canton, Cleveland, Rock Island and New York, the Indian proved an effective salesman for the pass. Knute Rockne and Gus Dorais, playing for Notre Dame against Army in 1913, had shown that the forward pass could be used successfully as the basis of an attack; the unknown Irish defeated Army, 35-13, with a shower of Dorais-to-Rockne passes. Rockne and Dorais played professional football, too, and added to the impetus provided by Thorpe.

The formations of the early days, with the exception of Warner's double wing, were

Indian Joe Guyon, Jim Thorpe and Pete Calac, all from Carlisle, made up three-fourths of the backfield of the Canton Bulldogs in the early days. Although Thorpe was the most famous, the other two were great backs.

designed primarily to provide a blocking escort for a ball-carrier, rather than a free route for a pass-receiver. Most of the attacking formations had evolved from the T formation, oldest of all. When Clark Shaughnessy, who was to have a major part in creating the modern, fast-striking and versatile T, played at Minnesota around the turn of the century, he spent part of his time as a fullback in the T.

"The pass was no part of the offense," he said. "If we ever used it, the ball was lobbed end over end in a desperate, last gasp play. You have to remember that the ball we used then looked more like a soccer ball than the modern football. I may have been the first man to try to throw a spiral with a football."

The old T did not last long. Warner invented and introduced first the single wing, then the double wing. Over the years—until 1940 and the re-establishment of the T as a universal offense—a dozen different arrangements of offensive players came and went. During most of the early days of professional football, the clubs used either the short punt or the Notre Dame box, shifting gradually to the single wing. Steve Owen, in New York, devised a variation of the single wing which he called the A formation. It was primarily a running formation and put terrible pressure on the defensive tackle facing the strong side of the line.

During these years, the area of attack gradually expanded. The single wing spread the striking zone toward the sidelines; although its principal strength was the weight of blockers it provided ahead of the runner, the presence of a back close to the line of scrimmage on the flank of the line meant that an additional receiver was in position for a quick foray into the secondary, so that the area to be defended was deepened as well. The double wing added another quick receiver — diffused the defense even more.

The rules of the game were gradually changed to favor the pass, too. The ball grew slimmer and easier to throw. In 1933, George Halas and George Preston Marshall lobbied to have the pass made legal from any place behind the line of scrimmage, instead of from five yards behind it. As important to the passing game was the adoption of the free-substitution rule in 1943, which meant that pass-catching specialists could be used without regard to their ability to play defense.

The 1933 rule, however, was to benefit Green Bay's Curly Lambeau more than it did its authors. In 1930, a rookie from Green Bay named Arnie Herber had joined the club. Using an unorthodox grip with the thumb of his short-fingered chubby hand on the laces of the ball, he could pass up to eighty yards in the air. More important, he could throw a football with extraordinary accuracy as far as sixty yards. The year before, Lambeau had hired John McNally, an itinerant Irish football player whose flamboyant career had led him from Notre Dame to St. John's College to the Duluth Esquimaux, to Pottsville and finally to Green Bay. McNally played under the name of Johnny Blood. He was a fast, slashing runner rather than an elusive one but, more important to Lambeau, he was a fine receiver.

Lambeau was the first of the pro coaches to make a proper evaluation of the forward pass. It had been an effective weapon for the Packers in Curly's days as player-owner and it was now to become the most fearsome weapon in the National Football League.

The Packers won league championships in 1929, 1930 and 1931. A tall, thin end named Don Hutson made an unforgettable debut in 1936. On the first play from scrimmage against the Chicago Bears, he caught a pass for eighty-three yards and a touchdown when Blood decoyed the Bear defense one way and Herber lofted a long pass to Hutson on the other side of the field behind the Bear defense.

That was the first of 101 touchdown passes Hutson was to catch before he retired. It

The Frankford Yellow Jackets against the New York Giants in 1926 demonstrate clearly the changes in pro football in the last three decades. Note the leather helmets and the canvas trousers; only one team wore numbers.

established the passing combination of Herber to Hutson, which was later to change to Isbell to Hutson when Cecil Isbell, one of the finest passers in history, joined the Packers in 1937.

The Packers were to win two more league championships during the Herber-Isbell-Hutson era and were to finish third or better in their division for the next sixteen years. Although Lambeau had a sound and even spectacular running game (with Clark Hinkle as the principal moving force) to supplement the passing, it was the incomparable ability of Hutson and the accuracy of Herber and Isbell in getting the ball to him which accounted for most of the Packer success.

If Thorpe, Rockne and Dorais had introduced the pass as an effective weapon in the arsenal of pro football, it was Lambeau directing the efforts of Herber, Isbell, Blood and Hutson who demonstrated that it was at least as potent a weapon as the run.

Lambeau's passers, however, were still throwing from the single-wing formation and taking a beating in every game. After Isbell joined the team, he would, on rare occasions, take a snap as a T quarterback, then hit Hutson immediately on a quick pass as a surprise, but the T did not take over until after the 1940 season.

Only one team had stuck to this formation from the beginning. That team, of course, was George Halas' Bears. The T, as practiced by the Bears, was a far cry from the high-scoring formation of today. In 1932, the Bears won the league championship, but did not score a touchdown until their fifth game and finished the season with six low-scoring ties on their record.

After that season Halas pushed through the rule changes which allowed a passer to throw from anywhere behind the line of scrimmage and which moved the goal posts back to the goal line. It may be coincidence that these changes were particularly beneficial to George in the next few years.

26

He developed the predecessor to what is now called a play-number pass to exploit the first change, which allows the passer to throw from anywhere behind the line of scrimmage. Bronko Nagurski, the massive Bear fullback, was a fair passer; Halas had used him earlier on a fake plunge into the line which turned into a pass when Nagurski straightened up and threw. Obviously, this play was much more effective when Nagurski could draw the defense farther in by stopping only a yard short of the line before passing.

George's wisdom in having the goal posts moved to the goal line paid off, too. The Bears beat the Giants for the championship in 1933 by virtue of three field goals by "Automatic Jack" Manders, Chicago's great place-kicker.

The next giant stride in pro football was taken in 1940. It involved a radical change in the use of the T formation. This change was to establish the trend of the offense for more than twenty years.

In the late thirties, the University of Chicago, deep in the doldrums of de-emphasis, was coached by an intense genius named Clark Shaughnessy. Shaughnessy had coached at Tulane, Maryland, Pittsburgh and Loyola College. His duties with the University of Chicago left him time and his inclination sent him to watch the Bears work out. He and Halas soon became fast friends.

Halas, Shaughnessy and Ralph Jones, the Bears' head coach in 1930-'32, began to work on variations of the standard T, designed to give it more and better striking power. They devised the man in motion, which sent one back trotting off toward one or the other of the sidelines. That worked for a while until defenses began overshifting to compensate.

In 1940, Shaughnessy left the University of Chicago to take over as head coach at Stanford. Shaughnessy had not won a game in 1939, but then neither had Stanford.

He brought with him the T formation, with variations.

"I thought he was crazy," says Hugh Gallarneau, one of Shaughnessy's halfbacks on the 1940 Stanford team. "We, like everyone else in college football, had always played the single wing. I was a halfback and when Shaughnessy diagrammed a play which sent the halfback into the line without a blocker ahead of him, I laughed."

Gallarneau and the rest of the Stanford team soon stopped laughing. The meticulous Shaughnessy drilled the team mercilessly on the intricacies of the T.

"He worked us twice a day, three hours at a time at first," Gallarneau says. "We were so tired at the end of the day we couldn't move but Shaughnessy had skull sessions at night."

Shaughnessy, working with backs who had never tried the fakes and maneuvers necessary to successful operation of the T, rehearsed his backfield endlessly, with the rest of the team watching, until none of the spectators could tell who had the ball after the fakes were finished.

And the Stanford team, which had not won a game the year before, went undefeated through the Rose Bowl.

Meanwhile, the Bears had won the Western Division championship. They faced the Washington Redskins, a team which had defeated them, 7-3, during the regular season, in the playoff game. The Redskins seemed to have solved the problem of stopping the T, even with the man-in-motion.

Halas called Shaughnessy back from the coast and Halas, Jones and Shaughnessy began an incredibly meticulous preparation for the championship game.

First, they studied the motion pictures of the previous game with the Redskins to the minutest detail. They discarded any play which had been stopped consistently and con-

This is John McNally, raconteur, bon vivant, halfback and coach. He is better known as Johnny Blood and he was one of the finest players in pro football history. Blood was a slashing runner and a sure-handed receiver.

centrated on plays which had been successful. From the successful plays, they devised new attacks which grew out of the sequences which had gained.

The Bear players, too, spent hours looking at themselves in action. They got an additional fillip of inspiration when news stories before the game reported the Redskins were calling the Bears front runners and cry babies.

Hampton Pool, who played end on that Bear team and was later to coach the Los Angeles Rams, says that the Bears did not do anything drastically different in setting up the ready list of plays for the game.

"The big thing turned out to be the counter series against the flow of the man in motion," Pool recalls. "But we had used the counter before. We found out in studying the pictures that the counter worked especially well against the Redskin defenses, so we put in more counters. Then Shaughnessy outlined three plays to be called the first time we got the ball so that we would know immediately if the Redskins were in the same defenses they had been in three weeks before when we couldn't score a touchdown on them and lost, 7-3."

As it turned out, the Washington defense was unchanged. The first exploratory play by the Bears resulted in an eight-yard gain for halfback George McAfee; the second was the most important play in football history, if you judge it by its subsequent effect on the course of the game.

The first play had clearly established that the system of Redskin coach Ray Flaherty for defending against the man-in-motion T was unchanged. The Redskin linebackers reacted to the direction of the motion; when McAfee started wide to the right, they shifted with him.

On the second play, Ray Nolting, the other Bear halfback, drove straight ahead on a fake into the right side of the Bear line and Sid Luckman feinted a handoff to him. Bill Osmanski, the Chicago fullback, turned to his right without moving his feet to carry out the fake to the left side of the Redskin defense, then turned back and took the handoff from Luckman as he headed outside the Redskin right tackle.

The hole was supposed to open there, but it was clogged and Osmanski, after dipping in toward the hole, bellied wide and outside the end and started down the sideline. The overshifted linebacker was blocked easily and suddenly Osmanski, a powerful and fast fullback, was alone with two members of the Washington secondary coming over to pin him against the sideline.

They were Ed Justice and Jimmy Johnston and Osmanski seemed sure to be stopped near the Redskin thirty-five. But George Wilson, the Bear right end (now coach of the Detroit Lions), had come across from his position and he hit Johnston with a blind side block so powerful that it hurtled the unfortunate Johnston into Justice and knocked both of them out of bounds, clearing the path for Osmanski's touchdown.

The score was 28-0 at the half, 73-0 at the end of the game and, within the next two or three years, football executed a major shift to the T formation, from high school to professional ranks.

Within the next few years, the ubiquitousness of the T formation began to produce the succession of great passers which has contributed to the marvelously accurate aerial offense of modern football. No longer did high school players dream of being great halfbacks; many of them took a leaf from the Sammy Baugh notebook and hung automobile tires from the limbs of trees in their back yard so that they could practice marksmanship.

Baugh, who had come to the Redskins as a single-wing tailback, was converted to a T

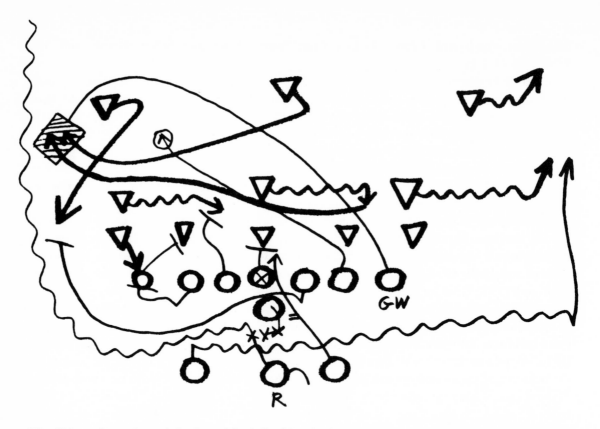

The Chicago Bears changed the face of football with this play, sending a back counter to the flow of movement. Bill Osmanski (R), the fullback, came back against the flow, scored with the help of George Wilson (GW).

quarterback, grumbling the while. Years later, when he had finished his career with a record sixteen years behind him, he admitted that the T formation stretched his career by years.

"For a while, I could have played in a top hat and tails," Baugh said. "The wear and tear on a T quarterback is about half what it is on a tailback. Or less."

In the high schools and junior high schools, youngsters were developing early into passers. Bobby Layne and Doak Walker played together at Highland Park High School in Dallas and together won a state high school championship with the T formation and the forward pass. The Waterfields and Christmans were sharpening their aim and the modern era, stalled briefly by the advent of World War II, was well on its way.

The great Bear team of 1940-41 was broken up by the war; it was, older and slower, to have a brief recrudescence in 1946, when Chicago won the league championship again.

It was in this immediate postwar era that the age of the quarterback really began. In 1945, Waterfield joined the Cleveland Rams and led the club to its first world championship with pin-point passing to a big, slow, but brilliant, end from Arkansas named Jim Benton. Otto Graham began his career in the All-America Conference a year later. One-eyed Tommy Thompson, from Tulsa, had rejoined the Philadelphia Eagles after two years in service.

Frankie Albert, who had been the first of the college T quarterbacks under Shaughnessy at Stanford, was using his left-handed magic for the San Francisco Forty-Niners. By 1948, two more superb products of the rebirth of the T were to join the league, both with the Bears. They were Johnny Lujack from Notre Dame and Bobby Layne from the University of Texas.

Paul Christman, from Missouri, joined the Chicago Cardinals in 1945, was to lead them to a championship in 1947. Norman Van Brocklin was at the University of Oregon and his passing took the Webfoots to the Cotton Bowl on January 1, 1949. Later that year, he joined Waterfield with the Los Angeles Rams.

The year after Christman won the championship for the Cardinals, a rather elderly college graduate from Mississippi named Charlie Conerly began his career with the New York Giants. Angelo Bertelli was with the Los Angeles Dons and so was Glenn Dobbs; George Ratterman was beginning his career with Buffalo.

This spate of great quarterbacks inevitably turned the pro game more and more toward the pass. From 1945 on, the world championship team invariably was led by a great passer. It was Waterfield in 1945; Luckman in 1946; Christman in 1947; Thompson in 1948 and 1949; Otto Graham in 1950; Waterfield and Van Brocklin in 1951; Layne in 1952 and 1953; Graham again in 1954 and 1955; Conerly in 1956; Layne again in 1957; Johnny Unitas in 1958 and 1959; Van Brocklin in 1960; Bart Starr in 1961 and 1962.

As the pass assumed more and more importance, the problem of the defense grew more and more difficult. First the offensive teams began splitting an end — lining him up far to one side or the other so that he would not be bothered by the traffic in the middle of the field in getting away from the line of scrimmage to run his patterns. Plays which began

In uniforms and pose typical of the era, the backfield of the 1933 Green Bay Packers prepares for a game with the New York Giants. They are, left to right, Arnie Herber, John Blood, Roger Grove and Clark Hinkle.

as a run, with line blocking suggesting a run, suddenly developed into a pass. Pass plays, too, suddenly developed into a run when the fullback, ostensibly back to block for the the quarterback, was slipped the ball and charged by the onrushing defensive linemen for significant gains.

The running back became less important and eventually one was taken from his position behind the line and moved to a spot far outside the end, as a flanker. Clark Shaughnessy, by now coach of the Los Angeles Rams, devised a diabolical variation of the old tackle-eligible play which flourished for two years until a frustrated George Preston Marshall, who had seen his Washington Redskins demolished by the play several times, had it declared illegal.

As the offense proliferated, the defense struggled desperately to adjust. Greasy Neale, coaching the Philadelphia Eagles, devised an intelligent, simple answer to the spread-end offense. He combed the boondocks for three massive men to protect the center of his line and found them. He found two big, strong and aggressive men to play corner linebacker and assigned them the task of preventing the opponents' ends from getting off the line of scrimmage, eliminating two receivers immediately.

He won championships with the Eagle defense in 1948 and 1949. By 1950, the inventive masters of the attack had devised a way to negate Greasy's ingenious defense. Actually, the beginning of the end for the Eagle defense came in 1949, when the Washington Redskins tried to borrow Neale's defense for a game against the Rams.

The Redskins imported an Eagle defensive specialist to inculcate the defense in the Redskin team; the Rams found out about it.

The Eagle defense, given the three big men in the middle to cut off any running threats, worked even against an offense with an end spread to one side and a back to the other. The two corner linebackers denied these widespread receivers any route over the center, so that the Philadelphia team did not have to worry about quick passes over the middle, which seemed the obvious riposte to this defense with no middle linebacker to protect against the short pass.

The defense overshifted toward the strong side — the side where there was an offensive end in close and a halfback flanked wide. That meant that a back moved up close to the line of scrimmage to cover the flanked halfback, while the corner linebacker played head-on the end on that side. The other linebacker played head-on the spread end. The halfback on that side moved over away from his linebacker to occupy the gap created when the halfback on the other side moved up to cover the flanked back.

The Rams, having suffered from the slings and arrows of this outrageous defense for two years, devised a simple way to beat the rotation of the defenders.

First, they kept both of their offensive ends in tight, so that the two linebackers, who played directly opposite them, were in tight, too. Second, they took a page from history and sent a back in motion, say to the right. This forced the secondary to revolve; that is, the defensive halfback on the side toward which the back was moving came up and out toward the back in action. The safety man on that side moved over to cover behind the defensive halfback. The other safety moved over to cover the gap left by the safety covering for the halfback. The halfback on the other side covered the gap left by the safety moving over.

Now the entire structure of the defense had rotated toward the side of the field where the Ram halfback headed when he went in motion. Remember, both linebackers were held in by the two ends playing close to their tackles. The secondary was overshifted to their left.

Had the Rams passed from this situation, the defensive coverage would have been

Prototype of all fullbacks was Bronko Nagurski, whose battering running animated the attack of the Chicago Bears. Equipped with tremendous power as a runner, Nagurski was a better than adequate passer as well.

more than adequate. But the Rams elected to run to the suddenly weakened right side of the defense. The halfback on that side had shifted over to his left to cover the gap left by the rotation; the linebacker was in close playing head-on the Ram end.

Now the ball is snapped. The Ram right halfback slants to his left, away from the direction of the left halfback, who has gone in motion to his right. The quarterback fakes a handoff to him and the linebacker on that side, who has held up the end so that he cannot get out to catch a pass, now reacts to the threat of a run to his inside, moving in, away from the flank.

But the quarterback only fakes a handoff. The Ram fullback has hesitated a moment, waiting for the linebacker to react to this fake, then started wide to his left. He is circling the flank of the defense earlier deserted by the halfback moving over to cover for the safety; the

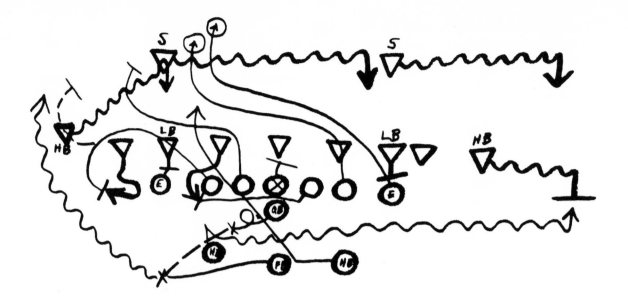

This Ram reverse did much to end the Philadelphia defense. The Eagle secondary (wavy lines) rotated to cover the Ram back in motion; a quick pitchout to the Ram fullback going the other way found a paucity of Eagles.

linebacker on this side has moved in, too, taking the fake; only the end is left.

The end's first movement on seeing the fake to his inside, is to close to his inside; when he does so, he leaves himself open to be hooked in to the middle by a guard pulling out of the line to lead the play.

Now the quarterback, after his fake, pitches wide to the fullback. The linebacker is too far to the inside to react, the end is hooked in, the halfback and the safety have revolved to the other side of the field to cover the threat of the pass. No one can stop the run.

No one did. The Rams, using a trio of the fastest backs in football, blew the Redskins out of the stadium with this play and stopped the Eagle defense from revolving. The defense still worked, however, without the rotation.

A year later, Paul Brown finished it for good.

The keystone of the Eagle defense against the run was the middle guard in a five man line. The middle guard was just what the name implies — a man in the middle, playing directly over the offensive center. With no middle linebacker to back him up, his was the sole responsibility for stopping any running play over center.

Obviously, this was a tremendous responsibility, demanding tremendous men. The middle guards were, in fact, tremendous men. Ed Neal of the Green Bay Packers weighed 324 pounds, broke empty beer bottles over his forearm to dispose of them. The Detroit Lions' Les Bingaman was about the same size and flipped the top off his beer bottles with his thumbnail.

After a while, coaches began to concede that it was well-nigh impossible to run up the middle and expect either to gain yardage or get your halfbacks back in operating condition. On each side of the middle guard, helping him seal off the belly of the defense, was a large, mean tackle. The three men in the middle of the defense constituted what was, for all practical purposes, an immovable object.

In the first league game of the 1950 season, the Eagles, twice champions of the National Football League, met the Cleveland Browns, four times champions of the All-America Football Conference. Most of the experts expected the Eagles to murder the upstart Browns. The Eagles also expected to murder the Browns.

They did not reckon with Paul Brown, one of the most inventive of pro football coaches. He had analyzed the problem of the impregnable middle and come up with what proved to be a perfect answer.

As long as you allow the three behemoths in the middle of the defensive line to operate as a unit, Brown reasoned, there is no way to penetrate them. But, if you can isolate any one of them, he can be handled.

Brown proceeded to isolate the middle guard, who was, by nature, more immobile than either tackles and hence more incapable of covering his flanks if they could be exposed, since he lacked lateral agility.

How to isolate the middle guard? Brown found a simple answer. The Eagle defensive linemen took station on the offensive player in front of them. Usually the middle guard played head-on the center, the tackles head-on the guards or in the hole between guard and tackle or head-on the tackle.

As the game got under way, the Cleveland offensive linemen took their normal stances. With each succeeding offensive play, however, they split wider and wider apart, almost imperceptibly.

As the game grew older, the wider splits began to tell. The Eagle tackles, stationing themselves by the position of the Cleveland offensive lineman, were led farther and farther from the middle guard. As the middle guard lost coverage for his flanks, he became vulnerable.

Then the Browns, given clean blocking angles on the middle guard, began doubling their blocking assignments on him, trapping one or the other of the Eagle tackles and run-

Cecil Isbell, the Green Bay quarterback more famous for his passes to Don Hutson than for his running, was nevertheless a good ball carrier. Here he gains eight yards against the Bears in upset 16-14 victory in 1941.

ning up the middle of the fearsome Eagle line as if it were made of tissue paper. Since pro football is so thoroughly scouted that today's innovation is tomorrow's play for every club in the league, the Paul Brown riposte to the Eagle defense was common property within weeks. Combined with the Ram stratagem which denied the Eagles the rotation of their secondary defense, the Brown line splits wrote the end of the Eagle defense.

The natural progression, since the middle guard had been rendered useless, was the abolition of the middle guard. It was now that the present four-three defense was born; the middle guard, thinner, faster and oriented to pass defense, was taken out of the line and became a middle linebacker. This relieved the pressure on the corner linebackers to prevent receivers breaking in over the middle of the line. The middle linebacker now took responsibility for any end or back in the short passing area over the center.

On October 30, 1949, against the Chicago Bears in the Los Angeles Coliseum, the Rams had introduced the three-end offense, which was also to contribute to the end of the Eagle defense. The Rams that year had acquired Elroy Hirsch, one of the finest of halfbacks. They had on hand two superb receivers in Tom Fears and Bob Shaw. Hirsch had suffered a severe head injury while playing for the Chicago Rockets and Shaughnessy, the coach of the Rams, wanted to get him away from the mob in the middle of the line, as well as to use his exceptional pass receiving ability to its fullest extent.

Here is the T formation as it was in the beginning. This is the 1941 Chicago Bears. Note how close together the offensive linemen played then. The modern T spreads an end and flanks a halfback and splits the linemen.

Since he wanted to retain the pass-catching talents of the two ends — Shaw and Fears — Shaughnessy simply moved Hirsch from the customary position of a halfback to a post far out on the flank of the Ram attack. With Fears spread far to one side, Hirsch far to the other and Shaw in close, the Rams in effect were using three ends. With Bob Waterfield and Norman Van Brocklin passing, they beat the Bears on that Sunday, 27-24, and the modern pro attack was born.

This three-end version of the T, with variations, has dominated the game since then. On occasion, some teams split both ends and put a halfback in the slot between one of the ends and the tackle, but this is still essentially the three-end attack, with the slot back taking the place of the tight end. Red Hickey, of the San Francisco Forty-Niners, experimented with the shotgun attack briefly. This formation leaves the quarterback alone some five yards behind the center with the other three backs and the two ends deployed on or near the line of scrimmage to give the passer five quick targets.

With the offense more or less stabilized in the three-end formation and the defense basically a four-three-four, the more recent innovations have been in the areas of nomenclature, tactics and strategy. Shaughnessy, who has had so much to do with the development of the attack, revised the Chicago Bear defenses a few years ago when he took over that department for George Halas.

This is one of pro football's most effective batteries: Don Hutson (left) and Cecil Isbell. Hutson is regarded as the best receiver of all time; Isbell was a superb passer who could throw long, short, soft or hard.

"One of the important things on offense or defense is nomenclature," Shaughnessy said, not long after taking charge of the Bear defense. "It is not hard to devise an offense which has two or three thousand plays. But if the quarterback does not have a signal system which allows him to name the assignment of each player on each play in a minimum of words, you'll never be able to call the play fast enough to miss a delay-of-game penalty. That's true on defense, too. What you do has to be done quickly."

Shaughnessy's signal system was a mathematical shorthand, numbering backs and holes in the line and giving special names, such as Ed, Tess, or Bluff, to blocking assignments in the line. He named defensive positions, too; the middle linebacker, for instance, became Mike. Pass patterns were descriptive — X, Y, Z in, Z out.

Since the modern defensive line's primary responsibility is to rush the passer, Shaughnessy discarded the old and inaccurate names of end and tackle for them.

"We changed the name of the front four men to 'rush men'," Shaughnessy said. "That indicates clearly to them what they must do. Now, you must be able to designate the other defenders and their assignments in a word or two in calling defensive signals."

Shaughnessy devised a football shorthand for the other defensive positions on the Bear

One of the three or four finest teams in the history of professional football was the 1942 Chicago Bears, just before the draft decimated the Bear personnel. They are: top line, left to right, Lotshaw (trainer), Artoe, Hempel, Famiglietti, Clarkson, Petty, Wilson, Pool, Stydahar, Doller; second line, Luckman, Anderson, Wager, Matuza, Morris, Berry, Turner, Clark, Fortmann, Musso, Halas, Johnsos; third line, Driscoll, Bray, Siegel, Akin, Osmanski, Kolman, Nolting, Drulis, Gallarneau, Brizzolara; bottom line, Fini, Hoptowit, Maznicki, Nowaskey, Geyer, McLean, O'Rourke, Kerasiatis.

team: the right outside linebacker, for instance, is Rob, the left safety is Les, the left half-back is Lou (for left outside) and the right halfback is Rose (for right outside).

Shaughnessy, too, split up the defensive signal-calling. Bill George, the excellent middle linebacker of the Bears, called the over-all defense; a lineman called the appropriate maneuver for the rush men and a back for the secondary defense.

The purpose of this rather complicated defense was, of course, to give the Bears a plus against the attack of the other teams in the league.

"There is no such thing as a good offensive play," Shaughnessy said. "The defense makes it look good. Against the three-end offense, you must attempt to assign a man and a half to cover each of the receivers. If your defense has sufficient knowledge of the habits of the offense, you should have a man and at least a half on the most dangerous receiver. That's the point of the game."

Shaughnessy's ingenuity on defense has been matched by the generals of the attack. Paul Brown first thought of calling all the signals for his team from the sideline and implemented his idea with messenger guards, who shuttled back and forth with plays from the sideline. For a few games, Brown even experimented with headphones in the helmets of quarterbacks so that he could talk to them directly, but this ploy was outlawed by the league.

Tom Landry, the canny young coach of the Dallas Cowboys, went Brown one better by shuttling quarterbacks Eddie LeBaron and Don Meredith in and out of the game. This gave him the advantage of consultation with the out quarterback on every other play and the system worked superbly until LeBaron was injured.

With the defenses spreading more and more to defend against the pass, Green Bay coach Vince Lombardi has returned to the running game with signal success. His "big-back" backfield of Paul Hornung and Jim Taylor has been emulated elsewhere in the league, but he was not the first to realize the value of a coterie of large backs. The forerunner of the modern big-back backfield was the "three-elephant" backfield of the 1950 Rams.

The elephants — Dick Hoerner, Dan Towler and Paul Younger — all weighed 225 pounds and were first used to negate a defense rigged by San Francisco coach Buck Shaw.

The Rams, with the three-end attack supplemented by a racehorse halfback named Vitamin Smith, who was also a good receiver, depended almost entirely upon the forward pass to move the ball. Shaw, realizing this, took out two of his big linebackers and replaced them with small, fast halfbacks to get more coverage on the Ram receivers.

His stratagem worked very well the first time the Forty-Niners played the Rams and the San Francisco team won handily. Unfortunately for Shaw, the two clubs played back-to-back in 1950. In the six days between the first and second game, the Ram coaches devised the elephant backfield and when Shaw sent his two small halfbacks into the game the second time, the massive Ram backs demolished them.

So it goes. Each year the game grows more complex and the demands upon the players and coaches grow more severe. Scouting is an exact science; each quarterback in the league is studied meticulously so that the defense learns his thought patterns and his play preferences even better than the quarterback knows them himself.

It is an endlessly exciting game and a completely fluid one. The players come up from college bigger and smarter each year. They must be, to match the game itself.

Bert Bell was the commissioner of the National Football League during the period of its major growth. He was a blunt, courageous man, fond of the telephone, whose leadership was invaluable to the league.

# THE CLUBS

## THE BALTIMORE COLTS

IN THE short and turbulent history of the Baltimore Colts, only one factor has remained constant since the city got its first pro club in 1947: the unabashed and violent affection for the Colts held by the Baltimore citizenry.

Baltimoreans have been afflicted, at one time or another, with some of the most ridiculous excuses for a professional football team in the history of the game. They have also had some of the finest teams in the modern era, but, to their credit, they loved the ugly ducklings almost as much as the swans.

Twice they were saddled with castoff teams from cities which had refused to support them and twice they welcomed the orphans of the storm and did their best to nurse them to health. Once they failed, through no fault of their own; the second time, they built the spindly, undernourished waif into splendid manhood.

The first edition of the Colts came to Baltimore in 1947, in the second year of the All-America Conference.

Robert Ridgway Rodenberg, who lived in Washington at the time and who had been a newspaperman, a public relations executive and a motion picture producer, conceived the idea of bringing the defunct Miami Seahawks to Baltimore, after discussing the matter with two of his newspaper friends, Vincent X. Flaherty and Shirley Povich.

Flaherty, a Hearst columnist, had been deeply interested in the formation of the All-America Conference and was anxious for it to succeed. Povich, a brilliant, caustic sports columnist in Washington, was later accused of persuading Rodenberg to back a group to bring AAC football to Baltimore purely out of spite toward George Preston Marshall, the owner of the Washington Redskins. The accuser, of course, was George Preston Marshall.

Whatever his reason, Rodenberg got the Seahawk franchise for Baltimore. He was a wonderful owner who threw post-game parties with equal verve after defeats or victories. This was fortunate for his guests since the Colts lost eleven, won two and tied one game in 1947.

Despite this record, nearly 200,000 fans watched the Colts play at home. Rodenberg, listening to the estimates of a general manager who proved to be more of an optimist than a mathematician, thought for a while he was making money. Then he suspected he was only going to break even. At season's end, he discovered that the Colts had lost $165,000.

All of it was not Rodenberg's loss — he had seven partners. Rodenberg might have been willing to try for another year, but his partners had had enough and the Colts, who were to change owners with the celerity with which most clubs change coaches, had a new set for 1948.

The group which took over grew out of a "Save the Colts Committee" set up by the

Probably the smallest and certainly one of the best of all pro football players was Buddy Young, who is shown here with the Baltimore Colts near the end of his career chasing a fumble very probably not his.

Baltimore mayor, Thomas D'Alesandro, Jr. The new president was R. C. Embry, owner of radio station WITH. On the board of directors were some of the top business men in the area.

Cecil Isbell, the old Green Bay quarterback, had coached the Colts in 1947. The new group wisely kept him. Isbell's most crying need in 1947 had been an adequate quarterback. He was given one by, of all people, Paul Brown, and he came within a few hours of signing another who might have ended the depression for the Colts. The Brown gift was Yelberton Abraham Tittle; the quarterback who got away was Bobby Layne.

A few years later, when he was with the old Dallas Texans as an assistant to Jim Phelan, Isbell recalled his effort to sign Layne.

"We offered him a hell of a deal," Isbell said. "We needed a quarterback in the worst way. I went down to Texas personally to talk to Bobby and I thought I had all the ammunition I needed to get him. I had ten brand new thousand dollar bills in my pocket and I spread them out on the bed in my hotel room for him to look at. That was going to be his bonus for signing. Then I offered him an escalator contract for three years, no cut, no trade. First year, $20,000, second, $22,500 and third $25,000. When he walked out of the room, I thought I had him."

Unfortunately for Isbell, Layne decided to discuss the matter with George Halas of the Chicago Bears, who had draft rights to him in the National Football League. Halas, a master salesman when it comes to landing football talent, must have outdone himself. Although the Bears already had Sid Luckman and Johnny Lujack at quarterback and did not match the Colt offer, Layne decided to go to Chicago.

The loss did not seem important immediately. Tittle, one of the great competitors in the game, led the Colts to a 7-7 record and a tie with Buffalo for the division championship, earning rookie-of-the-year honors.

Before the divisional playoff with Buffalo, a group of Colt players threatened to strike unless they were given a percentage of the gate as well as the customary game salary for the game. But the Colt management threatened to forfeit to Buffalo and play no game at all rather than accede to the players' demands, so the game was played.

The Colts had whipped the Bills easily enough in the last game of the regular season. They might have done so again, except for a questionable call late in the game. Chet Mutryn, a Bill receiver, appeared to have gained clear control of a pass when he was hit hard and fumbled, the Colts recovering. But the official ruled it an incomplete pass, the Bills went on to score and the Colts lost, precipitating a riot which had to be quelled by the Baltimore police.

Home attendance climbed to 224,502 and the financial loss dropped to $47,036.36. The future looked promising, but the club had to fight off an attempt by the AAC to jettison Baltimore as a condition for peace with the NFL as 1949 began. The Colts, although never directly approached with a proposal to cease operation, presented a strong front at the AAC league meeting. The league could not, in the face of antitrust laws, force the franchise out of business, and the bitter and costly battle between the leagues dragged on through 1949.

It was not a happy year for Baltimore. The club lost its first four games in a row, sending Isbell on his way. Walter Driskill, who had been general manager, replaced Isbell. Driskill managed to win one game and the season ended with a 1-11 record and a loss of nearly $100,000.

The owners initiated another "Save the Colts" campaign. Then peace was suddenly declared by the AAC and the NFL.

Baltimore was one of three AAC teams to survive, but the NFL wanted assurance that the club would have enough money to operate. Into the breach stepped one of the least qualified owners ever to enter pro football, a tall, enthusiastic, uninformed man named Abraham (Shorty) Watner, who had made a fortune operating a cemetery, a trucking company and a Wisconsin railroad.

Watner had made two or three abortive attempts to get into the NFL. Once, while talking to George Preston Marshall on the telephone, a vagrant breeze had swept some $10,000 in bills off his desk and out the window, to the vast satisfaction of passersby in the street below. He found, very quickly, that it was even more expensive to talk to Marshall in person.

The Colts had to agree to pay the Redskins $150,000 for invading Washington territory, the whopping levy to be paid in three $50,000 installments, the first due at once.

Marshall, divining that the Baltimore club was not long for the football world, offered Watner a $25,000 discount for cash on the balance of $100,000 but Watner, making one of the few wise decisions of his career as an owner, declined.

Clem Crowe, who had coached Buffalo the year before, was hired as head coach. His was a difficult job since the Colts, the thirteenth team in the league, were to play a

The perfectly balanced running style of Lennie Moore shows clearly here as the great Colt runner and receiver sets off on one of the weaving, sinuous excursions which make him a most potent attack weapon.

swing schedule, pitting them against every team in both divisions.

To add to Crowe's difficulties, Watner scheduled seven exhibition games, plus an intrasquad game. The Colts were exhausted when league play began. The only pre-season game they won was the intrasquad game. The most shocking walloping the club took was in Alamo Stadium, in San Antonio, Tex., when the Los Angeles Rams, at the time a great scoring machine, leveled them, 70-21.

"The only difference between the teams," Watner said later, "was four or five long touchdown passes."

When the Colts went to Los Angeles for a league game later, Crowe swore that the Rams would not humiliate his team again.

"They caught us on an off night," he said. "It will be a different story now."

It was only slightly different. The Rams beat the Colts, 70-27.

By mid-season, when the Colts finally won a game from the Green Bay Packers, the club had put together an eighteen-game losing streak, spanning the 1949 and 1950 seasons, and even the forgiving Baltimore fans were beginning to shun them. By season's end, it had become obvious that the franchise was in deep trouble. When Watner went to the league meeting in January, 1951, no one was quite sure whether the club would survive, or, if it did, whether it would survive under the same management.

Watner settled things by throwing in the towel on January 18, 1951, after the other clubs had refused his plea for player help. The towel he threw in was only partly his; most of it was owned by 202 shareholders, who later filed suit to have the franchise reactivated.

The league voted to pay Watner $50,000 for the twenty-five players remaining on the Colt roster. It was, considering the talent, a rather generous gesture.

Baltimore had no team in 1951. Early in 1952 it appeared Ted Collins' New York Yankees might be sold to Baltimore interests, but Collins sold the club instead to a Dallas group headed by Giles and Connell Miller, young sons of the owner of the Texas Textile Mills.

The Miller brothers outfitted their new team, called the Dallas Texans, in cowboy hats and fancy shirts and predicted a bright future.

They proved to be as inept as Watner in the operation of a team. Dallas fans were indifferent. The crowds, small from the start, dwindled to a handful by mid-season. The club folded before the end of the season and the franchise was taken over by the league, which made the Texans a road club based in Hershey, Pa.

Bert Bell, the commissioner, facing a suit by Baltimore stockholders for reinstatement of the franchise in that city, turned the club over to Baltimore in 1953.

This, of course, was as threadbare a team as the 1947 club Baltimore inherited from Miami. The Texans had won only one game in 1952, a contest with the Chicago Bears played in Akron, Ohio, in almost complete privacy. Moreover, Bell insisted that Baltimore sell 15,000 season tickets before he would grant them the franchise. Baltimore did it, during the Christmas season of 1952.

The season tickets were sold before the club was organized or the ownership agreed upon. Herb Wright, later to become assistant general manager of the club, quit an insurance job in 1952 to help promote ticket sales. The first purchaser asked him to whom his check should be made out and Wright had to answer honestly, "I don't know."

By the time the campaign ended, $300,000 was in the bank, awaiting an owner. Bell produced a good one: Carroll Rosenbloom, who had played in the backfield for Bert at the University of Pennsylvania in 1927.

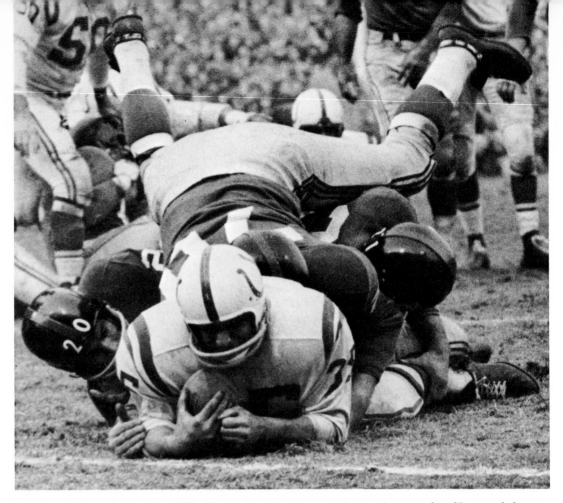

The three Giants pinning Alan (The Horse) Ameche represent the usual quota of tacklers needed to stop the powerful Baltimore fullback. Ameche was a superb blocker, as well as expert at pass protection.

Rosenbloom, an enormously successful business man, was not particularly interested in buying a pro football franchise. Only after repeated visits from Bell did he decide, reluctantly, to back the club.

Bell applied the coup de grace with a typical stratagem: he called Rosenbloom one night and said, "Carroll, you're the new owner. I just announced it." Confronted with a fait accompli, Rosenbloom went along.

At Bell's suggestion, he employed Don Kellett, a television executive who had been a college football and basketball coach and a star athlete at Pennsylvania, as general manager. Rosenbloom quickly reorganized the ownership, taking 51 percent of the stock for himself and distributing the rest among William F. Hilgenberg, Zanvyl Krieger, Tom Mullan, Sr. and R. Bruce Livie.

At first, Rosenbloom left the operation of the club entirely up to Kellett, who was a graduate of the Wharton School of Business at Penn and an excellent administrator with a good sports background.

This organization had nothing in common with the previous groups which had tried to operate a franchise in Baltimore. Adequately financed and intelligently led, the Colts rapidly developed into one of the most efficient organizations in the league.

The first season, understandably, was no great artistic success. Keith Molesworth was the coach, but he had little to work with. The club beat the Bears twice and added one more victory for a 3-9 record, but home crowds averaged a strong 28,000.

Rosenbloom, who had tried to stay aloof from the team, was won over in the first

46

league game, when the Colts upset the Bears. He retained an active role in club affairs from then on. By December of 1953, he and Kellett had decided the club needed a comprehensive scouting system and Molesworth was shifted from head coach to chief talent scout.

Rosenbloom and Kellett first tried to get Blanton Collier of the Browns as the new head coach, but Collier declined. They settled on another Brown assistant — short, stocky Weeb Ewbank.

"How long will it take to produce a championship team in Baltimore?" Rosenbloom asked Ewbank.

"Five years," Weeb said.

"That's too long," Rosenbloom answered.

Ewbank's time table was exact. The 1954 season was another 3-9 year, but the Colts began to move ahead in 1955, when the establishment of the comprehensive scouting system under Molesworth paid off with a draft of brilliant college talent.

Twelve rookies made the 1955 Baltimore team. Among them were some superb players: quarterback George Shaw of Oregon, the Colts' bonus draft choice; fullback Alan (the Horse) Ameche, the No. 1 pick from Wisconsin; a stumpy, quick halfback from Baylor named L. G. (Long Gone) Dupre; tackles Jack Patera of Oregon and George Preas of VPI, and a big center from Notre Dame named Dick Szymanski. All became regulars.

Only a few of the players acquired with the Texan franchise were left. The most effective of them were end Gino Marchetti, big Art Donovan and small but wonderful Buddy Young. All were of top-drawer caliber.

The improvement of the team was obvious; the season record was 5-6-1 and the Colts rose to a heady fourth place in the West.

Four more important additions were made in 1956, when Ewbank almost lost his job. Big Daddy Lipscomb was picked up on waivers from the Los Angeles Rams; Lenny Moore was a first draft choice; Billy Vessels, who had been a first draft choice in 1953 but elected to play in Canada, finally joined the club and a lanky, bony-faced young man who had had a tryout with the Pittsburgh Steelers, responded to an eighty-cent phone call from Don Kellett and understudied George Shaw at quarterback. He was John Constantine Unitas.

Big Jim Mutscheller, being dragged down here after taking a pass, helped animate both the ground and the air attack of the Colts. A sure short receiver, his forte was his blocking as the Baltimore tight end.

Despite this influx of talent, the Colts had an erratic season. Shaw suffered a severe leg injury against the Chicago Bears and Unitas, tossed suddenly into the front lines, made an inauspicious debut. His first pass was intercepted and he mishandled the ball so that Colt fumbles in the second half cost them the game.

By the last game, against the Washington Redskins, newspapers reported that Ewbank's job was as good as lost. Rosenbloom said no decision would be reached until the season was over.

The Colts won that last game, on a long Unitas-to-Jim Mutscheler pass and Ewbank, although still on shaky ground, was returned as coach.

By 1957, most of the personnel which was to carry the Colts to the heights had been assembled. Unitas, taciturn, unshakeable and with a gift for leadership, a remarkable arm and the peripheral vision of an owl, was settled at quarterback. Ameche, a thick-bodied, post-legged fullback who could block ferociously, gave the club a violent threat up the middle. The ends were Raymond Berry, bespectacled, skinny and studious; and Mutscheller, a tough blocker and second only to Berry as a receiver. The incomparable Lenny Moore operated from flanker back; Dupre was the dependable running halfback.

The offensive line had jelled and the defense was showing signs of becoming as potent as the offense. Donovan and Lipscomb were all but immovable in the center of the line. Gino Marchetti had established himself as the best defensive end in football and big Don Joyce was a respectable running mate for him on the other flank. Two rookies — Milt Davis of UCLA and Andy Nelson of Memphis State — joined veterans Carl Taseff and Bert Rechichar in the secondary. Don Shinnick, Jack Patera and Doug Eggers were capable linebackers.

They started fast, winning three straight under the daring guidance of Unitas. Then Taseff was hurt and a serious weakness developed in pass defense. This plagued the club the rest of the season. Still, the Colts left for the West Coast and their last two games tied for the lead with the San Francisco Forty-Niners and the Detroit Lions.

They had never been lucky on the coast and this season was no exception. They lost a narrow decision to San Francisco, then, out of the race, were whipped soundly by the Rams.

Unitas, however, was voted player of the year and the stage was set for a championship. In off-season trades, the club strengthened the linebacking corps by the addition of Leo Sanford from the Chicago Cardinals, and landed a third massive tackle, Ray Krouse, to help Lipscomb and Donovan. Three rookies made the 1958 squad: defensive backs Ray Brown and Johnny Sample and a sprint-fast halfback, Lenny Lyles.

This team won its first six games. The sixth victory was a 56-0 rout of the Green Bay Packers in which Unitas suffered fractured ribs and a punctured lung. The Colts lost the seventh game to the New York Giants, 24-21, although Shaw, replacing Unitas, threw three touchdown passes and played well.

The defense took over the next week against the Chicago Bears and the Colts won again, 17-0. The next week, against the Los Angeles Rams, Unitas was back again, wearing a special harness to protect his ribs. He celebrated his return by completing a 58-yard pass to Moore for a touchdown on the first play from scrimmage and the Colts went on to a 34-7 victory.

By the end of the tenth game, and before they had to make their trip to the jinxed West, the Colts had clinched the division championship.

They lost the two games on the coast, but it made no difference. Then they had a

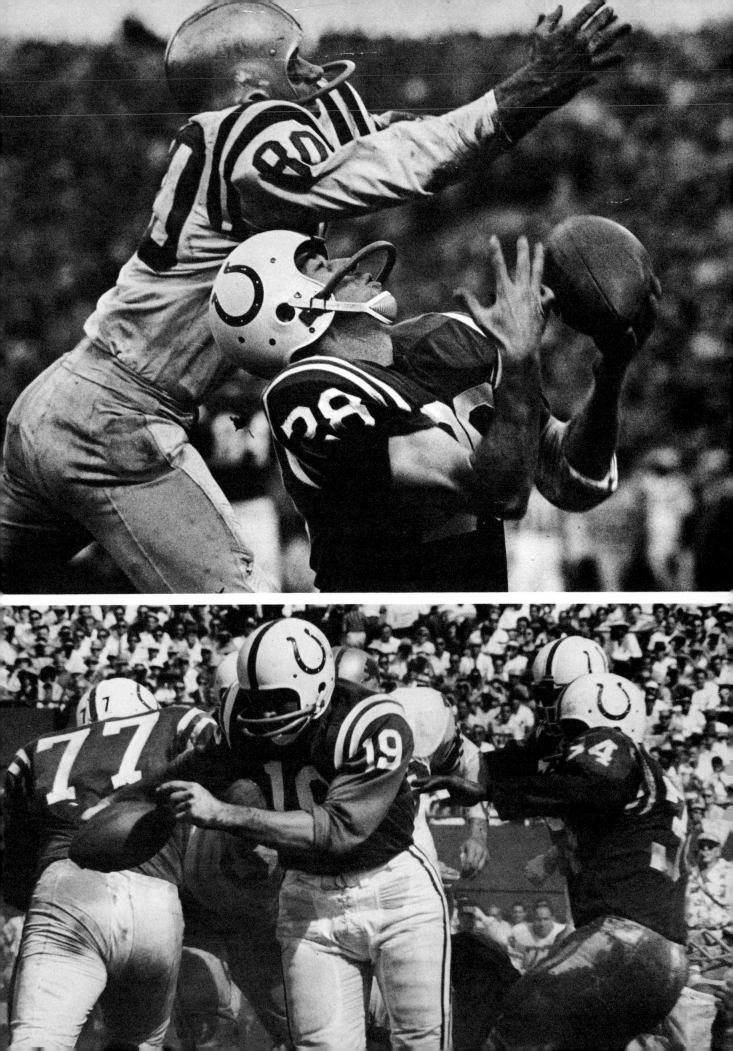

wait while New York and Cleveland played off a tie for the championship of the East, New York winning.

On Sunday, December 28, on a cold, overcast and blustery day in Yankee Stadium, they played the Giants for the championship. It was to be the most exciting and the best football game ever played and the first sudden death game in football history.

Unitas was well by now. Shaw had been the quarterback when the Giants had beaten the Colts during the season and had done well, but he was no Unitas.

In his pre-game talk to his team, Ewbank, a second choice himself as head coach, pointed out that fourteen of the players gathered around him had been rejected by other clubs before joining the Colts. The speech was a matter-of-fact one; its impact was tremendous.

The Colts, under the nerveless, precise Unitas, left the field at the half leading, 14-3. Early in the third quarter, they marched to the Giant one; had they scored on this drive, the game might well have been broken open. But the Giant line, one of the best, stopped four Colt tries and reversed the momentum of the game.

In one quick strike from their own thirteen, the Giants, who had looked beaten, moved to the Baltimore one. It was a long pass from Charlie Conerly to Kyle Rote, who had gone down the sideline, cut to the middle and caught the ball on the Colt forty-five. He carried it down to the twenty-five before he was hit and fumbled.

Alex Webster, the hustling Giant halfback, had trailed the play and picked up the ball, going on to the Colt one before he was stopped. The Giants scored and it was 14-10, with the Giants suddenly the dominant team.

Indeed, they were dominant for almost all of the rest of the game. They led, 17-14,

Having knocked down his blocker (lower left) Gino Marchetti (89), the Colts' perennial all-pro defensive end and captain, prepares to pounce on luckless John Brodie, quarterback for the San Francisco Forty-Niners.

when the Colts got the ball on their own fourteen with less than two minutes to play.

The Giants, worried about a long pass to Moore, conceded the Colts the short pass and Unitas made good use of the concession. Three times he threw to Berry, the lanky end with the most intelligent moves and the best hands in football. Three times Berry made beautiful catches, adding yardage with stubborn running. With only seven seconds to play, Steve Myhra sliced a 20-yard place-kick which curved through the goal posts and put the game into an overtime period.

The Giants won the toss and received and the Colts stopped them. Taseff took Chandler's long punt and the ball went over to the Colts on the Colt twenty-one. Time was no longer of the essence; the Colts had the rest of the cold night to score, if they needed it.

Unitas' first call was a sweep, with Dupre carrying, and the little halfback struggled to the thirty-one for a first down. Now Unitas coolly tried a gamble; he threw long to Lennie Moore down the sideline and Lindon Crow, covering Moore alone, barely tipped the ball away.

Knowing that the Giant middle linebacker, Sam Huff, was keying on fullback Alan Ameche, Unitas next called a draw play for Dupre, luring Huff away from the middle by faking Ameche wide. The play was good only for short yardage.

A flare pass to Ameche in the left flat was good when a Giant linebacker overlooked Ameche in covering Berry and the Colts had another first down on their own forty.

Unitas, always one to stick with success, went back to his first-down call which had begun the series and sent Dupre wide to the right and again the play succeeded, although not far enough for a first down.

This diving catch under strong pressure from a defender would be an impossible play for most ends. For Raymond Berry, probably the best informed and most skilled of all pro ends, it is an almost routine maneuver.

One of the most durable of all running backs is Joe (The Jet) Perry, the very fast, very strong fullback who played most of his 15 years as a pro with the San Francisco Forty-Niners before being traded to the Colts.

Dick Modzelewski, the squarely built Giant tackle, skidded off a block, barreled in to drop Unitas for an eight-yard loss on the next play, and Unitas made a mental note that Moe was blowing in very quickly. He capitalized on that later.

Unitas' next play was one of the keys in the drive. He brought the Colts out in a formation they had not used before, with Moore a slot back to the right and both ends spread. The play was meant to be a pass to Moore, but he was covered and Unitas looked for Berry. Unitas swung to his left, saw the halfback covering Berry slip, and waved to Raymond to go on down field, which he did. Then Unitas calmly completed the pass for the first down and the drive was still alive.

Two things prompted Unitas' next call. First, Modzelewski had been crossing the line aggressively and Unitas felt he could be trapped. Second, Huff, who had been keying on Ameche, dropped back off the line and to his left, obviously looking for a pass.

So Unitas called a draw to Ameche, a play which starts as a pass and suddenly becomes a thrust up the center. Art Spinney, the Colts' fine guard, dropped Modzelewski with a good trap block, tackle George Preas cut off Huff and Ameche shot through the gap for twenty-three yards to the Giant twenty-one yard line.

With first down again, Johnny went back to the Dupre sweep, but the Giants had recognized the pattern and stopped the play for no gain. But a quick slant pass to the ubiquitous Berry put the ball on the Giant nine-yard line, first and goal to go.

Ameche burrowed into the line for a yard, being careful to stay in the middle of the field so that a field goal could be kicked easily. Then Unitas came up with a daring, effective call.

The Giant team was bunched, expecting another routine smash at the center, preparatory for the field goal which could win the game just as surely as a touchdown. Noticing this, Unitas sent Mutscheller slanting wide to the sideline, tossed him a lofted pass over the head of linebacker Cliff Livingston and might have had his touchdown then except that he kept the ball too close to the sideline to insure against an interception. But the play carried to the one and then Ameche scored and the game was over.

Thirty thousand people greeted the Colts at the Baltimore airport. In their enthusiasm, they stove in the top of a police car and scrambled all over the buses which were to take the team into town. No one blamed them. They had waited a long time for glory.

The 1959 Colts won again and beat the Giants, 31-16, in Baltimore. They were a curious club; they seemed to play with an almost contemptuous languor until it became necessary for them to bear down. Then they would bear down viciously and successfully.

By 1960, though, some of the edge was gone. The superb defensive unit was growing slower with age. Unitas suffered a fractured vertebra high in his back early in the season and, while he could throw well enough, he was forbidden to run, so opposing teams could commit themselves more completely to rushing him. Ameche was benched, presumably for lackadaisical play. Then Unitas' three top receivers were injured — Berry, Moore and Mutscheller. It added up to a 6-6 season and a fourth-place finish.

The 1961 team rose to 8-6 and a tie for third. In 1962, they finished fourth, and at the end of the season, Rosenbloom replaced Ewbank with an old Colt hero — Don Shula, who had been an outstanding defensive halfback for the club. Shula had been instrumental in the building of the almost impregnable defense of the 1962 Detroit Lions.

Unitas once said, "The difference between a great passer and just a passer is about a second — the second it takes to get a pass off when you want to and not hurry it."

At the dawn of a new year, Baltimore fans hoped there would be a synchronizing of watches all around.

53

Busily engaged in trying to indicate to his quarterback that a kick is in order, George Halas, owner and coach of the Chicago Bears, demonstrates he is still as active and enthusiastic as when he started in 1920.

# THE CHICAGO BEARS

THE story of the Chicago Bears is the story of George Stanley Halas, an enormously enthusiastic, sometimes violent and always dedicated man. Halas may not have invented professional football but he contributed as much to its development since the formation of the National Football League as any single player, coach or owner in history — or more.

Legend has it that Halas grew interested in pro football when Bob Zuppke, the coach at his alma mater, Illinois, surveyed his graduating 1917 football team and said, ruefully, "Why do I always lose my football players just when they have learned to play the game?"

Halas had to wait two years to get into pro football. In 1918, he played with the Great Lakes Naval Training Station team which won a Rose Bowl game from Mare Island. Then, in 1919, after a brief fling at baseball, Halas played a few games with a pro team in Hammond, Ind.

In 1920, he was employed as the athletic director, among other things, of the A. E. Staley Starch Co. in Decatur, Ill. Although he played on the Staley baseball team in the summer of 1920, he devoted most of his time to scouting talent for the Decatur Staleys football team, which was formed just in time to join the newly-organized American Professional Football Association.

The 1920 Halas was tall and raw-boned, a better than average end, and a persuasive recruiter. The players he persuaded to come to Decatur to represent the starch works lost only one game that season. Halas' offer to the players was a job with the company and a share of the team profits, if any, at the end of the year. The profits turned out to be some $1900 per player. Among the players who pocketed the money was Charley Dressen, for many years a major league baseball manager and now coach of the Los Angles Dodgers.

A business recession cut into starch profits between the 1920 and 1921 seasons and A. E. Staley, the football buff who owned the company, reluctantly told Halas that he would have to forego a company football team in 1921. However, he did give George $5000 toward the 1921 season, with the proviso that the team, which Halas moved to Chicago, would retain the name "Staleys" that year.

Halas, finding that he lacked both the money and the time to operate the team as a one-man band, brought in one of his halfbacks, Ed Sternaman, as a partner. The two men worked out a deal with William Veeck, the owner of the Chicago Cubs, to play at Wrigley Field for a rental of 15 percent of the gross gate of each game. In 1922, George, a rabid Cub baseball fan, logically enough changed the name of the Staleys to the Bears. He also suggested that the league be called the National Football League. It was to be twenty-odd years before the Bears acquired the nickname "Monsters of the Midway" but the 1922

Bear club might easily have deserved it.

One school of thought has it that professional football teams clearly reflect the personality of the coach. The personality of the Bears as a club has been remarkably consistent over the years. The 1922 Bears, in their approach to a game and conduct during it, certainly resembled the later editions of the club.

At center was a big, black-haired, talkative Irishman named George Trafton, who had played briefly at Notre Dame before succumbing to Halas' blandishments in 1920.

Trafton's playing career with the Bears spanned thirteen years; he probably still holds the club record for conversation and for on-field violence. Typical of the era, the Bears, and of Trafton, the prototype of Bear football players since, was an incident in one of the early Bear-Chicago Cardinal games.

The Cardinals were using a young, enthusiastic rookie center from the West Coast; Trafton, in the old seven-diamond defense, was playing him head-on.

"Every play, he'd whack me on the head with his forearm," Trafton said, many years later. "Finally, I got tired of it. 'What do you call that?' I asked him. He laughed at me. 'That's a Southern California arm block,' he said, showing no respect. 'Don't you like it?' "

"I told him no," Trafton went on, doubtlessly editing his reply considerably.

On the next play, Trafton arranged for his guards, on the snap of the ball by the Cardinal center, to step on the big youngster's toes, pinning him in place. Trafton, thoughtfully backing away from the line of scrimmage a couple of yards so that he could get a running start, then carefully ran up the center from foot to head, leaving him badly in need of repair.

When he came to, he asked George groggily, "What was that?"

"That," said Trafton, cheerfully, "was a Notre Dame drop-kick. Don't you like it?"

It was Trafton, too, who devised a classically simple way to dispose of a guard who had been holding him inconspicuously and effectively on every play.

After Trafton had warned the player several times, he acted. On the next play, concealed by a pileup, George punched the guard smartly in the teeth, which was possible in those days before the universal use of face masks.

After the pileup had been untangled, George lumbered over to an official, holding his jaw, and said, "Watch that guy. He's punched me on the last two plays."

On the next play, the guard did indeed retaliate by punching George, with the official as an alert and interested watcher, and left the game forthwith. A small plus was, of course, a fifteen-yard penalty against the Bears' opponents.

Twice in his career Trafton played reluctant hare to the fans of the Rock Island team, who conceived an intense dislike for George in the course of an afternoon during which he incapacitated four Rock Island players. After that game, Trafton barely outfooted the fans to a taxi, into which he crawled thankfully, only to crawl out again on the other side when a barrage of rocks shattered the windows. Luckily, a passerby in a Mercer gave him a ride into town.

The next time the Bears played in Rock Island, George Halas capitalized on Trafton's speed born of terror. Halas had collected, in cash as usual, the Bears' share of the gate, about $7000.

As the game ended, he handed the sack with the money to Trafton and slapped him on the back.

"I'll meet you at the hotel," he hollered as Trafton, with the usual crowd at his heels, pounded away into the dusk.

56

Red Grange (partially obscured by goal post at right) starts a touchdown run against the Philadelphia Yellow Jackets during his first season with the Chicago Bears. Grange led pro game into sport limelight.

"I figured he'd be faster than I would," Halas said later. "He was running for his life. I would just have been running for the seven thousand."

But there was, of course, much more to the early Bears than George (the Brute) Trafton. The Sternaman brothers played in the backfield and in the line, besides Halas and Trafton, were players like Tarzan Taylor, a small but very aggressive guard, and Ed Healy, a massive tackle from Dartmouth whom Halas bought from Rock Island for $100.

In 1921, the club lost $71.63, although the overhead, by modern standards, was minuscule. The going rate for players was $75 to $100 per game and the league limit on rosters was sixteen. The following year, Halas and Sternaman managed a small profit — $1,476.92 — and the Bears did not lose money again until 1932, when the depression cut crowds and the club, although it won the league championship, dropped $18,000.

Strangely enough, although the Bears made money each year from 1922 to 1932, they never won a league championship during that period. They were usually close; in 1924, they finished only half a game behind Cleveland and Halas' sorrow was assuaged by a fat $20,000 profit.

In 1925, the advent of Red Grange saved a poor season for the Bears and turned a tidy profit for Halas, Grange and C. C. Pyle, Grange's manager. But Grange jumped to Pyle's outlaw league the following year, then played with the New York Yankees in the National Football League in 1927. It was during that season, in a game against the Bears, that Grange sustained a knee injury which was to keep him out of football entirely during 1928 and end forever the beautiful change of direction which made him so rare as a running back. His cleats caught just as he was hit by Trafton and his knee was irremediably damaged.

"I was just another halfback after that," Grange said some time ago, but this, of course, is not true. He lacked the maneuverability of the old Grange, but he served the Bears brilliantly as a pass receiver and as a defensive back for many years.

It took more than an injured Grange to help the Bears in 1929, when they managed only four victories in fourteen games and finished ninth in a twelve team league. In 1930, as a consequence, Halas and Sternaman fired themselves as coaches and hired Ralph Jones from Lake Forest Academy in Lake Forest, Ill. The tiny, bald-headed Jones had coached both Halas and Sternaman as an assistant under Zuppke at Illinois. He was an inventive, imaginative man who, with Halas and Clark Shaughnessy, was to have a major role in the refurbishing of the T.

In 1929, as a sort of afterthought to signing a quarterback named Walt Holmer from Northwestern, Halas had acquired a far more valuable property in end Luke Johnsos, who is still with the Bears as an assistant coach and who played superbly for the team for many years. The acquisition of Johnsos, although Halas did not realize it at the time, marked the beginning of an accumulation of talent which was, within the next five years, to produce the first, and what some old fans still consider the best, of the great Bear teams.

Jones, in his first season as head coach, had a rookie fullback from Minnesota named Bronko Nagurski and a rookie quarterback named Carl Brumbaugh who became the model for the T quarterbacks to follow.

Late in 1930, when the college season ended, Halas repeated the ploy by which he had signed Red Grange in 1925 and signed Notre Dame's Jumping Joe Savoldi, in a fanfare of publicity second only to Grange's signing. Halas was fined $1000 by league president Joe Carr for violation of the rule installed by the league after the signing of Grange. Although Halas protested that Savoldi had been expelled from school anyway when authorities discovered that he was secretly married, the fine stuck.

Savoldi, incidentally, played only four games with the Bears, all during the 1930 season. He faced difficult competition trying to break into the game at fullback on the same team with Nagurski.

Under the coaching of Jones and with the help of Nagurski, Brumbaugh, Johnsos and, briefly, Savoldi, the 1930 Bears improved significantly. They moved up to third in the standings on nine victories, four losses and one tie.

They finished third again in 1931, with an 8-4 record. In 1931, they acquired help in the line and, more important, Keith Molesworth, a small halfback who could punt, pass, return kicks and relieve Brumbaugh at quarterback when necessary. Garland Grange, Red's brother, played end. Late in the year Herb Joesting, another Minnesota fullback, joined the club.

In the 1932 talent race, the Bears added the finishing touches. They acquired from Michigan a superb end named Bill Hewitt who was to earn accolades as one of the finest offensive and defensive players ever. Joe Kopcha, who had played with the club in 1929, returned and became a magnificent guard. Bull Doehring, a sandlot player from Milwaukee, also came up in 1932. He was a competent back, but his principal claim to fame was his ability to throw a ball. He could and did throw a pass from one goal line to the opposite

This scene from the salad days of pro football was typical of the crowds and fields of the middle twenties. The Chicago Bears are playing against the Brooklyn Horsemen at the old Commercial Field in Brooklyn.

Trail of flattened tacklers was trademark of all-time great Bear fullback Bronko Nagurski (in 1933).

ten-yard line and, on one occasion, threw a 50-yard pass behind his back to Bill Karr for a touchdown.

Despite the talent which by now had accrued to the Bears, the 1932 team did not present an overwhelming offense. The team sidled into the championship with a record of seven wins, one loss and six ties, which gave them a percentage edge over Green Bay's 10-3-1, since ties are not counted in the standing.

After the 1932 season, Jones resigned as coach to go back to Lake Forest as athletic director. Deluged with applications for the head-coaching job, Halas decided finally to take it again himself, temporarily. He kept it until he went into the service during World War II.

The year 1932 had been eventful for Halas off, as well as on, the field. The club had lost money and, at the end of the year, Sternaman offered to sell Halas his half of the Bears for $38,000, which George did not possess.

He scraped the money together for a down payment, with other payments to come after six and twelve months, but by the time the last payment had come due, the depression had deprived him of four of his backers and he had to look desperately for more financial help.

Charlie Bidwill, long a close friend of Halas and soon thereafter to purchase the

Even with two New York Giant tacklers riding him during the 1934 championship game, Nagurski is still under way, churning almost irresistibly for extra yardage. But even with Bronk the Bears lost this one, 27-13.

Chicago Cardinals, came to his rescue by securing a $5000 loan from a Chicago bank for the beleaguered Bear owner. A group composed of Jim McMillen, a guard who had played for the Bears for seven years off and on before earning a small fortune as a wrestler; Ralph Brizzolara, a steel executive; and two mothers — Halas' and Trafton's — also put money in the pot for George and the franchise was saved. Halas never again needed to borrow money.

As 1933 opened, another influx of talent pushed the Bears over the edge of excellence into greatness. From Minnesota came "Automatic Jack" Manders, a place-kicker and full-back whose value was enhanced by the removal of the goal posts from the back of the end zone to the goal line. Link Lyman, one of the best of the many all-pro Bear linemen, was lured from a Nebraska farm to play again after a year's retirement. A young 260-pound tackle named George Musso, from Milligan College in Tennessee, had attracted Halas' attention in the East-West all-star game and reported to the 1933 camp. Another Nebraskan named Ray Richards played guard and Bill Karr arived from West Virginia to begin a brilliant career at end. That was the year, too, that Gene Ronzani came up from Marquette to become an extraordinarily adept jack-of-all-trades and one of the hardest blockers of all Bear backs.

In 1933, the league was separated into two divisions, with a playoff for the championship. The Bears, with the generous leavening of rookies, started slowly, coming from behind to win five of their first six games, then surviving a disastrous road trip during which they lost two games and tied one. But they finished with a rush to take the Western Division championship from Portsmouth by 3½ games with a 10-2-1 record.

The first championship playoff game was held in Wrigley Field on December 17, 1933, before some 26,000 people and the Bears defeated the New York Giants, 23-21. The two rules changes which Halas and George Preston Marshall had pushed through the

60

league meeting the year before were to stand Halas in good stead. Jack Manders kicked field goals of sixteen, forty and twenty-eight yards for the Bears; had the old rule been in effect, almost certainly the forty-yard field goal would have gone awry.

The two Bear touchdowns came as a result of the other rule change, which allowed a passer to throw the ball from anywhere behind the line of scrimmage rather than from at least five yards back of it.

Twice Nagurski rumbled up to the line of scrimmage, pulling the Giant defenders in close, then straightened up to lob a pass over the middle, once to Bill Karr, who scored by himself. Late in the game, on the same fake, Nagurski threw over the middle to Bill Hewitt, his other end. Hewitt added a spectacular touch by lateraling to Karr, who scored behind a bristling block thrown by Gene Ronzani on the Giants' Ken Strong. The play covered thirty-six yards and gave the Bears the championship.

The 1934 Bear team is the one most frequently ranked with the 1941 club as the finest of all of Halas' clubs. The addition of Beattie Feathers, a swift runner with uncanny balance, to the attack was the touch needed to complete a masterpiece.

Feathers did not have the driving power for the T quick openers, nor was he as jet-fast in his first few steps as he was after he had gained running room. Halas, realizing the value of his new back, tailored a new attack especially for Feathers, although he retained the T formation as well and used it much of the time.

But it was the single wing, with Bronko Nagurski a large, ominous convoy for Feathers on sweeps, which led the Bears to most of their twelve straight league victories that season. During the regular season, the club scored 238 points to eighty-six for the opposition. Beattie, swinging in and out behind Bronko's ponderous shoulder blocks like a fox terrier frisking on the heels of a St. Bernard, gained 1,004 yards before he was injured in the ninth game of the season, against the Chicago Cardinals. This was, at the time, a league record and the first time any pro had gained over a thousand yards in one season.

During the regular season, the Bears had had to come from behind to beat the New York Giants; now they faced the Giants for the second year in a row in the championship game, in New York.

December 9, 1934 was a bitterly cold day, with the thermometer hovering around nine degrees. The Polo Grounds, by game time, had become almost a solid sheet of ice. The footing, in cleats, was bad, but the Bears dominated the first half.

Twice Nagurski scored, only to have the plays called back for a penalty. Twice Jack Manders, who almost never missed from short range, missed field goals from inside the thirty yard line. Still, the Bears came off the field at the half leading by 10-3 and few of the 35,059 shivering fans had any hope that the New Yorkers could come back against the nonpareils of pro football.

As the second half started, nine of the Giants took the field in sneakers. Steve Owen had searched desperately for the shoes from early in the morning, when he first heard of the temperature. The nine pairs he finally located were delivered at the half; only Mel Hein at center and one of the Giant guards were forced to wear cleats.

Even so, the Bears added a field goal to their lead in the third period and had a seemingly comfortable 13-3 margin as the final quarter began.

The field goal had come after a Giant fumble deep in Giant territory. The Bears had been unable to advance the ball during the third quarter and, as the Giants began to find their balance in the sneakers, disaster hit suddenly in the final period.

Ike Frankian, a Giant end, snatched an intercepted pass out of the arms of Bear Carl

Brumbaugh on the goal line and the New Yorkers had their first touchdown. Then Ken Strong, moving sure-footedly, raced forty-two yards through the scrambling, slithering Bears for another touchdown.

The Bears, unable to secure purchase on the ice, watched helplessly as the Giants scored two more touchdowns and won the game, 30-13. Ironically, Halas, en route to the Polo Grounds in the morning, had commented that he had forgotten to bring along sneakers. It was a painfully serious mistake.

As suddenly as the Bears had blossomed, they faded. Nagurski and Feathers were hobbled by injuries in 1935 and Link Lyman, the massive tackle, retired for good. The Bears promptly fell from first to a tie for last place in the Western Division, although their won-lost record was 6-4-2. They were only a game behind the Detroit Lions, who won both the division and league championships.

The first draft in league history occurred in 1936 and Halas made two choices which were to begin building the Bears toward their second blossoming. His first choice in the draft was made on the good advice of two West Virginians, Carl Brumbaugh and Bill Karr, both of whom suggested that he pick Joe Stydahar, a tackle from Shinnston, West Virginia. Stydahar was, of course, to become the equal of Lyman as a Bear tackle.

Halas' last choice was a whimsical one, since, at that time, no club had the extensive, detailed scouting system which is standard all over the league now. By the time the first few rounds were over, most owners drafted more or less haphazardly. Halas, on his thirtieth round, liked the sound of the name of a guard called Daniel Fortmann, although he knew little of Fortmann's ability.

Fortmann, like Stydahar, was to be an all-pro lineman five times during his career with the Bears, until he retired in 1943 after obtaining a degree as a doctor of medicine.

Three of the players who helped make the 1939-42 editions of the Bears rate among the best teams in pro football: tackle Joe Stydahar (left), fullback Bill Osmanski (center), guard Dan Fortman, all all-pro players.

Beattie Feathers, shown here carrying the ball for the Brooklyn Dodgers in a scrimmage against the College All-Stars in 1938, was star of the 1934 Bear team, an eleven that is often ranked with the great 1941 club.

Outside the draft, Halas acquired Ray Nolting from Cincinnati, another integral unit in the great machines of the early forties.

The Bears moved up to second in 1936; the Packers, behind the receiving of Don Hutson and the passing of Arnie Herber, won the Western Division title. By 1937, the Bear rookies were blooded and Halas' club won nine, lost one and tied one for the Western title.

They made their first reluctant bow to Sammy Baugh, rookie tailback for the Washington Redskins, in championship competition. Only 15,870 people came out in near-zero weather to watch the game. The weather had little effect on Baugh, who finished the first of his sixteen years in pro football by completing seventeen of thirty-four passes against the Bears for 347 yards and a 28-21 victory. Baugh passed to a sophomore end from Notre Dame named Wayne Millner for touchdowns covering fifty-five and seventy-eight yards and thirty-five yards to Ed Justice for a third.

The Bears went into an unaccountable slump in 1938. It may have been because Nagurski was finally gone for what seemed to be for good. Too, Feathers had been traded to Brooklyn and Molesworth had quit to take a coaching post at the Naval Academy. But the bulk of the fine rookies of the previous two seasons was still on hand.

Indeed, one of them had learned so much that he undertook the instruction of a newcomer to the New York Giant lineup early in the non-league season.

Will Walls, a big, tough end who had played at Texas Christian University with Baugh, faced Joe Stydahar across the line of scrimmage as the two teams lined up after the kickoff, with the Bears in possession of the ball.

"I was pretty nervous," Walls says now. "But I wasn't afraid of the Bears. I just wanted to see how tough they were."

Will found out immediately. At the snap of the ball, Stydahar stepped across the line and hit Walls on the jaw with a fist as big as a Virginia ham and as hard as West Virginia coal.

The blow dropped the youngster on the seat of his pants, but he bounced up full of fight only to find Stydahar regarding him sorrowfully.

"I didn't mean to do that, kid," he said sincerely. "You got to believe it. I just get excited in the first game of the year. It won't happen again."

He draped a tree-thick arm over Will's shoulder and helped him back to the line of scrimmage, patting him on the back as he let him go.

63

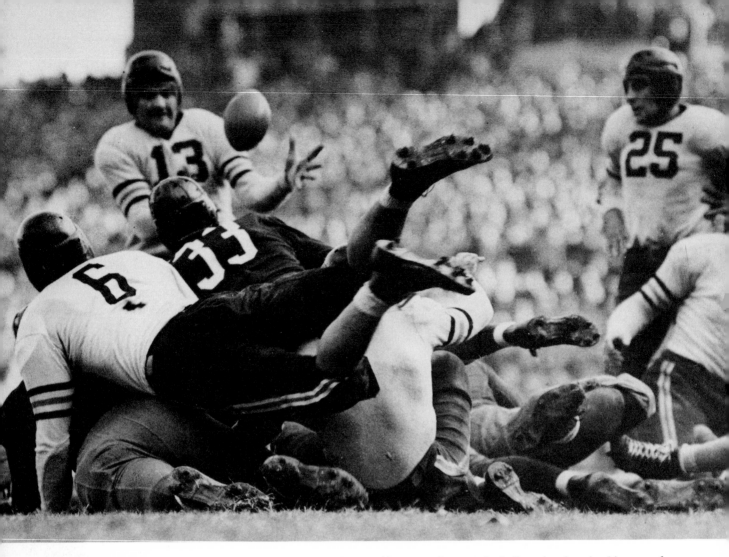

Jumbo Joe Stydahar, the massive all-pro Bear tackle, more often caught ball-carriers but, in this unusual picture of the 73-0 massacre of the Washington Redskins in 1940, he is shown catching a Baugh fumble.

"I remember thinking the Bears weren't so bad after all," Will says. "I lined up again and Stydahar smiled at me and then the ball was snapped and he stepped across the line and let me have it right on the chin again."

When the rookie finally wobbled to his feet, Stydahar looked at him and shook his head.

"You got to stay alert, son," he said.

The first of the definitive practioners of the art of the modern T quarterback joined the Bears in 1939 when Halas, after considerable difficulty, finally prevailed upon Brooklyn-born and raised Sid Luckman to join the club. Luckman had been a formidable tailback for Columbia. He had decided not to play pro football but Halas, who is as expert a psychologist and salesman as he is a coach, prevailed upon him to change his mind.

Bill Osmanski, a fullback from Holy Cross, joined the Bears in 1939, too. A year later, Osmanski and Luckman were to combine on a play which changed the course of football offense.

But the Packers, with Don Hutson, Clark Hinkle and Cecil Isbell, won the division championship, although the Bears were only a game behind, poised for their second giant step into excellence.

By far the most productive draft in the five years since the system had begun sent the Bears winging toward their 1940 explosion. Halas took a leaf from 1936 in his first choice, reaching into the small-college ranks for a lineman, just as he had plucked Joe Stydahar from West Virginia.

This was to be another of the Chicago perennial all-pros — a blocky, thick-necked center as fast as one of the road runners in his native Texas and as strong as a Texas steer. He was Clyde (Bulldog) Turner from Hardin-Simmons University. He quickly became a fixture in the middle of the Bear line.

But Turner was not the only super-star Halas came up with in 1940. He ranged all over the United States in his selections, going to the West Coast to pick a tackle, Lee Artoe, from Santa Clara and adding Ed Kolman, who later became an assistant coach for the New York Giants, from Temple in the East. Ken Kavanaugh, an end who also joined the Giant staff, came from Louisiana State, and Halas discovered Ray (Scooter) McLean at little St. Anselm's in New Hampshire. With Kavanaugh from LSU came a fine back named Young Bussey, who was killed several years later in one of the first actions by United States troops in the conquest of the Philippines in World War II.

The most exciting of all of Halas' acquisitions that year, however, was obtained in a trade with Bert Bell, the owner of the Philadelphia Eagles. Halas gave Bell three players for Bell's first draft choice — halfback George McAfee from Duke University. McAfee was to the Bear teams as much and more than Beattie Feathers had been in an earlier era.

McAfee ran ninety-three yards for a touchdown on the first kickoff he fielded in league play, against the champion Green Bay Packers; it was a fitting beginning for a great Bear year and for an unforgettable career.

The Bears slaughtered the defending champions, 41-10, in that opening game. They finished the season eight and three, with the championship of the West. One of their defeats had been by the Washington Redskins, 7-3.

The story of the championship game played in Griffith Stadium in Washington, D. C. on December 8 has been told earlier in this book. There were 36,034 fans in the stadium. They had come expecting a victory by a Washington team which had beaten the Bears already and had a better season record. They stayed to watch the most incredible perform-

Behind typical Bear blocking, quarterback Sid Luckman, known better for his passing prowess, sets off on a 10-yard run. Luckman, tutored by Clark Shaughnessy, was the prototype of all T quarterbacks in the game today.

ance by any team in the history of the game, as the Bears murdered the Redskins, 73-0.

During the long afternoon, ten Bears scored touchdowns; only Harry Clark scored twice. Six Bears tried conversions. Late in the game, with only one ball left after so many had been kicked into the crowd, the Bears tried passes for conversions, simply to make sure that the ball would be available for the next kickoff.

A little more than three weeks later, Clark Shaughnessy, who had had much to do with the imaginative Bear offense against the Redskins, sent another T team in action in a major bowl. Stanford, coming off a winless 1939 season, finished an all-winning 1940 season with a Rose Bowl victory over Nebraska and the T formation took over in football at all levels.

Halas added two backs from that Stanford Rose Bowl team to the 1941 Bears, who must be regarded as the finest Bear team and certainly one of the best teams in history. He acquired Norm Standlee, a fullback, and Hugh Gallarneau, a halfback. Neither had to spend much time learning Bear plays, since the Chicago and Stanford systems were almost identical.

That 1941 Bear team lost only one league game, to the Green Bay Packers, but the Packers lost one game, too — to the Bears. The Bears were trailing the Cardinals, 14-0, in the last game of the regular season when the teletype machines in the press box tapped out an urgent bulletin and the game became unimportant, although the Bears won it. The bulletin announced that the Japanese had attacked Pearl Harbor and the United States was at war.

The magic of a Packer-Bear game was proof even against the cataclysm of war: 43,425 people came to Wrigley Field to watch the first divisional playoff in the West. Gallarneau started the Bears on their way to a 33-14 victory with an eighty-one yard punt return for a touchdown.

A week later, the dread truth of war seemed to have soaked through to the Chicago fans. Although the Bears were playing the cordially hated New York Giants for the championship, only 13,341 hard-core fans turned out for the game. Two of the players on the field that day would die in action before war's end — Young Bussey of the Bears and John Lummus, an end from Baylor, who played with the Giants. Both were killed leading landing operations — Bussey as a Marine lieutenant at Lingayen Gulf in the Philippines and Lummus as an infantry lieutenant on the beach at Iwo Jima.

Midway through the 1942 season, Halas went into the Navy, leaving Hunk Anderson and Luke Johnsos, assisted by Paddy Driscoll, as a three-ply head coaching staff. Standlee and McAfee were in service by then, but the other clubs in the league had suffered service losses as well, and the Bears, even without Halas, were, for the second time in their history, undefeated in 1942. They ran their string of undefeated games in league play to eighteen, counting the Packer playoff and the championship in 1941.

But the same fate awaited the 1942 undefeated team as befell the 1934 champions: defeat in the championship game. This time it was the Washington Redskins, 1-to-5 underdogs.

The game, played in Washington, drew only twenty-eight fewer spectators than the 1940 contest, despite the tensions of war, and the 36,006 fans left this championship game much happier than their 1940 counterparts.

Lee Artoe picked up a Bear fumble and ran fifty yards for a Chicago touchdown in the second period, but that was all for Chicago. Sammy Baugh and Andy Farkas combined to whip Chicago, 14-6.

By 1943, the beautifully articulated, superbly equipped Bear juggernaut had begun

66

to decay. At the end of the 1942 season, Tuffy Leemans, the fine back for the New York Giants, had called the Bears the greatest football team ever assembled. In truth, they were.

But the attrition of war and time wore away the polish and, although they won another championship in 1943, the Bears had begun to go. Not long after the 1942 championship game, fourteen Bears were in service and this Bear team was destroyed for good.

The 1943 team lived comfortably on borrowed time. Nagurski, thirty-five years old, came back after a six-year absence. A transfusion of good players from the Cleveland Rams — notably a young, fiery halfback named Dante Alfredo Magnani and an unbelievably sure-handed and maneuverable, albeit rather slow, end named Jim Benton — helped Chicago to a championship in 1943.

By mid-season, though, with four more Bears gone to the wars, Halas, from his base in Norman, Okla., had to implore another ghost from the past to haunt the NFL gridirons. That was Ray Nolting, and he gave the team a brief lift. During the season, Luckman enlisted in the Merchant Marine and played on sufferance — and sometimes under orders — of his commanding officer. The Bears, who had been a violent, powerful running team, turned more and more to the pass, and, in one game against the Giants,

George McAfee, whom many still think was the best of all Bear runners, shows cut-back ability here as he runs with an intercepted pass in the Bears' 28-14 championship victory over the New York Giants in 1946.

Luckman set a league record for touchdown passing with seven, and for yards gained passing with 508.

The Bears reached their sixth championship playoff on the aging legs of Nagurski, who had spent the season acquitting himself nobly at tackle. They came into the last game of the season — against the Cardinals, as usual — needing a victory to avoid a play-off against the Packers and without a whole fullback on the club.

Nagurski came into the game at fullback in the fourth quarter, slammed into the Cardinal line over and over again, seeming, for that brief time in the dusk of the stadium and his career, to be the old Bronko. He scored at last to bring the Bears close at 21-24.

He came back again with four minutes left, the ball on the Cardinal thirty-three, the Bears four yards from a first down. He gained six. The Bears charged ahead to a 35-24 triumph.

He played one more game and scored one more touchdown in the Bears' upset 41-21 victory over the Redskins in the championship game on the day after Christmas in 1943. Then he retired for good and with him went much of the glory of the Bears.

The Packers won the championship in 1944 and, in 1945, the riddled Bears suffered through one of the worst seasons in their history. They won only three games. Their only consolation was that, at the end of the season, they heard that Halas would be back from his Navy duty to take over the club again in 1946.

Note the difference in the style of play of modern pro football. The attack has widened almost from sideline to sideline as Chicago quarterback Bill Wade starts a draw play against the champion Green Bay Packer club.

Most of the Bears had returned from service in 1946, but the All-America Conference, just beginning, drained away some of Halas' stars. Many others were beginning to slow down. Even so, Halas led the Bears to the championship.

The championship game was marred by the Mapes-Filchock scandal but the Bears won from the Giants, 24-14, on a Luckman run, before 58,346 in the Polo Grounds. Luckman ran a bootleg for the decisive score; this was to be the last flicker of greatness for the Bears for a long time to come.

The 1949 Bear team, with Johnny Lujack and Luckman available at quarterback, tied for the Western Division title with the Los Angeles Rams, but lost the division playoff, 24-14, as Ram end Tom Fears caught three Bob Waterfield touchdown passes in the Los Angeles Coliseum.

In 1956, the Bears were ostensibly under the direction of head coach Paddy Driscoll, who had taken over when Halas decided to give up the strenuous job of running the team from the sideline.

Again it was a bumper crop of rookies who sent the Bears up the standings. Rick Casares, a bull of a fullback from Florida, provided a semblance of Nagurski and J. C. Caroline gave the Bears tremendous speed.

Unfortunately, the championship game was played again in New York, this time in Yankee Stadium instead of the Polo Grounds. The conditions were the same as the tennis shoe game of 1934; the field was icy, the Giants wore sneakers, and the score was 47-7, New York.

Driscoll continued as head coach in 1957, but the Bears dropped to fifth in the Western Division, with a 5-7 record, and Halas took over again in 1958.

In the last five years, the fortunes of the Bears have fluctuated but, despite occasional flashes of the old Bear elan, the club has not been able to win another divisional title.

The acquisition of Billy Wade from the Los Angeles Rams in 1961 seems to have added punch to the Bear attack. In 1961, too, the Bears' first draft choice, a massive, mobile tight end from Pittsburgh named Mike Ditka, won rookie-of-the-year honors and seems destined to become another in the long line of great Bears.

Again, in 1962, the Bears made a fine first draft choice in Ron Bull, a strong and elusive running back from Baylor. On defense, the club still has tremendous talent, headed by one of the best middle linebackers of the modern era — Bill George.

Sadly, Clark Shaughnessy, who had so much to do with the success of the Bears, resigned at the end of the 1962 season after Halas had taken from him much of his responsibility for charting the defenses.

But Halas added one of his players from the great days as defensive line coach — Joe Stydahar, who retired after head coaching jobs with the Los Angeles Rams and the Chicago Cardinals.

The Bears, a young, strong team, are on the way back.

There is no indication now that Halas intends to give up the demanding head coaching job. He may in fact come up with something new, as he has so often before. He was the first coach to put an assistant in the stands to check plays during the game, the first to use movies to evaluate his players, the first to hold daily practice and the first to play in a major league baseball park.

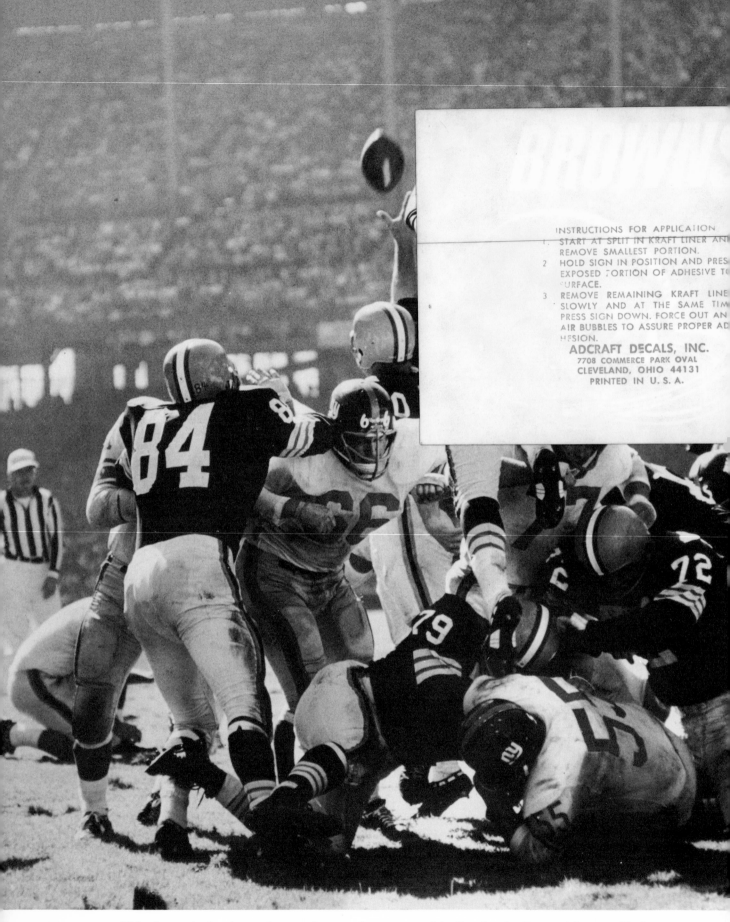

This almost classic picture shows a desperate but unsuccessful effort by the Brown defense to block an extra point attempt by the New York Giants. Note Bernie Parrish (30) using Giants as stepping stones.

# THE CLEVELAND BROWNS

IN the seventeen years of their existence, the Cleveland Browns have won more games and lost fewer than any other pro club. They started in the old All-America Conference in 1946 and won every championship in that league until it went out of business in 1949.

They moved into the National Football League and won the championship there, too, in their first year, although most of the mossbacks in the game had predicted that the upstart Browns would get their comeuppance once they started playing in the *real* major league.

They did all of this under the meticulous direction of a handsome, slender, brilliantly inventive man named Paul Brown, whose personal coaching career, through high school, college, service and professional football, has been inordinately successful. After winning the NFL championship in his first season, Brown went on to win six more divisional and two more world championships.

Brown was the first man to grade his players on each play in a game, the first to use messenger guards to send in plays on every call and the first to have a team named after him. He invented a face mask, used classroom techniques to teach and forced his players to take intelligence tests.

In short, Paul Brown has been as successful in his field as, say, Bob Hope in the field of comedy. At the end of the 1962 season, Brown was relieved of his duties as head coach of the Browns.

He was first hired for the job in 1945 by Mickey McBride, a Cleveland taxicab mogul who had never met Brown but who took the word of *Chicago Tribune* sports editor Arch Ward that Paul was the best coach around.

Brown had coached at Severn Prep in Maryland, at Massillon High School in Ohio, at Ohio State and at Great Lakes. He had been a winner in each place. When McBride had Ward call Brown about taking over the Browns, then in the planning stage, Paul was coaching successfully at the Great Lakes Naval Training Station.

Ward was the moving force in the foundation of the All-America Conference, which was organized in 1945 to go into operation as soon as World War II ended. Brown, who could have gone back to Ohio State when his service days ended, surprised many people by accepting McBride's offer.

Money, of course, had much to do with it. McBride offered Paul $25,000 per year, plus fifteen percent of the Browns, plus $1,000 a month during the rest of his service time if he would take the job.

Brown was not too happy at Ohio State. He had had differences with the athletic director and did not look forward to returning to what might develop into an unpleasant situation. He especially did not look forward to returning at a salary of $9,000 per year when he could more than triple that coaching the Browns.

He accepted McBride's offer and immediately set about securing talent for his club. It was a fortuitous time for the accumulation of players, since there was a vast store of seasoned athletes in service.

"I want lean and hungry players," Brown said. "I want amateur spirit. We may be the most amateurish team in pro football."

The nucleus of players he signed during the months remaining before the All-America Conference went into action won for him five straight league championships. They were lean, hungry and amateurish; they were also one of the best pro football teams of all time.

From Ohio State, Paul plucked Lou Groza, Dante Lavelli, Bill Willis, Lin Houston and Gene Fekete. Most of them were in service and had not yet been graduated from college. They were eligible to play pro football because their classes had been graduated, but Brown's picking them up did not endear him to Ohio State fans.

He raided the Chicago Bears for Edgar (Special Delivery) Jones and the Washington Redskins for a tough offensive tackle, Lou Rymkus. From Nevada came Marion Motley, a giant fullback Brown remembered from Motley's days at McKinley High School, Canton,

Thoughtful Paul Brown discusses game tactics with quarterback Jim Ninowski on sidelines. Brown had an unparalleled record of success as coach and general manager of the Cleveland club until his dismissal last year.

Ohio, when he had battered Paul's Massillon High line unmercifully.

Brown also remembered an end named Mac Speedie who had played on a service team against his Great Lakes club and signed him, too. Finally, he signed Otto Graham, who had been a great tailback at Northwestern University and had learned the T at North Carolina Pre-Flight. From the Cleveland Rams, who had won the National Football League championship and had moved to Los Angeles, Paul picked up a quartet of players who did not want to go to the coast.

By the time the AAC was ready to start, Brown had assembled by far the best club in the conference, as he proved forthwith. In the first year, Brown's team won twelve and lost two during the regular season, then beat the New York Yankees, 14-9, for the league championship. The Browns scored 423 points to their opponents' 137.

In 1947, they were 12-1-1; in 1948 they won fifteen straight, including the championship game; and in 1949, the last year of the league, they won ten, lost one and tied two before winning their fourth straight championship by beating San Francisco, 21-7.

In 1950, the Browns, with the San Francisco Forty-Niners and the Baltimore Colts, joined the National Football League as the All-America Conference went out of business.

"The two most satisfying victories of my career came in 1950," Brown said not long

A sight to chill the souls of enemy tacklers was fullback Marion Motley, a 240-pound sprinter who led the Cleveland ground attack from his position as fullback. For him, Paul Brown devised the potent Motley trap.

ago. He is a man who likes very much to win. "You remember the attitude of the National Football League toward us. They figured we had done pretty well with the teams in the AAC, but they also figured that the worst team in the NFL could beat us."

The first of the two victories came in the opening game of the 1950 season; the second came in the final game. The first game matched Cleveland and the 1949 NFL champions, the Philadelphia Eagles, in Philadelphia. There were 71,237 Eagle fans on hand for the game, most of them looking forward to watching the Philadelphia club's old pros teach the young Browns how to play.

They saw almost precisely the opposite. Brown, as explained earlier in this book, had devised a system of gradually increasing the spacing between his offensive linemen so that eventually he could nullify the middle guard in the Eagle defense. When he had accomplished this, the famous Motley trap, a bread-and-butter play for the Browns for four years, burst the big fullback up the center for good gains. When the Eagles tried to close up to stop Motley, Graham's accurate passes riddled their secondary defense. The Browns won, 35-10. No one, after that game, questioned that they could hold their own with the old pros of the NFL.

The Browns went on to tie the New York Giants for the Eastern Conference championship that year, with ten wins and two losses; in the West, the Rams and the Chicago Bears had tied with 9-3 records.

The Browns' two regular season losses were both to the Giants, but in the playoff game in Cleveland, the Browns won, 8-3.

The Rams had defeated the Bears, too, setting up a match between the former and the current Cleveland teams. The championship game was played in Cleveland, with the thermometer reading eleven degrees and a razor-edge wind blowing through Municipal Stadium off Lake Erie.

The game matched two of the most spectacular offenses in football. The Browns had Graham throwing to Speedie and Lavelli and handing off to Motley and Dub Jones. The Rams had Bob Waterfield and Norm Van Brocklin passing to Elroy Hirsch, Tom Fears, Glenn Davis and Vitamin Smith, and had a fullback the equal of Motley in Dick Hoerner.

The Rams, too, thought they had a secret weapon. They had ordered special abrasive for the soles of their tennis shoes so that they would grip on the glass-like ice of the field. Glenn Davis, testing the shoes on an ice-skating rink in Los Angeles, had found they provided almost perfect footing.

On the first Ram play from scrimmage, Waterfield passed to Davis for eighty-two yards and a touchdown and it seemed, for a moment, that this game might be a replica of the 1934 sneaker game in New York when the Giants used tennis shoes to whip the Bears. But the Browns came back strong to tie the score and when the first Brown was upended, the Rams discovered that Cleveland had precisely the same abrasive on its shoes as they did.

Lou Groza kicked a field goal from the Ram sixteen-yard line with twenty-eight seconds to play to give Cleveland the league championship, 30-28 in its first NFL season.

In their second year in the NFL, the Browns opened by losing to the San Francisco Forty-Niners, then won eleven straight games and took their second straight division title. They met the Rams again for the championship, this time in Los Angeles, but lost, 24-17.

For the next four years, the Browns dominated the East, with Otto Graham passing and Paul Brown calling the signals via messenger guards from the sideline. Brown controlled his team with iron discipline, but there were no complaints from the players. They knew that he demanded as much from himself as he did from them.

Dante Lavelli (56), shown carrying the ball after taking a pass from Otto Graham, was part of one of the best sets of ends in football when he teamed with Mac Speedie to provide Graham's favorite pass targets.

Otto Graham, a mechanically perfect quarterback, was the master of the quarterback sneak, which he is using here to score on the Los Angeles Rams in the 1955 championship game won by the Browns, 38-14.

He insisted that players wear jackets and watch their table manners. No one was allowed to miss a meal without a personal excuse from Brown. He did not tolerate drinking or dissipation and was quick to dispose of players he felt were not living up to what he expected of them morally, as well as on the field.

"We don't want any butches on this team," he would tell the players the first day of training camp. "Don't eat with your elbows on the table and don't make noise when you eat. Don't wear T shirts to the dining room. We intend to have good people on this football team because that's the kind who win the big ones. If you're a drinker or a chaser, you weaken the team and we don't want you. We're here for just one thing — to win.

"You must watch how you dress, your language, and the company you keep. When we're on the road, stay away from that stranger who may want to take you to dinner or

Enormous enthusiasm of the Cleveland fans is reflected in packed stands at Cleveland's Municipal Stadium on hand

talk to you in the hotel lobby. Maybe he isn't a gambler or after information, but stay away from him anyway."

Brown's rules for training camp and on the road were simple but rigid:

"In your room at ten, lights out at ten-thirty. Sometimes the coaches will make a bed check. There is an automatic fine of $500 for any player who sneaks out after bed check. The fines stick. I have never rescinded one for subsequent good behavior or meritorious performance."

The formula worked beautifully as the Browns won steadily. They lost championship playoffs to Detroit in 1952 and 1953, but exploded against the Lions in the 1954 championship game, winning by 56-10. In 1955, they met their old rivals, the Rams, in the championship game. This was Otto Graham's last game as a Brown and he made it a good one

'or the Browns' opening game against the New York Giants in 1962. Over 80,000 people watched rare win for Browns.

Most prolific scorer in Cleveland history, Lou (The Toe) Groza concentrates as he waits to try a field goal. Groza, a fine offensive tackle early in his career, was a deadly marksman from almost any range.

as Cleveland demolished the Rams, 38-14, in Los Angeles.

In 1956, his first year as a pro coach without Otto Graham, Brown suffered his first losing year. He had a small, eager quarterback named Tommy O'Connell, but O'Connell was no Graham and the Browns finished fourth in the East with a 5-7 record.

Paul revised his attack for 1957, fitting the Brown aerial game to O'Connell's abilities, and came back. Another major factor in the resurgence of the Browns was their first draft choice — Syracuse All-American Jim Brown, who led the league in rushing his rookie year and continued to lead it each year until 1962, when he finished fourth. The combination of Brown's fleet and powerful running and O'Connell's short, deft passes carried Cleveland to the championship of the Eastern Division. However, the Detroit Lions gained revenge for the lopsided beating Cleveland had given them in the 1954 championship game by walloping the Browns, 59-14, as Detroit linebacker Joe Schmidt dominated a defense that held Jim Brown to a negligible gain on the ground.

A young quarterback from Penn State, Milt Plum, replaced O'Connell in 1958. Plum, a brilliant short passer, later began to resent Brown's sending in all the plays. But in 1958, Plum took Cleveland to a tie for the Eastern Division title with the New York Giants, helped by a giant-sized assist from Jim Brown.

Jim set a league record of 1527 yards gained rushing in 1958 and scored eighteen touchdowns, seventeen on the ground. He established himself as one of the finest running backs in the history of the game, but it did him no good against the Giants.

The Giants beat the Browns, 10-0, in the playoff for the Eastern Division title as Sam Huff, playing middle linebacker, keyed on Jim Brown throughout the game and held him to little gain.

Paul Brown never again won a division title for the Browns. After the 1958 season, his backfield was set with Plum at quarterback, Brown at fullback, Bobby Mitchell at halfback and Ray Renfro, a talented pass-receiver from North Texas State, as the flanker back, but the club failed to win the championship each season, for a variety of reasons.

The defense was in a state of flux, for one thing. While a spectacular offense was responsible for most of the adulation gained by the Browns during their good years, it was primarily a sound, experienced defense which won the championships. Now age had begun to erode this unit and replacements for a team finishing consistently near the top were not easily come by.

The Browns finished second in 1959 and 1960, third in 1961 and 1962. Players who had submitted to Brown's discipline when the club was winning and they were getting

Regarded by many experts as the strongest running back ever to play football, Jim Brown has been the star and the workhorse of the Cleveland backfield ever since he joined the team from Syracuse back in 1957.

championship checks began to grumble. Cleveland fans and newspapermen charged that Brown's offense was stereotyped and that every club in the league, especially the Giants, could read the Brown attack like a book.

This was not true. Brown was as inventive as ever. If his offense was limited, it was limited by personnel, not by the scope of Brown's imagination. Paul had been criticized before for his complete control of the offensive pattern of his team through the messenger guards.

"Brown," Otto Graham said, "maintains that a quarterback gets stereotyped in his calls and that's right. You don't even realize it. I remember when San Francisco used to have the ball down on our twenty. With Frankie Albert in at quarterback we knew he would call the bootleg and he always did. But Paul doesn't realize that his own calls get stereotyped, too."

But Brown's calls were limited by the competence of the men under his command. He had no confidence in Milt Plum's ability to pick up deep receivers in the intricate, delicately-timed patterns of the Cleveland pass plays, which break receivers open at one-second intervals deeper and deeper downfield. Plum's tendency, Brown felt, was always to throw to the first or second receiver, who were the closest.

He had Bobby Mitchell at halfback. Mitchell was a brilliant openfield runner, as elusive as any back, but he habitually fumbled when called upon to carry the ball into a hole inside the ends. Jim Brown, of course, could go inside or outside.

"The limitations of the players simplified the problems of the defense," Brown explained. "It simplifies your defensive strategy when you know that you never have to worry about the halfback carrying the ball inside the ends or the quarterback passing deep. It narrows the area you have to defend. It's easy to guess with the offense, then."

Before the 1962 season, Brown made a desperate effort to gain diversity for his attack. Knowing that he could not do any more than he had with the personnel on hand, he traded Plum to the Detroit Lions for Jim Ninowski, a quarterback he hoped would be able to find the deep receivers, and run a bit as well. He sent Mitchell to the Washington Redskins for the draft rights to Ernie Davis, another big Syracuse back who seemed likely to be nearly as good as Jim Brown and who could certainly run inside or out. Davis became ill and could not play in 1962.

A trade with the Los Angeles Rams brought Tom Wilson and Frank Ryan. A tall, strong-armed quarterback with the IQ of a genius, Ryan had a natural aptitude for the Brown system.

Ninowski was injured early in 1962 and it took Ryan a couple of games to become

Baleful glare reflects Jim Brown's determination as he starts one of the long runs which have given him the league rushing championship in an unprecedented five of his first six years in the National Football League.

acclimated. The Browns, beginning with a victory over the eventual division champions, the Giants, slipped badly at mid-season and finished fourth, barely over the .500 mark.

McBride had long since sold his interest in the club to a combine headed by Dave Jones. Jones, in turn, sold the Cleveland team to a young television executive from New York, Art Modell, who raised $4,000,000 to buy the team.

Bright and personable, with a deep and abiding love for pro football, Modell brought an imaginative, resourceful mind to the league. In his second year, he promoted a pre-season doubleheader. Many other club owners regarded it an unwise promotion, but Modell brought off a resounding success. Over 80,000 fans attended, the games were exciting and Modell paid the visiting teams $5000 more than their guarantee.

When Modell took over, he gave Paul Brown a complete vote of confidence and a contract which stipulated that Brown would have unrestricted control of the club so far as football was concerned.

It was a long-term, $75,000-a-year contract with stock options which increased its value to close to $100,000 per year. Brown seemed assured of the right to operate the team he had created for at least eight more years.

But after the 1962 season, in a move which rocked the pro football world, Modell relieved Brown of his coaching duties and appointed long-time Brown assistant Blanton Collier to take over the team.

The wisdom of Modell's decision will be up for regular audit as the years roll by.

# THE DALLAS COWBOYS

IN late January of 1960, in the plush Kenilworth Hotel on the beach in Miami, the National Football League owners, in long and bitter conclave, finally reached two momentous decisions, one of which grew out of the other.

They argued for a week about a successor to Bert Bell as commissioner of the league. One faction wanted to retain Austin Gunsel, the league treasurer, who had served as pro tem commissioner after Bell's death. The other group, whom you might call the young lions, were adamant in their support of Marshall Leahy, a San Francisco attorney whose sympathies, supposedly, might lie with the younger clubs in the league.

A third party watched the week-long struggle carefully, did not vote one way or the other and nursed his own project, which had nothing to do with the election of a commissioner.

The third party was George Halas of the Chicago Bears, who wanted the league to vote for expansion and give franchises to Dallas and Minneapolis-St. Paul. He refrained from voting on the commissioner question in order not to alienate anyone on the expansion question.

His forbearance was rewarded when the warring factions, weary of butting heads, finally made a fortuitous compromise. They discarded both Gunsel and Leahy and settled on young (38) Pete Rozelle, who was general manager of the Los Angeles Rams and had vast experience in dealing with recalcitrant owners. Rozelle was elected on the first ballot after his name appeared. There had been twenty-three ballots during the week of argument.

Now Halas made his move. He got Dallas and Minneapolis-St. Paul admitted as new members, Dallas to begin operation in 1960 and Minneapolis-St. Paul in 1961.

The putative owners of the Dallas franchise had spent the long week of argument waiting to learn their fate. They had wandered restlessly from lobby to bar to pool to beach and back again. Texas E. Schramm, already hired as general manager, and a high-strung, restless man, lost five pounds during the week.

The American Football League, which was preparing for its first season, and which had both its headquarters and a team in Dallas, reacted with something less than enthusiasm to the news that the NFL had granted owners Clint Murchison Jr. and Bedford Wynne a a competitive franchise in Dallas.

Said AFL Commissioner Joe Foss, an ex-governor of South Dakota: "This is an act of war. We will go to the court or to Congress to prevent the NFL from putting the AFL franchise in Dallas out of business. You have antitrust laws to take care of such situations."

"They moved into our territory in New York and Los Angeles and San Francisco," answered Rozelle, in one of his first public statements as NFL commissioner. "Why shouldn't

tars fell on the Giants' Joe Morrison at the end of this run, the stars in point being carried on the helmets of the Dallas Cowboys, youngest but one of the league's franchises. The Cowboys have already begun to move up in the standings.

we be allowed to move into Dallas?"

Lamar Hunt, owner of the rival Dallas Texans and founder of the AFL, had an answer for that.

"It's not the same at all," he said. "In our case it's just like a little dog going into the big back yard of a big dog. But in their case it's the big dog going into the little back yard and asking the little bitty dog if there's not room for him. It's the size of the back yard that counts."

Hunt and the owners of the Cowboys then proceeded to put on a whale of a dog fight over possession of a back yard which seemed, for two years, to be too small for one dog of any size.

The populace of Dallas, in the first year the two teams battled for attendance, regarded the pair with equal boredom. Schramm had been trained in one of the best pro football schools in the country as assistant to Dan Reeves, president of the Los Angeles Rams, but he found that running a last-place club was a far cry from operating a team like the Rams. Nevertheless, he set about building for the future with a dogged, if some times almost

Typical Dallas combination of youth and experience is exemplified in this picture. Young Don Meredith (17)

hopeless, persistence. The Cowboys, coming into the NFL after the completion of the 1960 draft, had no chance to pick players from the crop of 1959 college seniors. The older clubs in the league made some of their players available to them for draft, but these were often *has beens* or *never weres*.

Tom Landry, the young, brilliant coach hired from the New York Giants to run the club on the field, found himself equipped with a ragtag, bobtail assortment of players. He decided to do as much as he could to provide Dallas fans with an exciting offense and let defense, the core of a championship team, go by the boards temporarily.

"I figured we were bound to lose," he said. "If we could score a little while we were losing, maybe we could make some friends."

As was expected, the Cowboys finished last in their maiden season and did not win a game. Even Landry, as capable as he proved to be, could not make a silk purse of this collection of sow's ears.

Schramm had, meanwhile, installed Gil Brandt as talent scout to locate the best of the college seniors, using a system based on the best in the league — that of the Rams. The

watches as 10-year veteran Bill Howton (81) leaps high in the air to catch his pass against the Pittsburgh Steelers.

system began to pay off in 1961, when the Cowboys, for the first time, participated in the annual draft.

Their first choice became a steady and more than competent performer. He was Bob Lilly, a giant (6-4, 251 pounds) end from Texas Christian. The scouting system also turned up Amos Marsh, who was not picked by any club. He became a fine fullback for the Cowboys. Another first-line Cowboy running back, Don Perkins, was also located and reported in 1960 but missed all of that season because of a chronic foot ailment.

Diminutive Eddie LeBaron cooly prepares to hand off to Amos Marsh, disregarding giants around him.

Beleaguered Don Meredith's face reflects despair as he is hauled down by a pair of tacklers in game.

Newest ploy in football strategy is shuttling quarterback system devised by Cowboy coach Tom Landry, who uses this method to send in each play called on offense. System worked until LeBaron was hurt.

The Cowboys, fortunately, had two fine quarterbacks — Eddie LeBaron, the tiny veteran obtained from the Washington Redskins, and Don Meredith, who had played at Southern Methodist and who was rated by most scouts as certain to become a star in pro football.

The 1961 season began auspiciously. The Cowboys beat the Pittsburgh Steelers, 27-24, in their first game, then whipped an even newer team, the Minnesota Vikings, 21-7, in their second. They won four games in their second season, one of them against the mighty and long-established New York Giants.

Dallas fans, who had first favored the AFL Texans, seemed to turn toward the Cowboys in 1961.

Tom Landry, the young Dallas coach, is regarded as one of the finest football brains in the business. Although he was considered a defensive specialist with New York, he has given Cowboys a fiery attack.

Don Perkins, a young halfback from New Mexico, has combined with Oregon State's Amos March to give Dallas a versatile, hard pounding running game. Here Perkins breaks through the line for gain against the New York Giants.

The losses for both teams were astronomical. The AFL filed suit on antitrust charges against the NFL, using the situation in Dallas as one of the major points in their allegations. The suit was lost on all counts, then appealed, but it had little effect on the battle to the death going on in Dallas.

Landry, by 1962 going into his third year as the head coach of the Cowboys, had improved his team bit by bit. It was a long way from being a contender, but now he could begin to spend some time on his first love, defense. The third season began almost as well as the second.

Amos Marsh as fullback, Don Perkins at half and Frank Clarke, an end picked up from the Cleveland Browns in a trade, had developed rapidly. The defense was beginning to learn the maneuvers carefully and perfectly planned by Landry and the team seemed to grow in confidence through the pre-season games.

Landry tried something new. He had always been a believer in Paul Brown's system of messenger guards, but he felt it could be improved upon. With two fine quarterbacks in Meredith and LeBaron, he decided that instead of shuttling guards in and out of a game to call plays, he would shuttle quarterbacks. The system was an instant success.

"It gives you the opportunity to discuss what happened on the previous play and what to expect on the next with the quarterback," Landry said. "The quarterback standing with you on the sideline knows what play is being called on the field. If it fails to work, he knows why. Sometimes a quarterback may call a play which fails simply because of a blown assignment or a breakdown in the blocking. If he stays on the field, he may not realize this and he may junk a perfectly good play when it would work later, with good blocking. If he's on the sideline with me, he realizes this."

The system also provided invaluable experience for Meredith, who got a good deal of game action without the responsibility for the whole game resting on his shoulders.

"I think I've learned a lot," Meredith said. "Landry's a genius. He knows just what he wants to do and just how he wants to do it. Not many people do."

LeBaron, who is one of the smartest quarterbacks in the league and who is in his thirteenth year at this position, has endorsed the system for another reason.

"It's hard to have a bad day in this system," he said. "Some days, if you're in all by yourself, you get into a bad pattern or things go wrong and it's impossible to start over again. With this system, if you start going off, Landry's there to put you back on the right track."

After the eighth game of the 1962 season, the Cowboys still had an outside chance in the league race. They faced the Giants, the division leaders, in the Cotton Bowl. A victory would leave Dallas only a half-game out of first. The Cowboys had just come home after a convincing victory over the Steelers in Pittsburgh.

"This game tells it," Schramm said before the kickoff. "If we don't do over 30,000, Dallas doesn't want pro football."

The Dallas Texans, leading the Western Division of the AFL, had played natural rivals the week before in the Houston Oilers, the Eastern Division leaders. The crowd had been 29,000 for the most attractive game possible in the AFL.

Over 45,000 turned out for the Cowboys-Giants game. Unfortunately, early in the game, LeBaron injured his Achilles' tendon and was forced to leave. The Giants, intent on locking up the division championship, handed the Cowboys their worst defeat of the season. The Cowboys finished the 1962 season respectably, even though LeBaron was out for most of the rest of the games.

The future looked bright. LeBaron, associated with club owner Bedford Wynne in Wynne's law office, planned to play again in 1963. The Cowboys picked up one of the best college quarterbacks in the 1962 draft in giant Sonny Gibbs of Texas Christian. Meredith, beginning to fulfill his promise, prepared to shoulder the responsibility as No. 1 quarterback in the event LeBaron retired.

In 1960, when the National Football League granted the Dallas franchise to Murchison and his associates and the American Football League complained bitterly, someone asked Senator Estes Kefauver, head of the Senate Antitrust subcommittee, his views on the problem.

"I'm for expansion of football," Kefauver said. "But it is not a question of rights. It is a question of who has the better product in a city, if he produces it fairly without monopolization and without pushing anyone around."

Early triple-threat star of the Detroit team was Dutch Clark, runner, kicker, passer. He blocked, too.

# THE DETROIT LIONS

A MOUNTED policeman was run over by a fullback in what was probably the first pro football game ever played in Detroit. No one remembers the name of the policeman, but the fullback was Dutch Maulbetch, who was playing against the Detroit Heralds. The cop, obviously too close to the sidelines, was on hand to hold back the overflow crowd; neither he nor his horse nor Maulebesch was hurt in the collision.

That was just after World War I. The crowds thinned considerably after that first game and pro football disappeared until 1925, when Jimmy Conzelman rented Navin Field, guaranteeing $1000 a game for ten games, then suffered through ten consecutive rainy home dates. His club was an artistic success — it finished third behind the Chicago Cardinals and Pottsville with an 8-2-2 record — but a monumental financial failure.

Conzelman tried again in 1926, when the weather was better but the team worse. The club finished twelfth in a twenty-two-team league and Conzelman gave up the franchise in the general reshuffling which reduced the league to twelve teams in 1927.

Benny Friedman tried again in 1928, but found no enthusiasm among the Detroit fans and turned his team into a road club before the end of the season. The depression hit in 1929, and pro football did not return to Detroit until 1934, when a radio station owner, Dick Richards, bought the Portsmouth Spartans for the bargain price of $21,500.

Richards was a showman on the order of Washington's George Preston Marshall. He conducted a contest on his radio station — WJR — to select a new name for the Spartans and settled on Lions as a logical corollary to the Detroit Tigers baseball team. His players wore matching sports coats, ties and slacks off the field. They were required to race in and out of the game at top speed.

The club Richards bought was a good one. In its inaugural season in Detroit, the team won ten games and lost three, two of them to the Chicago Bears, who went undefeated.

Bronko Nagurski had been the prime mover in the Bears' two victories over the Lions and Richards, over drinks at the end of the season in a New York restaurant with George Halas, Nagurski and some other players, figured out a way to dispose of the Bear fullback.

He wrote out a check for $10,000, made out to Nagurski, and offered it to him.

"Here," he said. "This is for you not to play next season. I'm not trying to sign you. I just don't want you to play."

Nagurski, of course, refused the offer, which turned out to be unnecessary, anyway. In 1935, the Lions won the Western Division championship with a 7-3-2 record and beat the New York Giants for the championship in Detroit University Stadium, 26-7. This game was notable chiefly because Raymond (Buddy) Parker, who coached the Lions during their best years later, scored the last Lion touchdown.

Parker played fullback and halfback in a backfield with Ace Gutowsky and the wonderful Dutch Clark, who could thread his way delicately through the maze of a broken field or slam headlong through a mass of tacklers with equal facility.

The Lions established a league record for ground gained by rushing in 1936, but finished third to the Green Bay Packers and the Chicago Bears. The impatient Richards fired Potsy Clark, who had been head coach, and installed Dutch Clark as a playing coach.

With a radio executive's consciousness of the public image, he hired Steve Hannigan, the top press agent in the land, as Dutch's personal publicity man. Dutch, for the sixth time, made all-pro as a back, but it is doubtful that Hannigan was of any material assistance to him in the achievement.

Despite the coaching change, the Lions, who were beginning to feel the erosion of age, slipped still more in 1937. In 1938, they were second to the Packers, only a game out of first place, but the club lost four of the eleven games played and Dutch Clark quit as head coach.

Richards replaced him with "Gloomy Gus" Henderson, who had had a long and successful tour as head coach of various colleges, but very little pro experience. Henderson could do nothing to stop the slide. His team won six and lost five and finished third.

Meanwhile, Richards had had trouble with the league and with George Halas. Halas had drafted Clyde (Bulldog) Turner from Hardin-Simmons after the 1939 season. Richards, who had heard about Turner and wanted him very much, contacted the big center before Halas did, gave him $200 to have his teeth repaired and was surprised when the league, at Halas' outraged howl of protest, slapped a $5000 fine on him for tampering with another club's player.

The fine was imposed on February 2, 1940. On February 10, the indignant Richards, who had been in failing health for a couple of years, sold the Lions to Fred Mandel, a Chicago department store owner. A probably apocryphal story has it that Richards, who was a good hater, erected tombstones to his pet enemies in the back yard of his retirement home in Palm Springs. Prominent among them was one with "George Halas" lettered on it.

Richards turned a neat profit on the Lions. The club he had purchased for $21,500 in 1934 sold for $165,000 in 1940, nearly a 700 percent profit in six years.

Although Mandel proved as generous as Richards in pouring money into the team, he had as little success. He paid Pittsburgh $5000 for the contract of Byron (Whizzer) White, who had returned to the United States after a year in England on a Rhodes scholarship. White, a quick-thinking, ingenious runner, responded by winning the league rushing championship, just as he had done for Pittsburgh in 1938. White played only two seasons for the Lions, however, before embarking on the law career which carried him to a seat on the United States Supreme Court.

White was especially effective on punt returns. One of his most successful ploys was to plant himself three or four yards to one side or the other of where the punt was to fall, luring the defensive players toward him. At the last moment he would sprint to the side, take the ball on the dead run and, like as not, be off on a long return.

Mandel also brought Potsy Clark back as head coach, but Potsy went out faster under Mandel than he had under Richards. He left at the end of the 1940 season after the club had won five, lost five and tied one.

Bill Edwards took over for 1941 and 1942, achieving the dubious distinction of coaching the Lions to their first all-losing year in 1942, when the club lost eleven straight.

Flat-footed Frankie Sinkwich, one of the slowest great runners of all time, joined the

Massive Leon Hart (82) played fullback and end at Notre Dame; when he came to the Lions, he was one of the biggest as well as the best offensive ends in club history. Here he reaches high to get a pass.

club in 1943, as John Karcis took over as head coach. Sinkwich, who could run, pass and kick superbly, began a small resurgence as the team won three and lost six, not quite a good enough record to keep Karcis in his job.

In desperation, Mandel raided the University of Detroit for his next head coach — Gus Dorais, who had combined with Knute Rockne to set passing records at Notre Dame during his playing days.

Although Sinkwich surpassed his fine rookie year by winning the most valuable player award in 1944, Dorais posted another 3-6 record. Dorais, however, had a long-term contract and Mandel kept him. Gus reached his high-water mark with the Lions in 1945. A fine line and a corps of hard-running backs headed by Bob Westfall of Michigan accounted for a 7-3 record and a second place in the West behind the Cleveland Rams.

Pre-season injuries riddled the 1946 team and it skidded to last place with a 1-10 record. The Lions remained at the bottom of the heap for the next two years.

By 1947, Mandel had had enough. The team was not drawing fans or winning games and he could see no future in Detroit for pro football. The All-America Conference was providing competition all over the league, so Mandel sold out to a syndicate of Detroit business men headed by an electrical contractor, D. Lyle Fife, and a brewery executive, Edwin J. Anderson.

Fife was elected president and Anderson vice-president. The syndicate moved quickly to dismiss Dorais and hire Bo McMillin. Bo was no magician; the Lions finished last in 1948, improved by only one place in 1949; and the syndicate lost money just as lavishly as had Mandel.

In 1949, Fife was deposed as president and Anderson was elected in his place, a move which precipitated a bitter fight for control of the club in the next few years. In 1950, the fight had not yet flared and Anderson, with the help of an ebullient, aggressive and efficient general manager, Nick Kerbawy, moved quickly to build up the Lions.

The most important acquisition Anderson made in 1950 was Bobby Layne. Bobby had come into the league in 1948 and spent one year sitting restlessly on the bench for the Chicago Bears and another trying fruitlessly to get a pass away behind the weak-blocking New York Bulldogs.

To go with Layne, the Lions acquired two of the most highly-publicized collegians of the decade — Notre Dame's massive end, Leon Hart, and Southern Methodist's all-everything halfback, Doak Walker, who had played with Layne at Highland Park High School in Dallas.

A third Texan also joined the club in 1950, and eventually proved to be as important to the Detroit success as Layne or Walker. He was Buddy Parker, who came from Chicago, where he had been released as head coach by the Cardinals.

From the now-defunct All-America Conference came Bob (Hunchy) Hoernschemeyer. The Lions, too, reaped a bumper crop of rookie linemen in 1950. With this influx of talent, the club managed a break-even season, splitting twelve games and finishing fourth in the National Conference, the new name for the Western Division since the "merger" of the two leagues.

On December 20, 1950, Parker replaced the ailing McMillan as head coach and the last ingredient in a winning formula had been added. Wry, sometimes humorous, always moody, Parker fit the personality of the Lions like a glove. He was particularly at home with the flamboyant, violent and talented quarterback — Layne.

Jack Christiansen, a little-known back from Colorado A&M, began his career in 1951.

96

He was to mold about him one of the best sets of defensive backs in league history in the next few years.

Two exceptional rookie ends reported that year, too. They were Dorne Dibble from Michigan State and Jim Doran from Iowa State. Leon Hart, of course, had begun his career the year before.

All of this added up to an explosion which carried the Lions to second place in 1951. The colorful, long-gaining team almost doubled its home attendance figures, attracting 237,161 fans as against 133,331 in 1950, and put the Lions firmly on the road to solvency.

Layne, who had led the league in 1950 in passing attempts and in yards gained passing, led in 1951 in three categories: attempts, with 332; yards gained, with 2403, and

Doak Walker (left) and Joe Schmidt were key players on the great Detroit clubs. Walker, a small man, nevertheless was one of the top scorers in pro football history; Schmidt was a superb linebacker.

touchdown passes, with an awesome twenty-six. Parker, in order to give the Blond Bomber more time to throw, had traded for fullback Pat Harder of the Cardinals before the season began and Harder, combining with Hoernschemeyer and Walker in the Lion backfield, had given the Lions a thunderous ground game to supplement Layne's aerial didoes.

In 1952, a tall, crane-like end named Cloyce Box, who had come to the team as an oversize quarterback from West Texas State, returned after a year's layoff and became Layne's favorite touchdown target. The opening of the season was dismal enough. Box, suffering from his layoff, could not get untracked and the Lions opened on the West Coast, losing to San Francisco, then squeaking by the Rams.

The third game, the Lions' home opener, was pure disaster. The club could do

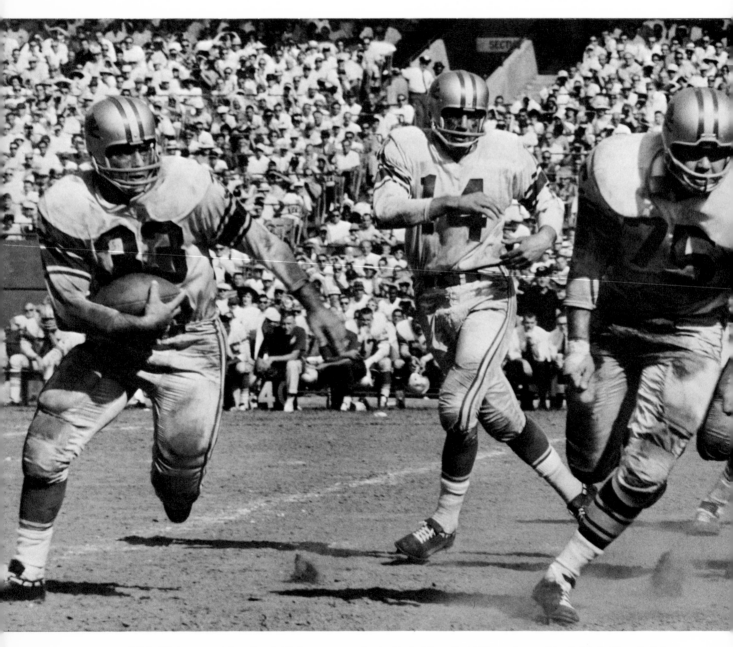

Nick Pietrosante takes handoff from quarterback Earl Morrall (14), swings wide behind Guard John Brody on start of off-tackle slant. Rugged Pietrosante provided much of the punch in Lion ground game.

nothing right in the face of an inspired Forty-Niner team and lost, 28-0, before a capacity crowd of 56,822.

From then on, though, the Lions began to move, urged by the high-pitched, irascible voice of Layne at quarterback and the quiet leadership of Doak Walker. Layne's philosophy is summed up in a remark he once made, jokingly.

"I've never lost a ball game," Bobby said. "But sometimes time has run out on me."

Time ran out on him only once more during the 1952 season, when the Bears managed a 24-23 victory in Chicago. Layne got his revenge two weeks later in Detroit by crushing the Chicagoans, 45-21.

The club finished the season with a 9-3 record, good enough to put them in a tie with the Los Angeles Rams for the National Conference championship. They had whipped the Rams twice during the regular season. They made it three in a row in the playoff for the conference championship by beating them again, in a deep fog at Briggs Stadium, 31-21. Pat Harder was the Ram nemesis, scoring nineteen points on two touchdowns, a field goal and four extra points.

The Lions had whipped the Cleveland Browns during the regular season, 17-6. They came within a point of duplicating that score in Cleveland Municipal Stadium in the championship game, winning by 17-7. The key play came early in the second period when Walker, who had been hurt much of the season, popped through the center of the Cleveland line on a counter play, cut sharply to his left to avoid a linebacker, and sped sixty-seven yards to a touchdown which put the Lions out of reach. Earlier, Layne had set up a touchdown with a long pass to Bill Swiacki and scored it himself on a two-yard quarterback sneak through the hefty Cleveland line. Harder added a field goal after Walker's run.

The 1953 season was almost a replica of 1952, except that the Lions did not have to play off with the Rams for the division championship, although the only two games they lost that year were to the coast club. Layne by now was making almost as many headlines off the field as he did on, but his night life had little effect on his play. He was still the leader of the Lions, goading them into furious play by roundly berating any player who blew an assignment.

"I don't care if a guy tries to make a block and gets beat," Bobby said once. "But I can't stand a guy who forgets an assignment. They get paid good money to remember."

This time the Lions met Cleveland in Detroit. They scored their usual seventeen points against the Browns, but Cleveland managed sixteen in this game, ten points on three field goals and an extra point by Lou Groza. By now, Detroit home attendance had rocketed to 315,549 for six home games, not including the championship, which attracted 54,577. The Lions were the toast of Detroit; season ticket sales soared.

The honeymoon lasted one more year. The Lions won their third straight division championship in 1954, losing one game each to San Francisco and Chicago and being tied by the Philadelphia Eagles. Pat Harder had gone, but a tough young back from Arkansas named Lew Carpenter, who had come up the year before, took up the slack, leading the club in ground gaining. The indestructible Layne was as good as ever. Walker, who had doubted his ability to play as a pro because of his size, scored 106 points, second highest total in the league and the Detroit defense, built around Christiansen's crew in the secondary, was as tough as ever.

The 1954 championship game, played in Cleveland, was a portent of things to come. The Lions had held a seemingly unbeatable jinx over the Browns for three years. That jinx ended in a superlative one-man show as Otto Graham ran for three touchdowns, passed for three more and led Cleveland to a 56-10 victory.

In 1955, the Lions did one of the most spectacular nose dives in league history, plummeting from first place to last. Many of the 1954 stars had retired. Les Bingaman, the mountainous guard who had been all-pro in 1954, decided to quit, as did linebacker Lavern Torgeson, defensive back Bob Smith, and Thurman McGraw, who had been an all-pro tackle.

Hoernschemeyer and Walker were playing their final seasons. Many of the Lions were beginning to feel the twinges of age. It all added up to catastrophe; the club lost six games in a row to begin the season and finished with a 3-9 record.

By the next year, the club had bounced back. David Middleton, who had come up as a rookie offensive end from Auburn in 1955, learned the intricacies of playing pro football and caught thirty-nine passes. Gene Gedman, a bouncy halfback from Indiana, provided some running punch and a rookie named Hopalong Cassady from Ohio State proved to be a real find.

The defense, led by linebacker Joe Schmidt and Christiansen, was one of the best in the league. The club won nine and lost three, finishing only a half-game behind the Chicago Bears.

Just before the 1957 season, Buddy Parker made a dramatic exit as head coach. At a banquet two days before the first pre-season game, Parker, who had been expected to respond to his introduction with the usual platitudes such an occasion calls for, dropped an atom bomb instead.

"I am quitting," Parker said, morosely. "I can no longer control this team and when I cannot control it, I can't coach it."

The reasons behind Parker's sudden resignation never were made clear, but certainly a cocktail party given by some of the club owners for some of the players just before the banquet had much to do with it.

Parker quit on August 12. On August 13, one of his assistants, an old Chicago Bear named George Wilson, was named to succeed him. Wilson is a big, gentle, easy-going man, soft-spoken and friendly. He had some good rookies available for the 1957 season: Steve Junker, a big, tough, red-haired end from Xavier; John Henry Johnson, a thumping fullback from Arizona State; and Gary Lowe, a fine defensive back from Michigan State. He also had picked up Tobin Rote to back up Layne at quarterback.

Wilson's first team won the division championship, finishing the regular season in a tie with the San Francisco Forty-Niners, then winning the playoff with a brilliant comeback.

The playoff took place in San Francisco. The Forty-Niners, cheered on by a full house, rushed to a 24-3 lead at the half and upped that to 27-3 shortly after the beginning of the third quarter.

The turning point of the game came early in the third quarter when Hugh McElhenny, the magnificent San Francisco halfback, carried the ball on a long run down to the Detroit two-yard line. Had the Forty-Niners scored, the game might well have become a rout. But four times the Lions turned them back, then took over the ball and reversed the tide of the game. They won, 31-27.

The championship game, against Cleveland, was almost anti-climactic. Layne was out of the game with a broken leg, but Rote was a more than adequate substitute. He threw four touchdown passes and scored once himself before 55,263 in Briggs Stadium. Many fans had stood in line all of the cold, windy night before the game to get tickets.

Layne was traded to the Pittsburgh Steelers in October of 1958 and with him went some of the spark of the attack. Rote was a good quarterback, but under his guidance the club dropped from first to fifth with a 4-7-1 record. Wilson began a rebuilding program in 1959.

The only bright spot of that season was the performance of a rookie fullback, Nick Pietrosante, from Notre Dame, who led the club in rushing. Earl Morrall, obtained from Pittsburgh in the Layne trade, replaced Rote at quarterback, but the team stayed mired in the lower echelon in the west, winning three games, losing eight and tying one.

In June of 1958, Edwin J. Anderson had taken over as general manager of the Lions. Nick Kerbawy, who might have remained as his assistant, decided instead to accept an offer from Fred Zollner to become general manager of the Detroit Pistons basketball team.

This, eventually, set off a bitter proxy fight for control of the Lions, which came to a head in the spring of 1961, when a group headed by D. Lyle Fife, who had been deposed as Lion president in 1949, when Anderson was elected, tried to wrest control of the club from the Anderson faction.

Their effort was unsuccessful. Anderson resigned as president, was succeeded by William Clay Ford, of the automotive Fords, and is at present the successful general manager of the Lions.

Wilson, in the meantime, built a sturdy defensive team. Alex Karras, a bespectacled cat-quick tackle of 270 pounds, and Roger Brown, almost as quick at nearly 300 pounds, anchored a line whose flanks were protected by Darris McCord, an all-pro end, and Sam Williams, who performed exceptionally well in 1962.

Joe Schmidt, a perennial all pro, directed the defense intelligently from his middle backer post. Wayne Walker and Carl Brettschneider filled out a superb trio of linebackers. The secondary defense approached the Christiansen crew in effectiveness. Good pass defense had become a trademark of Detroit football.

For three straight years, from 1960 through 1962, the Lions won the annual second place playoff in Miami. They appeared ready to move up.

## A DAY IN THE LIFE OF A PRO

Nick Pietrosante is a pro fullback. His is a demanding job and it takes, during the season, almost all of his time to prepare himself for it. He must work out hard (right) to perfect himself in the intricate maneuvers which are a part of his job. But, for him, as for most professional players, football is more than a business. When he comes home in the evening, he is still ready to work out with the neighborhood children, who idolize him. His family is important to him, and the moments he can steal for a quiet stroll through the neighborhood streets with his wife and his two small children make the sacrifices worthwhile. His teammates call him Petro for short; like most of them, he is using pro football as a way stop en route to a career. Pietrosante works for a Detroit steel company during the off season. When his football career ends, as all must, he will be ready to take his position in the non-athletic world in a good job with a lucrative career ahead. The determination and team work he learns as a player carry on into later life.

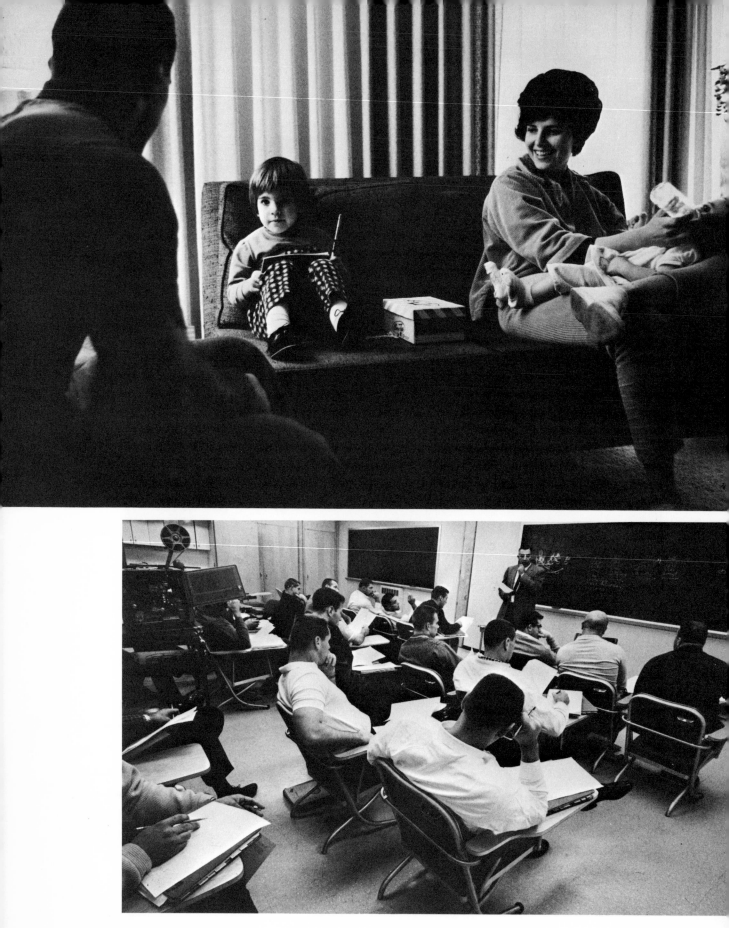

Lessons takes up a good deal of Nick's day. He helps daughter with hers (upper left), sits in on the never-ending classes where he learns his own pro football lessons (lower left). But there is time for relaxation, too, when he can help his wife in the kitchen or play a tough and competitive game of bridge with friends in his comfortable den at home.

With Mrs. Pietrosante involved with their younger child, Nick finds that some of the marketing devolves on him and he gets assistance from his older daughter. Pietrosante is aware of his responsibility as a father as well as a player; he devotes as much of his time to his family as he does to his work. His employer in the steel company, Detroit tycoon Harry Levine, considers Nick one of the brightest young men in his organization. "He is quick and aggressive and we feel we are lucky to have him," Levine says. "He's a credit to professional football." Pietrosante is typical of the modern professional player, who considers the game as a stepping stone to success in other fields of endeavor. The day of the football bum is over; pro football has become, in the last twenty years, a desirable helping hand to the young men who are capable of playing during the years just after their college careers. "Pro football has done more for me than I can ever repay," says Pietrosante. "The contacts you can make as a player are invaluable and the income is far more than most college graduates can expect to earn in the years just after they finish school. My family enjoys more comforts now than I could have given them in any other profession this soon after leaving Notre Dame. By the time I finish playing, I'll be established in the steel business. If I hadn't been a pro player, I would never have met Harry Levine." Pietrosante's future is sure, as is that of his wife and his children.

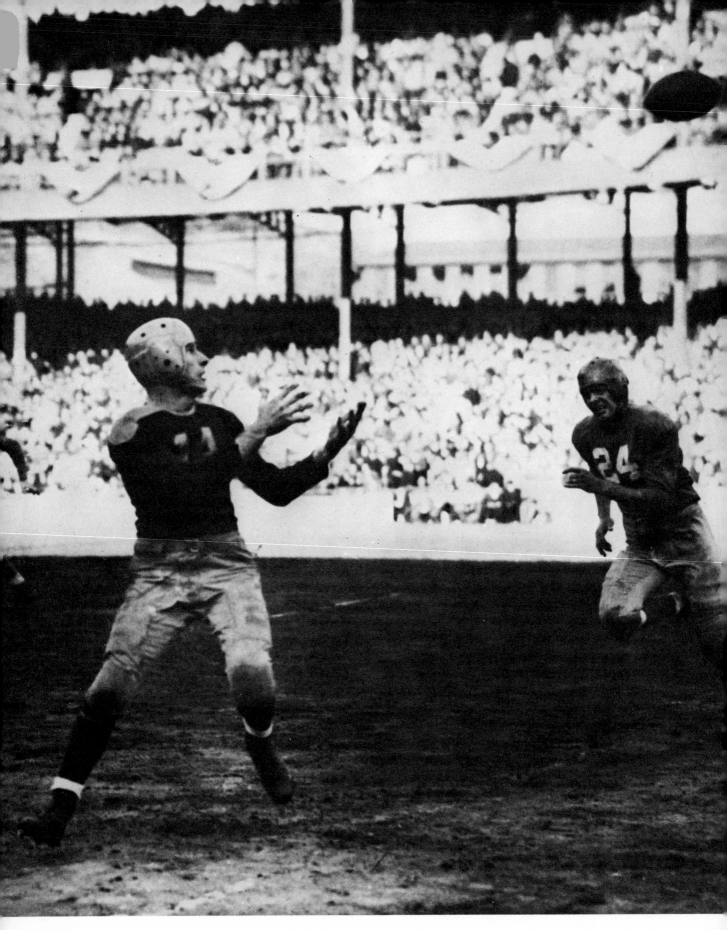

Don Hutson, the first of pro football's great pass catchers, shows clearly his talent for getting in the clear in this picture. He is yards away from the defender as the pass is dropping into his hands.

# THE GREEN BAY PACKERS

JUST after World War I, a young man named Earl Louis Lambeau lost his tonsils; Knute Rockne, who had just taken over as coach of Notre Dame, lost a back, and Green Bay, the oldest city in Wisconsin, gained a professional football team.

Green Bay lies in the never-never land between large and small. In 1919, its population was about 30,000. In 1962, the population had just about doubled, but the city remained much the same. It would be indistinguishable from any other city of 60,000-odd population in the United States if Lambeau had not contracted tonsilitis some forty-five years ago.

The city itself lies athwart the Fox, a rather nondescript river, but it is, nonetheless, an engaging town. The town folk are friendly and it is not difficult to engage them in conversation. All you have to do is mention the Green Bay Packers, order a beer at Speed's or the King's X, and listen. Green Bay's heroes are many and, as the old song has it, well-known to fame, and the least of Green Bay's citizens can tell you all about them, beginning of course, with Earl Louis (much better known as Curly) Lambeau.

Curly was the son of Marcel Lambeau, a Belgian-born building contractor. Curly was a high school football star in Green Bay during World War I; in his senior year, when the coach went off to the wars, Curly coached as well as played.

He played well enough to get a scholarship to Notre Dame, where he began, unpromisingly, as a substitute for George Gipp. But, because he could pass very well and because Rockne had a certain affinity for passers, Curly was moved to quarterback after one game and remained there until he had to leave school for six weeks because of the troublesome tonsils.

He never went back, because the Indian Packing Co., hard up for help during the war years, offered him $250 a month to work for them, a job which seemed to offer the riches of Croesus to a young boy in those days.

Curly, of course, took the job. Then, as football season drew near again, he felt the urge to play and solved his problem by organizing his own team. The organization took place on August 11, 1919. Green Bay has had a professional team continuously ever since, which, as the inhabitants will point out to you at the drop of a free beer, is longer than in any other city in the United States, including Chicago, New York, Philadelphia or any place you care to mention.

The packing company provided money for jerseys and stockings and the players hailed from the vicinity of Green Bay and were paid nothing, so the overhead for the first Green Bay Packers was small. The packing company had just moved to town from Providence, where the owners were familiar with the redoubtable Providence Steamrollers, which explains why they were willing to part with $500 for the privilege of having their names

Obviously (and not very well) posed publicity picture shows Green Bay star Clark Hinkle leaping dramatically through hole in line during scrimmage as the Packers worked out for Giant game in 1937.

displayed on the jerseys of the new pro football club.

Their confidence was justified. Curly's first team scored 565 points to six, which is better than any other Packer team has been able to do, since the competition has been stronger.

The six points, unfortunately, accounted for Green Bay's lone loss of its inaugural year, to a team from Beloit, Wis., which represented Fairbanks-Morse and labored under the unrealistic and difficult name of the "Fairies."

Lambeau scored three times on the Fairies, on successive plays, in this game, but twice was called back for being offside. On the third attempt, he told his club to stand perfectly still while he ran the ball over, which they did and he did, and the official called the play back again.

"Now what?" asked Curly.

"You were in motion," said the official, who was working in Beloit and well aware of which side of the bread his cheese was spread on.

In that first season, no admission was charged to Green Bay games. George Calhoun, who handled publicity for the team, would pass among the spectators with his hat out and collect donations. At the end of the season, Calhoun thoughtfully doled out $16.75 to each of the Packers as their share of the season's profits, then went off and bought himself a new car.

This prompted Lambeau to have his father build a fence around Hagemeister Park, where the Packers played, and erect stands seating some 3000 people. Now Curly charged fifty cents for a ticket and dispensed with Calhoun as a solicitor.

With people in the stands, the Packers were 9-1-1 in 1920, but lost again to the Fairies,

110

Curly Lambeau, who *was* the Green Bay Packers for many years, goes over game strategy with Hutson (right) and assistant coach Walter Kiesling. Lambeau's departure from Green Bay was a bitter one.

who beat them, 14-3, without the help of the official's good will. It was just before this season began that the famous meeting took place in the Ralph Hay automobile agency in Canton, Ohio, where the first pro league was formed, but Lambeau was not invited to attend. The Acme Packing Co., which had bought out the Indian Packing Co., put up $50 for Curly in 1921 and he bought the Green Bay franchise then. In 1921, there were thirteen teams in the league and the Packers won six games, lost two and tied two to finish fourth. They began their long and bitter rivalry with the Chicago Bears by losing, 20-0.

The league, flexing its muscles, asked Green Bay to forfeit its franchise after the 1921 season, on the charge that the Packers had used college players playing under assumed names, which, indeed, they had. So had almost every other club in the league; Joe Carr, the new league president, simply chose the Packers as a convenient whipping boy.

However, all Curly Lambeau needed to get back in the league was $50 for another franchise fee and transportation to Canton, Ohio, where the next league meeting was scheduled in June, 1922. He had the $50 and prevailed upon a friend, Don Murphy, to sell his car to raise the transportation money. Murphy asked only that he be allowed to start for the Packers in the first game of the 1922 season, and Lambeau agreed.

Murphy's pro football career lasted for one play, which, although it is not carried in the league record book, is certainly a record.

Curly had to be bailed out after the first game in 1922, when the Packers had accumulated an astronomical debt of around $2000. He was rescued by a civic-minded man named A. B. Turnbull, the publisher of the Green Bay *Press-Gazette*. Turnbull organized a group which supported the Packers for nearly a quarter of a century. Next to Curly, the group was most responsible for the survival of the Packers.

Tough, intelligent Vincent Lombardi (shown here with Linebacker Ray Nitschke), has led the Packers to two straight world championships. As both coach and general manager, he has complete control of club.

Turnbull's group consisted of himself, Lambeau, a grocery store owner, Leland H. Joannes, Dr. W. Webber Kelly, and an attorney, Gerald Clifford. With their help, Lambeau struggled through 1922, finishing seventh in an eighteen-team league with a 4-3-3 record. When the season ended, it became apparent that no five men could support the club. In August of 1923, the Packers, in effect, became a community project, with new articles of incorporation, 1000 shares of stock issued, and profits earmarked for the American Legion post of Green Bay.

From 1923 until 1929, the Packers fielded a team regularly, but with only fair success, except in 1923, when they finished third behind the Canton Bulldogs and the Chicago Bears, and in 1927, when they were second to the New York Giants.

There were some fine players on the club. Verne Lewellen, an officer of the team now, came from Nebraska. He holds the distinction of having been the only pro player to have been a playing halfback and a district attorney at the same time, which he was from 1924 through 1928. Eddie Kotal, chief talent scout for the Los Angeles Rams, was a good halfback during those days, although he was handicapped early in his career by playing behind Lambeau.

There was no draft during these salad days and no option clause in contracts. As the 1929 season began, Lambeau picked up three disaffected players from other clubs in the league: a giant tackle from the New York Giants, Cal Hubbard; a small, tough guard from the New York Yankees, "Iron Mike" Machalske; and an uninhibited combination of scholar,

112

esthete, bon vivant and halfback from Pottsville, John McNally. McNally conducted his life by rules formulated by himself.

"He wasn't a particularly elusive halfback," one of his teammates from the old Green Bay team recalls. "He wouldn't give you much dipsy-doodle. But he had a long stride and completely deceptive speed and he was a slasher. He could run through you, although he wasn't a big man. And he had wonderful hands. He would have been a great receiver today; he was a great receiver then, when no one threw much."

He was also strikingly handsome, attractive to and attracted by the ladies, and a fount of conviviality. He called himself Johnny Blood, a name he ran across on a theater marquee while trying to decide what pseudonym to use to play a pro game for Minneapolis while he was still an undergraduate.

The Packers were undefeated in 1929, as they won their first league championship. They played their first five games in Green Bay, then went on the road for the last eight, first waiting for forty-five minutes for Blood before their train left Green Bay. They won seven of the eight road games; only a tie with Frankford kept them from an all-winning season.

The same team returned in 1930 and 1931, and won two more championships. Blood was the sparkplug; he paid no attention to training rules and played at top speed only when he felt it necessary. Lambeau tried to curb him with numerous fines, all of which Blood accepted docilely before skipping another meeting or ignoring curfew again.

One season, Lambeau refused to sign Blood until he had promised not to take a drink until the season ended. Blood agreed and, in fact, did not drink. He spent his free time in the library of the editor of the Green Bay newspaper, sipping milk and reading omnivorously. He had a magnificent year, but he never took the pledge again.

In 1930, Arnie Herber joined the club. Within a few years he teamed with Don Hutson in one of pro football's most famous passing combinations. In the beginning, his principal targets were Lewellen and Blood.

Only a weird season by the Chicago Bears kept Green Bay from its fourth consecutive title in 1932. The Packers won ten games, lost three and tied one but the Bears won seven, lost one and tied six. Since ties were not counted, it was a 7-1 season and it gave the Bears the championship.

The 1933 season was disastrous on the field and off. The club recorded its first losing season with five victories, seven losses and a tie. A fan fell out of the stands and sued for $25,000, which was more than Lambeau had at the time.

The liability insurance company covering the Packers against contretemps of this kind went bankrupt and so did the Packers, although the receiver appointed for the Packers was a friendly one, as, indeed, any receiver appointed from the population of Green Bay would have been.

Another stock sale was organized and sufficient financial backing arranged to keep the team in operation. Within a year and a half, the club was on its feet again and out of receivership.

The indefatigable Lambeau went doggedly to work, rebuilding the club on the field and in the front office. A big help was a rookie who reported in 1934 — Clarke Hinkle, a fullback from Bucknell.

Cecil Isbell, who joined the team in 1937, had this to say of Hinkle: "He did not have the pure brute power of Nagurski, because he didn't have Bronk's size. But he had the knack you see today in a runner like Jim Taylor of exploding at the point of impact. He was a compact runner and he had the same kind of balance Taylor has — he could take the shock of a tackle, bounce sideways and keep going. And he never quit. He wanted to win more than anyone I ever saw."

Hinkle's collisions with Nagurski were noteworthy; over the years it was just about a standoff between the two fine fullbacks. Once, meeting Bronko head-on along the sideline under full speed, Hinkle exploded as Nagurski came in for the tackle, dropping his shoulder and smashing it into Nagurski's face. He ran right through the Bear fullback, leaving Nagurski lying on the field with a broken nose, broken hip and seriously bruised feelings.

Another time, bursting through a quick hole in the Bear line, Hinkle met Nagurski head-on, bounced backward through the hole from the impact, lit running and came back through the same hole for a considerable gain.

George Musso, the big Bear tackle, had watched Hinkle shuttling back and forth, his head shifting from side to side like a spectator at a tennis match.

"That's the only time I ever saw a back go by me three times on one play," he said.

By 1934, the Packers' fortunes perked up on the field and at the box office. They climbed back over .500, winning seven games and losing six and finishing third in the Western Division.

The tall, skinny Hutson joined the Packers from Alabama in 1935. With his coming, the Green Bay team was almost ready to move into its second championship era. The frail-looking Hutson played end without pads, in order to keep all of his speed, and despite his appearance, was as durable as cured leather. He was the first and one of the best of the pass-catching specialists, and he played beautifully on defense as well.

Isbell, who was to work with him for years, says: "He was the first end with all the moves. He had good head and shoulder fakes and he had an endless series of changes of pace. It was impossible for one man to cover him and almost impossible for two. He had absolute concentration on the ball; he never heard a footstep in his life, and he'd catch the ball in a crowd almost as easily as he did in the open. And he ran like a halfback after he got it."

The 1935 Packers, with Herber completing seventeen passes for seven touchdowns to the rookie Hutson, won eight games and lost four and finished second to the Detroit Lions. But the 1936 team, with the Herber-to-Hutson combination operating at full effectiveness, lost only one game and won the Western Division championship easily. The Packers met the Boston Redskins for the championship. George Marshall, piqued at Boston fans because they had not supported his champions as wholeheartedly as he thought they should, took the game out of Boston and into the New York Polo Grounds, where the Packers won, 21-6.

An injury slowed Herber in 1937 and the Packers faded a little, finishing second to the Bears. But in 1938, Lambeau found a more than adequate replacement for Herber in Isbell, who had been a great tailback at Purdue and who was an even better passer than Herber.

Isbell was an excellent runner, sturdy and stubborn, and was one of the most accomplished passers ever. He had complete mastery of the throwing game; he could drill a rifle-shot pass to a hooking end between defensive backs, throw a flat, hard long pass or lift a long, soft one far downfield for Hutson to run under.

He and Herber played in the same backfield at first and the double-barreled threat posed problems for Packer opponents which have not been duplicated since. On a few occasions, when the other team concentrated on Hutson or Joe Laws or Milt Gantenbein,

114

Versatile Paul Hornung, a deadly blocker, resourceful and strong runner and good passer, was the sparkplug of the 1961 champions but sat out much of the 1962 season with a series of leg injuries.

who played the other end from Hutson, or on Hinkle, Isbell would pass to the now portly and slow Herber or Herber would pass to Isbell. It was an effective play, although not a long-gaining one.

The Packers moved to another division championship in 1938. The club was strengthened not only by Isbell, but by two rookies, end Carl Mulleneaux and halfback Andy Uram. Carl's brother, Lee, was obtained from Pittsburgh at the same time.

A knee injury to Hutson hobbled him for the championship game against the New York Giants in the Polo Grounds, and he limped on the field for only a few plays. Still, the Packers nearly won. They led, 17-16, in the third quarter on a field goal by Tiny Engebretsen, one of the greatest of Green Bay guards. But the Giants came back with a long pass before the quarter ended and won, 23-17.

The 1939 team was probably the strongest Lambeau ever had. The addition of husky Larry Craig at blocking back on offense and end on defense made Hutson's chores lighter. Don moved off the defensive line into the defensive backfield, where the going was not so punishing.

The Packers again won the Western Division championship and again met the Giants for the league title. After some consideration, Lambeau moved the title game from Green Bay to Milwaukee and charged $4.40 per ticket, a new high for pro football prices. The price did not affect the attendance; the stadium was sold out in two days.

On a chill, windy day, the Packers nearly blew the Giants off the field, 27-0. Herber passed to Gantenbein for one touchdown, then Isbell hit Laws for another. Tiny Engebretsen and Ernie Smith contributed field goals, and a double reverse, with rookie end Harry Jacunksi winding up with the ball, set up another touchdown. It was an enormously satisfying afternoon for the Green Bay fans.

For the next four years, the Packers had almost as good a team as the 1939 group. They had the misfortune, however, to be in the same division as the Chicago Bears, who had by then built their super team. For four years, the Packers could whip any team but the Bears, and for four years they finished second to Chicago.

Cecil Isbell retired after the 1942 season to take a coaching job at Purdue. Isbell, a level-headed young man, had no desire to stick around until he had outlived his usefulness.

Years later, when he was an assistant coach for the old Dallas Texans, Isbell said, "I saw the Turk call for some good ball players, including Arnie Herber. I didn't want to get the news from Curly when I was through. So I quit while I still had some good time left."

The Packers won another world championship in 1944, Lambeau's last. Irv Comp was now the passer, and a new fullback named Ted Fritsch provided tremendous power. Hutson was playing his penultimate season at end; Craig and Laws were still in the starting backfield.

Rock-hard, brutally powerful Jim Taylor, the Packers' all-pro fullback, is one of the most painful men in pro football to tackle. His extraordinary balance makes him nearly unstoppable for one tackler.

The Packers beat the Giants 14-7 in the Polo Grounds for the championship, with Hutson contributing two extra points and Fritsch scoring both touchdowns.

Now a long and bitter period began for the Packers. With the organization of the All-America Conference at the end of World War II, the cost of football talent soared. Green Bay, with a smaller war chest than almost any other club in the National Football League, suffered particularly in bidding for topflight college seniors. The rocketing salaries were reflected in the amount of money demanded by the veteran players on the Packer roster.

Finally, Lambeau had to change from the single-wing attack, with which he was thoroughly familiar and which he operated better than anyone else in the league, to the unfamiliar T, where he was uncomfortable and inept. The 1945 Packers slipped to third, with a 6-4 record; in 1946, they were third again, with 6-5.

The diffuse ownership of the Packers began to hurt. The thirteen-man board of directors took sharp issue with Lambeau, curtailing his authority off the field. They were unhappy over a $50,000 lodge he bought for the club to use for a training camp. They criticized him for his personal life (he had been married three times, divorced twice, and spent his summers in Malibu). They called him the "Earl of Hollywood" and studiously ignored him in club functions.

From 1945 through 1950, the Packers never had the talent they needed. They had fine individual players in quarterback Tobin Rote, who came in 1950, and in a small greying halfback named Tony Canadeo, who was as capable a runner as any the team ever had. Tony became so emotional over playing against the Bears that he cried after every Bear game, win or lose. There was Bob Forte, a big linebacker from Arkansas and Clayton Tonnemaker, an all-pro linebacker from Minnesota. But there were never enough good players for a division championship.

Even so, Curly's 1947 team might have won a championship had it not been thoroughly snakebitten. The club lost its first four games by an average of less than a field goal and wound up the season at 6-5-1.

During this season, while Lambeau was on the road, the board of directors set up a series of operating subcommittees, in charge of almost every phase of running the club. When Lambeau returned and was confronted by this accomplished fact, he was furious, but there was nothing he could do about it.

Thus began the inefficient and almost ludicrous rule by committee which hamstrung the Packers until the arrival of Vince Lombardi in 1959.

The 1948 Packers slid to 3-9 and fourth place in the West, only a game out of last. The 1949 team made it to last place with a 2-10 record and suddenly the Packers were again in deep financial trouble.

An intrasquad game on Thanksgiving Day of 1949 raised over $50,000, which helped, but it was obvious that another thorough reorganization was needed. This was proposed by attorney Jerry Clifford, one of the members of the board. The new grouping would not include Lambeau. Lambeau's lodge burned down not long after that; it was to be symbolic of the end of the Lambeau regime.

This came suddenly. Lambeau, beset on all sides by friends turned enemies, appeared before the executive committee on February 1, 1950, and resigned. He had taken a job as head coach for the Chicago Cardinals.

With his going, a long, colorful and indispensable chapter in the history of pro football came to an end. Whatever his shortcomings, Lambeau, in the early, difficult days of the game had provided unfailing determination, a lively imagination and an eternal optimism. It is not to the credit of the Green Bay organization that he left on so dour a note.

"If Lambeau had stayed two more years, we would have gone completely busted," said Clifford.

Buckets Goldenberg, who for twelve years was a superb guard for the Packers and later served on the board of directors for the club, said, "I don't see how the club can go on without him. He was the Packers."

The truth lay somewhere in between the two opinions.

The first coach hired to replace Lambeau was Gene Ronzani, who had played with the Bears. Young, intelligent and personable, Ronzani worked under the same handicaps that had restricted Lambeau: not enough money to bid for the top players, and rule by committee. The first problem had been lessened, since the All-America Conference had folded and there was no longer an all-out competition for talent. But the second problem was even worse, if possible.

Ronzani and the team had to face the executive committee each Tuesday in a meeting at the YMCA in which the previous Sunday's game was taken apart piecemeal, a heaven-sent opportunity for Tuesday morning quarterbacks. When Ronzani finished his explanations, the committeemen then cornered individual players to talk over the situation.

If there is a cardinal rule in professional football on player-management relationships, it is that under absolutely no circumstances should an owner or a general manager discuss the coach or the team with a player. This rule was broken freely.

Ronzani's first season produced a 3-9 record. The second was no better, but by 1952, he had hauled the Packers up to even (6-6), no mean feat with the talent at his disposal.

He was not allowed to finish the 1953 season. The executive committee fired him with two games to go, and Hugh Devore and Scooter McLean coached the club through its final two defeats, on the West Coast.

In another organizational shakeup, Verne Lewellen was named general manager and Lisle Blackbourn, a successful college coach at Marquette, was hired as head coach. It appeared for a while that the executive committee, at long last, was going to keep its fingers out of the pie.

This, however, proved to be an illusion. The committee soon stripped Lewellen of any authority beyond that of a business manager. They did let Blackbourn alone — for a while.

Blackbourn responded by producing a minor miracle in 1954, although the club won only four games and lost eight. With inferior material, he kept the Packers close in almost every game they played. In 1955, Blackbourn managed a 6-6 season. It seemed the Packers were on the road back, and the executive committee was at least quiescent.

Injuries to fullback Howie Ferguson hurt Blackbourn during 1956 and it was during 1956, too, that his quarterback, Tobin Rote, announced that he was considering retirement and criticized Blackbourn for calling him inconsistent.

Blackbourn needed offensive linemen in 1957. He traded Rote to Detroit for a defensive back, a running back and three offensive linemen. Unfortunately for Blackbourn, Rote, with Bobby Layne, led Detroit to the world championship while the Packers dropped limply into last place, with a 3-9 record. Blackbourn was criticized for disposing of the quarterback and also for not using the Green Bay bonus draft pick enough. That bonus choice was Paul Hornung.

As expected, the executive committee moved hastily. While Blackbourn was out of town on a scouting expedition, the committee fired him. His replacement was Scooter

McLean, who had been an assistant under both Ronzani and Blackbourn.

McLean lasted one horrendous year, during which the Packers won one, lost ten and tied one. Familiar with life under the committee system, Scooter did not wait around for the inevitable firing. He quit to take a job as a Detroit assistant coach.

By now it was obvious, even to the executive committee, that the Packers could not survive without a firm hand at the controls.

In searching for a new head coach, they received two strong endorsements for the same candidate from intelligent football men. One was from Paul Brown of the Cleveland Browns, the other from Commissioner Bert Bell. Both recommended a stocky, determined assistant coach for the New York Giants, Vincent Lombardi.

Lombardi took the job with the understanding that he was to have complete control of the club. When he arrived in Green Bay, he underlined that understanding: "Let's get one thing absolutely straight right now. I'm in complete command here."

He had a five-year contract as coach and general manager and he set about rebuilding the team with characteristic meticulous attention to details.

Lombardi believes that championships are built on defense, so he started work on the Packer defense at once. From Paul Brown, he acquired three defensive linemen: Bill Quinlan, an end; Willie Davis, an offensive tackle whom Lombardi converted to a superb defensive end; and Henry Jordan, a defensive tackle. The three combined wtih veteran Dave (Hawg) Hanner to give the Packers the sine qua non of a good defense: four men

Lombardi corrals the other National League football coaches in a picture that is as much fact as fiction.

to line the barricades. Behind them Lombardi had Dan Currie, the Packers' first draft choice in 1958, as one corner backer and Bill Forester, an excellent veteran, as the other. The middle linebackers were steady, reliable Tom Bettis, and Ray Nitschke, a bull of a man but a player who needed discipline in playing his position.

The unwieldy thirteen-man executive committee was streamlined to seven but its contract with Lombardi placed it in an advisory capacity only. Vince ran the show. Occasionally he discussed his programs with the executive committee, but the old rule by committee was disposed of for good. Lombardi, like Lambeau in the old days, *was* the Packers.

Practice sessions before the 1959 season were a far cry from what they had been in preceding years. Lombardi, a driving, unrelenting worker, demanded the same dedication from his players and got it.

Lombardi obtained Lamar McHan, an in-and-out quarterback, from the St. Louis Cardinals and used him very well. The Packers began play in the best condition in years. More important, Lombardi, helped by the ex-Cleveland players who brought with them the taste of winning, had convinced the Packers they could be winners.

With almost the same club which won only one game in 1958, Lombardi won seven and lost five in 1959. McHan was injured and Bart Starr, who had been an understudy to Rote and McHan, led the club through the last four games. Given his first real chance, he performed adequately, if not brilliantly.

In 1960, the Packers won eight, lost four and took the Western Division championship. New Packer heroes began to take hold. Hornung, who had been tried at quarterback and fullback by previous Packer coaches, settled gratefully into a halfback position, where he became one of the most spectacular halfbacks in the league. Hornung was a kind of latter-day Johnny Blood, handsome and high-living, with an enormous talent for playing football and enjoying life.

The 1960 Packers lost the league championship to the Philadelphia Eagles in Philadelphia, 17-13. The game ended as a Packer drive ran out of time on the Eagles' nine-yard line with Chuck Bednarik tackling Jim Taylor. The Packers spent the off-season berating themselves for losing a game they felt they should have won easily.

By 1961, when the league season began, Lombardi had molded what must rank as one of the finest teams ever. The defense, under the intelligent, quiet direction of Phil Bengtson and Norb Hecker, was one of the stingiest in the league; it was a perfect blend of size and speed, caution and daring, calculation and inspiration.

The four front men — Davis and Quinlan at the ends, Jordan and Hanner at the tackles — were not the biggest in the league but they worked as though born to the task. Behind them was the best trio of linebackers in the league: Currie and Forester on the corners and a chastened and more orthodox Nitschke in the middle. The secondary, with Henry Gremminger, Jess Whittenton, Willie Wood, John Symank, Emlen Tunnell and a rookie, Herb Adderley, was deep and blended the sagacity of the veteran with the daring of the young.

The offense was set, too. One of the best blocking lines ever had taken the field in 1960. The tackles were Bob Skoronski, Forrest Gregg and Norm Masters. One guard was Fred (Fuzzy) Thurston, who had been released by four clubs before he came to the Packers to find a niche as a deadly blocker ahead of the ball carrier or in the line. The other was big, blond Jerry Kramer, who teamed perfectly with Thurston and was a devastating blocker, as well as a better than average field goal kicker. Jim Ringo, playing his ninth year for the Packers, was at center; he was small but quick and a sure, consistent blocker. He was named

120

all-pro for the fourth year in a row in 1961.

The ends were Max McGee, a fast, sure-handed receiver, and massive Ron Kramer, who was deceptively fast for his bulk and a brutal blocker from his tight end position.

Behind this formidable line was a versatile, powerful backfield. Taylor, the concrete-hard, violent fullback, could slash into the line or veer outside of it. Hornung, one of the best blocking halfbacks, was a runner with almost as much power as Taylor and a little more elusiveness. Boyd Dowler, a tall, gangling ex-hurdler from Colorado who had joined the Packers in 1959 as a third draft choice and won rookie of the year honors, was the flanker back.

Running the club was Bart Starr, a quiet, scholarly young man who needed only this opportunity to prove he belonged among the top quarterbacks.

"Football is not a subtle game," Lombardi said, as the season began. "It is two things: blocking and tackling. The winner is the team which blocks and tackles best."

After watching the Packers in action in 1961, one of the league scouts unconsciously parroted Lombardi. Looking over his notes on the uncomplicated Packer offenses and defenses, the scout shook his head sadly.

"How do you scout blocking and tackling?" he asked

The Packers won the Western Division championship again in 1961, then, in a display of pure power, blasted the New York Giants out of City Stadium in Green Bay for the championship, 37-0. Hornung, running beautifully, blocking with precision and sparking the team, scored nineteen points. The Packer line punched gaping holes in the heralded Giant line. It was a rout.

The 1962 season was more of the same, although the Packers, winning thirteen games and losing only one, had to stand off the stubborn challenge of a rugged Detroit club, which beat them on Thanksgving Day in Detroit and nearly beat them in Green Bay before that.

Taylor, improving with each season, led the league in ground gaining in 1962. Hornung, unfortunately, suffered a knee injury in mid-season which was to keep him out of action almost until the championship game. He was replaced capably by Tom Moore, another of the big backs Lombardi likes so well.

This time the championship game was played in Yankee Stadium on a wind-swept, icy afternoon. The field was rock-hard and slippery. The gusty winds nullified, to some extent, the threat of Giant quarterback Y. A. Tittle's long passes, but the slippery turf handicapped the power-running Packer backs.

This was a far more bitter contest than the 37-0 game in Green Bay, but the Packers, clearly the better team, won again, this time by virtue of three field goals by Jerry Kramer. The only Packer touchdown came on a seven-yard slant by Jim Taylor through a hole opened over the left side of the Giant line by the Packer guard and tackle on that side.

The Packers, who had had to carry the tension of a long winning streak through most of the campaign, looked tired toward the end of it, but they seemed fresh and strong for the championship game. Age did not appear to have withered nor custom to have staled this fine team as the season ended.

Kenny Washington, the first Negro to play modern professional football, was one of the Rams' best runners despite the fact that by the time he joined the club, he was operating on two bad knees.

# THE LOS ANGELES RAMS

THE Los Angeles Rams have been a team of superlatives. From 1937, when a cartoonist named Damon H. (Buzz) Wetzel became the first general manager of the club in Cleveland and selected "Rams" for a name so that it would fit comfortably into headlines, until 1963, the Rams have compiled a notable list of mosts, firsts, bests and worsts.

Slices of the club sold for the least (one dollar for thirty percent in 1947) and the most ($4,800,000 for two-thirds in 1962). The team scored more points in one game or in one season than any other in the league. The club held the record, an unenviable one, for total number of head coaches on the payroll at the same time: one active, three turned out to pasture. It played before more people in one game, or in one season, than any other team.

The Rams were the first team to decorate their helmets. Fred Gehrke, a Ram half-back who was a commercial artist in the off-season, painted the original rams horns on the helmets, setting off a wave of imitation. The Rams were the only team to change home cities the year after winning a world championship and the only team to televise its home games.

The group which was granted a franchise in Cleveland in 1937 was a syndicate of Cleveland businessmen headed by Homer Marshman. The first Ram club, coached by Hugo Bezdek, won one game and finished fifth and last in its division.

When the Rams opened the 1938 season by losing four in a row, Marshman discarded Bezdek and hired the youngest head coach in pro football, Art Lewis. A tackle, Lewis promptly set the club off on a three-game winning streak. Stars of the streak were Bob Snyder, the quarterback who was later to become, briefly, Ram head coach, and a big and slow but sure-handed end named Jim Benton, from Arkansas. Despite this spurt, the Rams finished the season at 4-7 in fourth place and Lewis gave way to Dutch Clark, remaining with the club as Clark's assistant.

Clark, blessed by the acquisition of Parker Hall, a halfback from Mississippi who was the most valuable player in the league in his rookie year, pulled the club up to 5-5-1. Hall, Johnny Drake from Purdue, Benton, Corby Davis and Riley Matthesen, a fine linebacker from Texas School of Mines, got the Rams off fast in 1940. They won the first two games but bogged down quickly, finishing at 4-6-1.

Marshman and his associates had had enough by then. In June, 1941, they sold the Rams to Daniel Farrell Reeves, who became the youngest owner in pro football. Reeves, whose older brother, Ed, had owned a part of the Washington Redskins, had long been a rabid fan. The price for the Rams was $100,000. When he bought the club, Reeves had already decided to move it to Los Angeles, if the Memorial Coliseum there were ever

Jim Benton, a sure-handed end from Arkansas, made a habit of diving catches such as this one he made against the Philadelphia Eagles. Coming up too late to stop the pass is Eagle Steve Van Buren.

opened to professional football.

Reeves was the son of the founder of the Reeves chain of grocery stores, which were sold to A&P in 1940 for $11,000,000. A resident of New York with no affection for Cleveland, Dan commuted back and forth while the club was operating in Cleveland.

When Reeves and his partner, Fred Levy, Jr., took over the club in 1941, they installed Billy Evans as general manager. The partners retained Clark and his coaching staff. The first game they saw their new club play seemed to justify their faith in the coaches.

The Rams were playing the Pittsburgh Steelers in Akron, Ohio. Dante Magnani, a halfback from St. Mary's University in his second year with the club, took the kickoff all the way for a touchdown.

"Is it this easy?" asked the overjoyed Levy. He was soon to find it was not.

The Rams won their second league game in 1941, too, then lost nine in a row, finishing last in the Western Division and nearly ending Clark's tour of duty. Clark was retained, however, and before he was fired, his four-year tenure set a record for longevity which held up until Sid Gillman lasted a year longer in the late fifties.

Reeves had already begun the exhaustive draft system which was to set a pattern for the rest of the clubs in the league. It was simple by contrast with later Ram systems, but it gave the club a clear edge in drafting. The 1941 Ram selections were good, but the war intervened before they could take effect. In 1942, still under Clark, the club won five, lost six and tied one.

124

By the end of 1942, Reeves and his partner were in service and so were many of the players. Levy sold out to Reeves and Dan obtained the permission of the league to suspend operations in 1943. Clark resigned and the Ram players were distributed among the rest of the clubs for the year.

Chile Walsh, who had been an assistant under Clark, was head coach in 1943, with no team to coach. He was promoted to general manager in 1944, when the franchise was reactivated. He was the only Ram coach never to lose a game.

When the Rams were re-grouped in 1944, the head coach was Aldo (Buff) Donelli, who did reasonably well to win four and lose six.

Donelli went into service after that season and was replaced by Chile Walsh's brother Adam, who had been the center on the Notre Dame team featuring the Four Horsemen.

Adam Walsh found the 1945 Ram team loaded. One of the most versatile and talented quarterbacks in the game joined the club from UCLA: Bob Waterfield. He could run fairly well, punt, pass and place-kick superbly and he was a cold, brilliant strategist and leader. Gil Bouley was a rookie tackle from Boston College. Milan Lazetich, a small but fierce guard and linebacker, joined the club from Wyoming.

Fred Gehrke, a sturdy, quick back from Utah, rejoined the club after four years in service and Walsh acquired a tackle, Eberle Schultz, from the wartime Card-Pitt combination. The fullback was another rookie — big Don Greenwood, who had played at Missouri and Illinois. Benton and Pritko were the ends.

The 1945 Rams lost only one game and met the Washington Redskins for the championship in Cleveland on a day so cold that the musical instruments of the famous Redskin band froze and the band was unable to play. Bill John, business manager of the Rams, bought six boxcar loads of straw with which to cover the field, but the surface was still ice-hard when the game began.

The Rams won, 15-14, on the passing of Waterfield. Sammy Baugh had the misfortune to provide the Rams with their edge, however, when his pass from behind the Redskin goal line hit the goal post. In those days, this meant an automatic safety. Because of this play, the rule was changed the next year to make such an occurrence an incomplete pass.

After the championship game, Reeves learned that the Coliseum in Los Angeles had been thrown open to pro football. Since the league had promised him first call on putting a franchise in Los Angeles, he petitioned the other owners at the league meeting in January for permission to move.

The crusty league veterans turned him down and Reeves stormed out of the meeting. He vowed he would sell the franchise and get out of football. After considerable deliberation, the other owners, faced with the dissolution of the championship club, reluctantly agreed to let Reeves move to Los Angeles. Reeves made a telling point in his argument: in winning the championship in Cleveland, the club had lost $50,000.

The league meeting was in New York. The announcement of the shift from Cleveland to Los Angeles was in the papers before Dan could reach home to tell his wife that they were moving to Los Angeles.

Vitamin Smith's real name was Verda Thomas. The blazing fast little halfback from Abilene Christian College was part of the fastest backfield in football when he was a member of the Ram champions.

"All I have to do now is get enough votes at home to ratify the move," Reeves said wryly when he saw the headlines.

The same year Reeves made his move to the West, the All-America Conference began operation. From 1946 through 1949, the Rams competed for the then-elusive pro fan with the Los Angeles Dons. The losses were huge on both sides. Reeves had dropped $82,000 in the four years he operated the Rams in Cleveland. In his first four years in Los Angeles, he looked back wistfully to the Cleveland days as an era of prosperity.

Pro football was relatively new in Los Angeles and the two college teams in town — UCLA and USC — had the corner on the football market. In 1946, their first year in Los Angeles, the Rams lost $161,000. The club tailed off on the field, too, winning six, losing four and tying one and prompting a most unfraternal act by general manager Chile Walsh, who fired brother Adam as head coach. Reeves soon thereafter fired Chile Walsh as general manager and took over the operation of the club himself.

Bob Snyder, who had been one of Walsh's assistant coaches, was made head coach and the club responded with a 6-6 season, not good enough to wean away many fans from

126

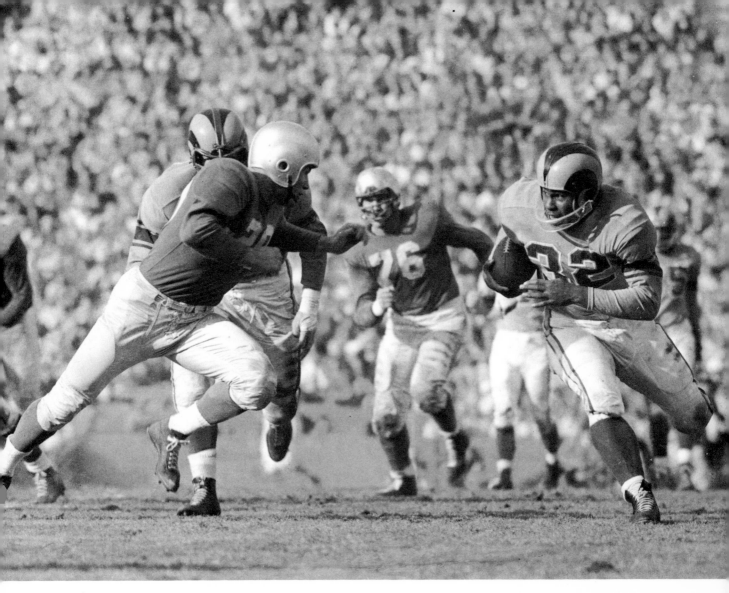

Deacon Dan Towler, now a minister in the Los Angeles area, was the club's leading ground gainer during his career. A 9.8 sprinter, Towler was big (228 pounds) and also very agile for his heft.

the rival Dons. The loss in 1947 climbed to $201,500.

As the losses mounted, Reeves sought additional financing. He had a large personal fortune but could not stand the drain alone. Moreover, the Internal Revenue Department, which looks tolerantly on a losing business for five years, expects a business man to make a profit after that or consider the whole thing a hobby and quit taking tax losses. Reeves decided to take in partners.

Paul Schissler, who had owned a minor league football team in Los Angeles and had once been coach of the Chicago Cardinals, introduced Reeves to Ed Pauley, a wealthy oil operator and a power in the Democratic party at the state and national levels. Pauley and his brother Harold and Fred Levy, who had been Dan's original partner in the Rams, bought shares for a nominal payment and agreed to shoulder a proportionate share of the losses.

They got one of the best buys in sports history. For one dollar, Ed Pauley bought 30 percent of the stock. He had to help cover only two more losing seasons.

The 1948 team opened the exhibition season by losing to the Washington Redskins,

127

21-10. Reeves' dissatisfaction with the head coach, Snyder, boiled over. Snyder was at home packing for a trip to Honolulu, where the Rams had two exhibitions scheduled with the Honolulu Warriors, when he got a call from Reeves, who informed him that he was fired for lacking diligence. Three hours before the plane left for Honolulu, the assistant coach, Clark Shaughnessy, was named head coach.

Shaughnessy, who had done so much to revitalize the T formation, took the team to a 6-5-1 record but the financial losses continued to grow as the costly fight with the Dons went on. The Rams set a club record for red ink in 1948, with a loss of $253,300. Only the presence of the new partners kept the club alive.

The 1949 season was crucial for the Rams and the National Football League. The war with the All-America Conference had fattened payrolls. On the key battleground, Los Angeles, the Rams needed a spectacular season to capture the fancy of the populace. For three years, the Dons averaged almost 10,000 more spectators per game than had the Rams.

The comprehensive scouting system which Reeves had installed and supervised continued to pay off in 1949. Eddie Kotal, who had been a halfback for the Green Bay Packers, was the chief talent scout. In his small room in the Ram headquarters, he had voluminous, accurate files not only on the well-known college players of the time, but on players from obscure teams who were potential stars.

In 1949, the Rams brought in one of the finest crops of rookies ever harvested. Verda Thomas Smith was a small, compact, pigeon-toed halfback from Abilene Christian College who, off the field, moved with all the alacrity of a three-toed sloth. Tank Younger was a big, awkward player from Grambling College, a Negro college in the South where he had scored twenty touchdowns in his freshman year — as a tackle on a tackle-around play. Jerry Williams and Gabby Sims, small but wink-quick halfbacks from Washington State and Baylor, gave vital aid to the Ram pass defense.

Tommy Kalmanir arrived from Nevada. He was another small, lightning-fast halfback who could thread his way through a broken field as though equipped with radar to warn him of approaching tacklers. Elroy Hirsch was obtained from the Green Bay Packers. The Rams suddenly had most of the talent necessary to create the most devastating attack in history.

In 1949, too, the scouting system turned up the information that Norman Van Brocklin, the brilliant Oregon quarterback, could graduate a year ahead of his class if he so chose and would be eligible for drafting.

The Rams drafted him, amid loud protests from the other owners, and signed him when he got his degree early. He saved four games during the 1949 season. The club also had the best third-string quarterback in the league in Bobby Thomason from VMI. He might have been a starting quarterback on any other club, but he saw almost no service behind Waterfield and Van Brocklin.

The crafty Shaughnessy devised an offense to take advantage of the blinding speed and uncanny passing and the Rams vaulted into the championship of the West. They became the most exciting team in football to watch.

They opened the season with six straight victories, then staggered home with two wins, two losses, and two ties, enough for a fifty-percentage-point edge over the Chicago Bears, who finished at 9-3.

They met the Philadelphia Eagles for the championship. The Eagles had been a jinx team for the Rams for years. The jinx held good for the championship game.

The heaviest rains in years made the Coliseum in Los Angeles a shallow lake. The

All pro for three straight years, big Dick Huffman was one of the best Rams' defensive tackles. He is looping arm around Clyde Scott here, in the Rams' 14-0 loss to Philadelphia in 1949 title game.

Rams, whose success depended on speed and the forward pass, were helpless on such a field, but Steve Van Buren, the formidable Eagle halfback, found the gooey footing no handicap. His 196 yards rushing in the game was a league record and was more yardage than the entire Ram team could record. Van Buren scored no touchdowns, but his teammates managed two as the Rams lost, 14-0.

Shaughnessy, a perfectionist irked over the time lost in sleeping, had driven the club and coaches ruthlessly. Some critics blamed the so-so second half of the season on his relentless tactics, but he had, nevertheless, brought the club its first championship since the move to the coast.

He was a giant in the technical development of football. His one fault was that he expected everyone to devote eighteen hours a day to the theory and practice of advancing a football across a measured field. By the end of the 1949 season, his assistants were rebellious and his players exhausted. After the defeat in the championship game — which certainly was no fault of Shaughnessy's — the deep-seated dissatisfaction surfaced.

Shaughnessy, who had made a notable achievement in bringing the club to a division championship in the most crucial year of its existence, was fired on a rather vague charge of "internal friction."

It was a shock to the old man, who retired to his home in Santa Monica and, with Los Angeles *Times* columnist Braven Dyer, composed bitter statements about the Ram ownership. Joe Stydahar, the big, likeable ex-tackle for the Chicago Bears who had been on the point of leaving the Rams to take a job as line coach for the Green Bay Packers, was named head coach. He was a beloved figure to the players. When Shaughnessy said, from the depths of his despair, "I'll take a high school team and beat any team coached by Joe Stydahar," the sentiment of the team, fans and sports writers shifted suddenly to Stydahar.

With the death of the All-America Conference, the Rams fell heir in 1950 to a great tackle from the Dons — Bob Reinhard. They already had a two-time all-pro on the squad, the squat and powerful Dick Huffman of Tennessee. Huffman and Reinhard gave the Rams the best pair of defensive tackles in the league.

Deacon Dan Towler, a 225-pound fullback from Washington and Jefferson who could run the 100-yard dash in 9.8 seconds, joined Younger and big Dick Hoerner at fullback, giving the Rams the most potent set of fullbacks since the Osmanski-Famiglietti-Maniaci trio of the 1940 Bears.

Paul Barry, a wild, rough halfback from Tulsa who ran with reckless abandon, beefed up a backfield which had been long on speed but short on muscle. To a plethora of scatbacks such as Vitamin Smith and Tommy Kalmanir was added Glenn Davis, the great Mr. Outside of West Point, who had finished his service duties. Bob Boyd, who had won the NCAA sprint championship with a 9.4-second 100, joined the club as an end, but played very little behind the two great ends already on hand — Fears and Hirsch. Woodley Lewis, another sprinter, joined the secondary defense.

Stydahar hired Hampton Pool, an assistant coach at Santa Barbara Junior College who had played with him on the Chicago Bear super teams of the late thirties and early forties. Pool was a Shaughnessy as a tactician, innovator and strategist and as inept as Shaughnessy in dealing with players and coaches.

For two seasons Stydahar and Pool were as compatible as ham and eggs. Stydahar kept the boys happy. Pool, the intellectual, devised more and better ways for this great machine to score.

The 1950 Rams broke nearly every offensive record. They gained 5420 yards, 3709

Concentration and tension show on the face of Rams' Jon Arnett as the fine back crouches on sidelines at game.

by passing. They made 278 first downs and completed 253 passes, thirty-one for touchdowns. They scored 466 points, seventy in one game against Baltimore. In one quarter, they scored forty-one points against Detroit. All were league records.

The individual Rams ran wild, too. Tom Fears caught eighty-four passes, eighteen in one game against Green Bay. Both were records. Van Brocklin and Waterfield split the quarterbacking. Alone, either could have set records in passing that year.

They were scored on freely, too. They beat the New York Yanks by 45-28 and 43-35. They lost to Philadelphia by 56-20. They lost twice to the Chicago Bears and finished in a tie with the Bears for the division championship with nine victories and three losses.

The Bears had beaten them by 24-14 and 24-20 during the season. In the divisional playoff, the Rams won, 24-14.

Bob Waterfield brought the Rams a championship in his rookie year in 1945 with his passing, but he was an adequate runner, a superb kicker and a good defensive back, too. He was a leader most of all.

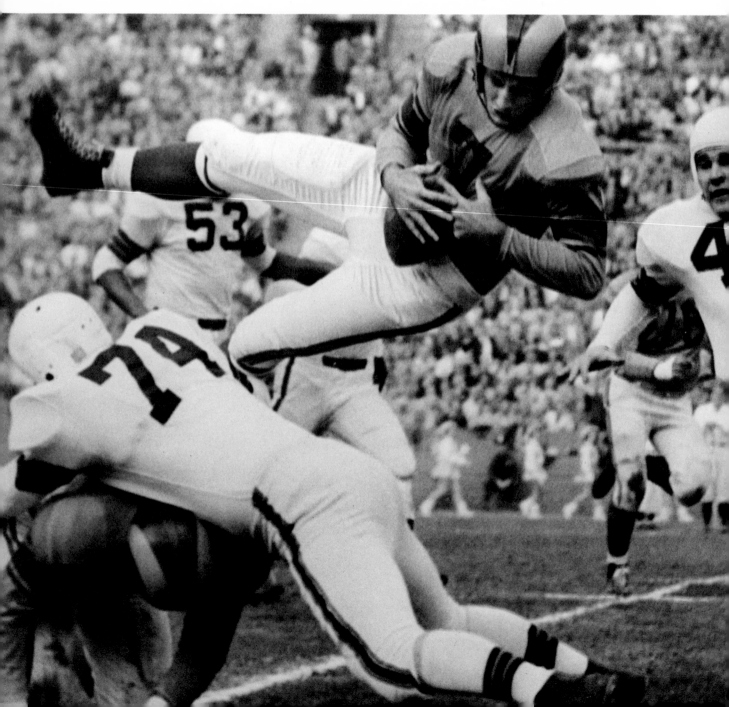

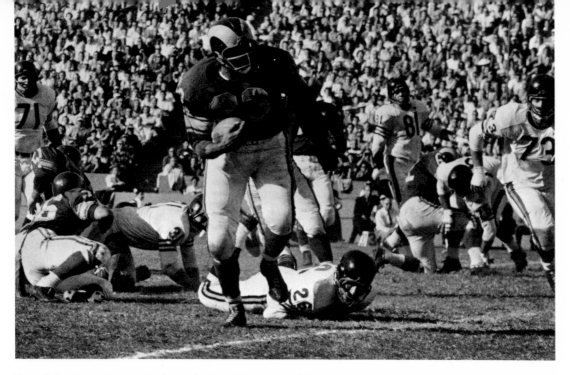

One of the finest all-around players in Ram history was Ollie Matson (33, shown leaving a trail of Chicago Bears as he takes off on a 36-yard run. Rams traded almost an entire team of eleven players for Matson.

The 1950 season was a resounding artistic success, but very few people went out to the Coliseum to see the Rams. The club televised its homes games and the fans stayed home to watch. The television sponsors, who agreed to pay the difference between the actual gate and what would have been a break-even gate on each home game, were presented with a bill for $307,000 and the Rams broke even at the gate for the first time. The fans were enthralled by the hell-for-leather, exciting football they had watched for nothing but the next year, with the TV sponsors taking cover, they had to go out to the Coliseum and put up $3.90 for a ticket. They did. Home television had created a large and enthusiastic group of fans which grew year by year.

The 1950 championship game matched the Rams, a club which had left Cleveland after winning a championship, with the Cleveland Browns, a club which had filled the void left by the Rams in 1946 and had won four straight championships in the All-America Conference. Even though Cleveland early in the season had walloped the 1949 NFL champions, the Philadelphia Eagles, many die-hard NFL fans felt the Browns were not really that good.

The Browns, on a last-minute field goal by Lou Groza, won the game, 30-28, after trailing most of the afternoon on the icy field of Cleveland Municipal Stadium.

A measure of the intensity with which the pros play could have been taken in the Ram dressing room after the game. Stydahar, who had waited until the team left the field before going to the dressing room, stopped before the door to warn a Ram official with him: "Don't act like you're taking it hard. The kids will be way down. Let's try to cheer them up."

Then he opened the door and walked in. The dressing room was deathly still. Most of the players sat dully before their lockers, many of them weeping. The massive Stydahar took one look around the room, then retired to a corner as tears trickled down his craggy face.

Stydahar was an emotional man. The tensions of coaching tore at him unmercifully. During the 1951 exhibition season, he lost his temper one night in Little Rock, Ark., after

133

the Rams had managed one of their rare victories over the Philadelphia Eagles. The players were slow returning to the hotel. By 2 a.m., big Joe was furious. Canvassing the night spots of Little Rock by telephone, he finally got Jack Finlay, one of the Rams' veteran guards, at a night club.

Impersonating a player, Joe asked Finlay if anyone was with him.

"Sure," said Jack, happily. "We're all here. Come on."

"Listen," Stydahar roared. "This is Stydahar! You guys have got thirty minutes to get to the hotel. And you're fined a hundred bucks each. And another hundred if it takes you longer than thirty minutes to get here!"

Stydahar exacted $7400 in fines that night for a league record. Not long after, he rescinded all the fines.

Stydahar and Pool continued as a winning combination through the 1951 season, with almost exactly the same personnel. The club won eight and lost four, squeaking by Detroit and San Francisco to the division championship.

The team had the same scoring punch as the 1950 club. Hirsch, well-adjusted as a spread end, broke the league record for yards gained catching passes and tied Don Hutson's old mark for touchdown passes caught, with seventeen. Towler, the big, swift fullback, led the club on the ground. In one cataclysmic afternoon against the New York Yanks, the Rams gained 731 yards, 554 on passes.

They met the Browns again for the championship, this time in Los Angeles. The key to the Ram attack now had become the long pass from Waterfield or Van Brocklin to any of the Ram race-horse receivers. This game was won on a beautiful seventy-three yard play from Van Brocklin to Fears, who caught the ball at midfield between two Cleveland defenders and outran them to the goal line.

As the 1952 season began, a rift which developed between Pool and Stydahar widened. Once during 1951, Stydahar had been tempted to fire Pool, but had been dissuaded. Now he was convinced that Pool was working behind his back to get his job, so he went to Reeves again.

He had relieved Pool of many of his responsibilities. The club had lost its last three exhibition games and been dumped, 37-7, in its first league game. When Stydahar gave Reeves a blunt ultimatum: "Pool goes or I do," Reeves stuck with Pool. Big Joe, who had been the most popular of all Ram coaches with fans, writers, and players, was through.

Under Pool, the club tied for the division championship again, winning nine games and losing three, then lost a division playoff game to the Chicago Bears.

Pool's tenure as head coach was brief, stormy and unproductive of championships. He was, in his way, even more intense than Stydahar. An intellectual giant of the game, he spent eighteen hours a day working on offenses and defenses. He was a perfectionist who used biting sarcasm to flay players who were not as quick as he thought they should be in comprehending his plays. Before long, an undercurrent of dissatisfaction was working against him.

Pool drove himself, his staff and his players mercilessly. He was eager to experiment. He tried to devise a series of aptitude tests for rookies which would reveal the extent of their aggressiveness. Once, on learning that an ultrasonic tone could be used to key up human emotions, he had such a tone piped into the Ram dressing room before a game. He found that it was more irritating than inspiring to the players.

The offenses he devised were ingenious and effective. He set up pass patterns which broke four of the gifted Ram receivers into the secondary simultaneously, precluding double

134

**Young Harland Svare,** thrust into a head coaching job after only part of a season as an assistant, has the demanding job of rebuilding the Rams. Quarterback Roman Gabriel is listening in on the phone.

coverage on at least one. The Rams scored profusely with this tactic.

In 1953, although the Rams won eight, lost three and tied one, they dropped to third. The following year, with a 6-5-1 season, they skidded to fourth.

Four of Pool's assistant coaches resigned after the 1954 season. Players were free with criticism of him in the Los Angeles papers, which printed the criticism happily. So, early in 1955 and very reluctantly, Reeves let Pool go.

"Hamp had too many strikes against him," Dan said.

When he made the decision to dismiss Pool, Reeves, who under his contract with his partners was the operating head of the Rams, was unable to advise Ed Pauley, off on a hunting trip, of the move before it reached the papers. Pauley, who had no veto in any case, was enraged. A rift developed among Reeves and his partners.

Pool was given six months' pay and left philosophically. Of his tenure as Ram head coach, he said, "I enjoyed every miserable minute of it."

For thirty-nine days after the firing of Pool, the Rams conducted a widely publicized, flamboyant search for a coach. Almost every coach of any stature was mentioned, among them Eddie Erdelatz of Navy, who was immediately given a better contract by the service school, and Jordan Olivar of Yale, who got a salary increase.

The Rams settled on Sid Gillman, well-known to other coaches and highly respected by them, but almost a total stranger to Los Angeles. Gillman had been spectacularly successful at Cincinnati University and was regarded as a brilliant student of football.

Gillman was the originator of the belly series, of ingenious blocking improvements and of a system of substitutions which was a forerunner to the two-platoon system. He had never coached pro football before. He was a tireless student of game movies and as industrious a worker as any Ram coach who had preceded him.

In his first season, Gillman took the Rams to a division championship, relying heavily upon the veterans in his lineup. He lost the championship game to the Cleveland Browns, 34-14, but no one seemed to mind.

During Gillman's first year as head coach, the simmering feud among the Ram owners boiled over and Reeves was divested of his authority to run the club. He had counted on Fred Levy, Jr., an old friend from the Cleveland days, to vote with him. Levy shifted his vote to the Ed Pauley faction and, on November 1, 1955, over lunch at Scandia's, Dan was informed that he was being relieved of the directorship of the team.

For the next seven years, after a series of compromises arranged by Bert Bell and later Pete Rozelle, as commissioners, the Ram ownership was divided. Neither Pauley and his men nor Reeves had clear-cut control and the club staggered under the divided, quarrelsome rule.

After his first successful year, Gillman began to run into trouble. He and Van Brocklin were never compatible. More and more Gillman turned to Billy Wade, who had been the Rams' first draft choice in 1951. The veterans soon became disenchanted with Gillman; Fears quit in an atmosphere of bitter recrimination.

In the next four years, the Rams made a series of signally unfortunate trades, most of them apparently based on the theory that a young player with the same potential as a veteran is preferable to the veteran. Texas Schramm, the general manager, had as much to do with the trades as did Gillman.

Schramm, who became general manager of the Dallas Texans when they entered the league, said much later: "I have, in the last couple of years, gone over my thinking on the Ram trades. I had a part in most of them and, naturally, I've tried to analyze where we

Powerful Les Richter, Ram linebacker for nine years, was once called a 245-pound acrobat by an opposing coach. For most of the nine years he spent with the Rams, Richter was named to Pro Bowl teams.

California weather in Washington as Ram fullback Bass storms Redskin defense on Indian summer day in "Skins" new stadium.

went wrong. And I think it's this. We discounted the plus of experience. The extra efficiency you get from keeping, say, a defensive unit together for years. Maybe one cog in that unit is not — in speed or size — as good physically as a rookie two or three years younger. It's hard, then, to resist the temptation to trade away a player you know you can get a first draft choice for and keep the guy who may, in a year or two, be better. If you evaluate our trades purely on a man-for-man basis, we were right. But if you evaluate them on the resulting efficiency of the team itself, I guess we might have been wrong."

The Rams had only two reasonably good seasons under Gillman after the first. They finished fourth at 6-6 in 1957. In 1958, they moved up to second with an 8-4 season.

Van Brocklin went to the Philadelphia Eagles, where he won a championship in

1960. Eleven players, including three capable linemen, were traded to the Chicago Cardinals for Ollie Matson. This prompted Red Hickey, the coach of the San Francisco Forty-Niners, to ask Gillman, over their cups in a coffee shop, to do him a favor.

"Please," said Hickey. "When you feel like making a trade, call me first."

The scouting system continued to produce sparkling players. During the seven-year drought, from 1955 through 1962, the Rams had Wade and great running backs like Matson, Jon Arnett, Skeets Quinlan, Joe Marconi and Dick Bass. Red Phillips, a small but immensely capable end, was another Fears. Del Shofner, fast, long-legged and maneuverable, looked like another Hirsch but he too was traded and became a star for the New York Giants. Les Richter was one of the best middle linebackers in the league, but he was never able to reach his full potential because he customarily played with strangers all around him.

Gillman's last year was 1959, when the team won two games, lost ten and finished last. Pressure from Reeves' partners forced Gillman out even though Dan still had confidence in him.

He was succeeded by Bob Waterfield, the nonpareil quarterback. Unfortunately for Waterfield, the battle among the owners became fierce during his regime. The club was never able to get untracked. It won four and lost ten in 1961 and dropped to a low of 1-11 in 1962 for another last-place finish.

At the end of the season, Harland Svare, brilliant young defensive specialist from the New York Giants, was made head coach. He had served for the last four games of 1962, taking over when Waterfield resigned.

Reeves regained control and moved into the Ram headquarters to resume direction of the team. For the first time in eight years, no intramural battles were going and the Rams were once again under the direction of one of the ablest executives in football.

Reeves developed some of the top executives in the National Football League. Schramm, general manager of the Cowboys, was succeeded as general manager of the Rams by Pete Rozelle, who sprang from that job into the commissionership of the league. Bert Rose, who was Ram publicity director, became general manager of the Minnesota Vikings.

# THE MINNESOTA VIKINGS

MINNEAPOLIS and St. Paul share several things: the Mississippi River, the University of Minnesota, the Minneapolis-St. Paul Twins, and most recently and most enthusiastically, the Minnesota Vikings, the lustiest baby ever born into the National Football League.

There had been the usual town pro teams in one or other of the cities before the arrival of the Vikings. John McNally was blooded as a pro and picked up his nom de football in Minneapolis. But the true history of pro football in the Twin Cities began with the Vikings.

It began before the Vikings came into being with a major league sports committee that had been formed in Minneapolis in 1951. Bill Boyer, a big, dynamic owner of two automobile agencies in Minneapolis, was one of the prime movers on the sports committee.

"We hired a market research firm in Chicago to find out for us what we could expect to draw in the Minneapolis-St. Paul area with a major league baseball club," said Boyer, who became president of the Vikings.

The report indicated that the area could easily support major league baseball. The ten-year projection was for 770,000 spectators in 1955 and over a million by 1965. As it turned out, the Twins were well over the projection for 1965 by 1961.

Emboldened by the optimistic forecast, Boyer and his group decided to build a stadium and then lure a major league baseball team to inhabit it.

The stadium was built, diplomatically, in Bloomington, which is equidistant from Minneapolis and St. Paul, forming an equilateral triangle with the Twin Cities, which in fact are not twins but rather disparate entities. The Twin Cities got their baseball club. With it ensconced in the new stadium, Boyer and his associates began to cast about for another tenant for the rest of the year, to help pay off the cost of the big, handsome park.

Since Minnesota is the epicenter of the football earthquake which rocks the United States each fall, they turned naturally to professional football. The University of Minnesota, over the previous twenty years, had averaged nearly 50,000 per game, although only once during the two decades were the Golden Gophers good enough to win the Big Ten championship and make the trip to the Rose Bowl.

Boyer's group first made eyes at the Chicago Cardinals. The Cards were the logical beloved of any group trying to woo a pro football team, since they were living in joyless juxtaposition to the Chicago Bears, were unloved by Chicago fans and were unprofitable.

The Cardinals were interested but not eager. Meanwhile, the American Football League was born and Boyer's group plumped, tentatively, for an AFL franchise.

"It would have given us a pro club," Boyer says. "But we were more interested in a

By the time the club entered its second year (1962), young Fran Tarkenton had established himself solidly as the quarterback. Unlike his coach, Tarkenton was a scrambler, but a fine leader as well.

A pro football team is being born here as Minnesota Viking coach Norman Van Brocklin (center) works with the first Viking team (left, right) in training camp. Team won surprising three games.

National Football League franchise. George Halas, who was head of the National Football League expansion committee, let us know that a franchise might be available, so we hesitated before we committed ourselves absolutely to the new league."

This hesitation proved to be a thinking man's falter. At the same session where Pete Rozelle was elected NFL commissioner and the Dallas Cowboys were granted an immediate franchise — in January, 1960 — the Vikings were given a franchise to become operable in 1961. They were not, of course, the Vikings at the time. The name was the brainchild of the Viking general manager, Bert Rose, Jr.

143

The delay between the granting of the franchise and its date of effect was helpful. The unfortunate Dallas club was forced to rush into action without the benefit of a draft and with only a ragtag collection of players picked up from the culls of the rest of the league and a few free agents.

The five owners of the Minnesota team were Boyer, H. P. Skoglund, president of and principal stockholder in the North American Life and Casualty Co., Max Winter, a sports entrepreneur who formerly owned the Minneapolis Lakers basketball team, all from Minneapolis; Bernie Ridder, Jr., publisher of the St. Paul papers, and Olaf Haugsrud, from Duluth, where he once owned the Duluth Esquimaux and now owns a wholesale candy and tobacco business.

The first order of business for the new club was preparation for what would be, for them, a dual draft: the annual league draft of college seniors and a draft of players to be made available to them by the other clubs, with the exception of the new Dallas Cowboys.

To scout the college and pro players, the club, at the suggestion of Rozelle, hired Joe Thomas, who had been an assistant coach in Canada and for the Rams and who had a wide familiarity with both kinds of players.

Class work and homework played a big part in the development of the young team as Van Brocklin introduced them to a new offense and a new defense. This was 1960 and Van's first head coaching job.

Thomas proved to be a wise choice. When the Vikings took the field in 1961, they were equipped with much better personnel than the Cowboys had been for their maiden year.

The owners next looked for a general manager. Since none of them had either the time or the qualifications for running a team, they were sadly in need of a competent director. At the recommendation of almost everyone they consulted, they hired the young, intelligent and energetic Rose, who had been publicity director of the Los Angeles Rams.

Rose had a deep and thorough knowledge of the operation of a pro football club and he had been trained by one of the ablest executives in the business — Dan Reeves. He had also worked under two exceptional general managers — Tex Schramm and Rozelle.

"We turned the whole thing over to Bert," Boyer said. "We leave all the decisions to him and to the coach. We only want to be informed."

Rose took over the organization of the new team with a sure hand. He made a list of the things to be done. By the time the club went to training camp at the end of the summer of 1961, he had written down and crossed off over 150 items, including such details as the selection of jackets for linesmen.

Trying to build up confidence in his collection of veterans and grass-green youngsters, Van Brocklin ran a happy camp the first year. Workouts were light-hearted, as these hopeful Vikings demonstrate.

His first problem, however, was the sale of 25,000 season tickets, which had been made a condition for the team being granted a franchise. Rose spent seven weeks preparing his campaign. When he had finished with it, it was the most successful season ticket sale for a new club in the history of sports.

He organized booster groups in St. Paul and Minneapolis and conducted whirlwind campaigns in both cities, then sent other groups on safari throughout the state. By the time he was finished, the Vikings had sold over 25,000 season tickets, an almost incredible figure for a team which had not yet been in action.

While he worked on the ticket campaign, Rose had also to decide on a head coach. The list of applicants was long; it required a good deal of courage to settle, at last, upon Norman Van Brocklin, who had just led the Philadelphia Eagles to a league championship, then retired. Van had never coached. He had a quick temper and a sharp tongue and some people thought he would not be able to control either well enough to last as a head coach.

The King — Hugh McElhenny came to the Vikings after a long and illustrious career with the San Francisco Forty-Niners; he retained enough of his speed and all of his guile to life offense.

There was no question of his football acumen or of his leadership qualities.

The Dutchman brought with him a young staff. He and Rose selected Bimidji, Minn. as a training camp site and the Vikings began their first season with a makeshift but carefully selected team.

From the other clubs in the league, they picked veterans who still were sprightly: Hugh McElhenny, the incomparable running back who had grown old but not elderly with the San Francisco Forty-Niners; Mel Triplett, a powerful runner and fine blocker at fullback with the New York Giants; Don Joyce, a tough end from Baltimore, and Mike Rabold, a good young guard from the Washington Redskins. They traded the Giants a first draft choice to get veteran quarterback George Shaw.

Their first draft choice was a big, quick halfback from Tulane who looked like a young McElhenny — Tom Mason. They backed up Shaw with a young quarterback from Georgia, Fran Tarkenton. They surprised the draft meeting by selecting a future on their

The Crown Prince—First draft choice Tommy Mason from Tulane looked like a young McElhenny in his rookie season and gave promise of even greater brilliance both for himself and the team in the future.

fourth round — a player who would not be available for another year.

The Vikings were not, of course, a first-division team. They figured to finish in last place — and did so. Van Brocklin, realizing that he was building a team around players who had been rejected by the other teams, conducted an easy training camp, devoting himself primarily to building up the confidence of his players. The material was not devastating. Almost everywhere, except in a few backfield positions, there was much to be desired.

Stan West, the big Oklahoman who coached the Viking line, surveyed his charges sadly one afternoon in Bemidji and said, "Well, they're not big, but they sure are slow."

The club won three games; at the beginning of the season Van Brocklin, an optimistic minority of one, had predicted they might win four. Almost no one else in the league conceded them as many as two victories.

Tarkenton took over as quarterback during the first season and he was firmly established as the No. 1 man when the 1962 season began. He is a scrambler, unlike his coach, who once said seriously, "A quarterback should never run unless it is from sheer terror."

As the weeks rolled by, the team began to shake down. Fran Tarkenton, a youngster from Georgia, worked at quarterback and had trouble learning to stay in the cup. Here he prepares for handoff.

Terror may have had something to do with developing Tarkenton's elusiveness. In his first year, he tried for a while to stay in the protective cup formed by blockers, but time and time again, the cup had runneth over so that Fran was forced to run for his life.

The problems in the first season were multiplied by the loss, for all or part of the season, of three star rookies by injuries in the College All-Star game. Mason, the halfback, suffered a jammed neck. Ed Sharockman, a good defensive halfback, broke his leg, and Rip Hawkins, a good linebacker from North Carolina, suffered a knee injury, but played most of the season.

The 1962 Vikings did not improve on the record of the maiden team but some strong additions were made to the team. Sharockman moved in to be as promising a defensive back as Van Brocklin had expected. A big rookie center named Mike Tingelhoff bolstered the offensive line. Mason, healthy all season, turned in successive 100-yard-plus running efforts in the last two games. Tarkenton, gaining confidence and poise, was one of the league's better quarterbacks by season's end. Chuck Lamson, who was the surprise future draft choice on the fourth round in 1961, proved a good defensive back, even as a rookie.

With Tarkenton established as the No. 1 quarterback, the Vikings let Shaw go in order to keep a surprise — John McCormick, a free agent from Massachusetts who became the No. 2 thrower.

It takes at least five years to build a championship team in the tough pro ranks. After their second year of operation, the husky young Vikings appeared to be well ahead of schedule.

A perfect block protects a perfect punt as Phil King (24) takes out a Green Bay defender to let Don Chandler get the Giants out of trouble with one of the booming punts which are his specialties.

# THE NEW YORK GIANTS

TIMOTHY J. MARA, a respectable bookmaker in the days when it was legally possible to be one, bought the franchise for the New York Giants football team in lieu of an interest in Gene Tunney. This was in 1925. As it turned out, Tunney would have been a more profitable short-term investment, but the Giants have paid off better over the long haul.

Mara had gone to the office of Billy Gibson, the heavyweight contender's manager, to see if he could buy a part of Tunney's contract. Instead, he ran into Joe Carr, the president of the National Football League and Dr. Harry March, a pro football *aficionado*. They were trying, unsuccessfully, to persuade Gibson to buy a franchise for New York. Gibson, who had all he could handle in managing Tunney, was not interested.

"How much is it?" asked Mara.

"Five hundred dollars," said Carr.

"Any New York franchise is worth $500," said Mara and wrote out a check forthwith. He knew nothing about professional football at the time, which probably accounts for his casual willingness to become involved in it.

Mara hired Dr. March to operate the franchise. From the August afternoon when he so offhandedly bought the club until the October afternoon when the Giants opened their home season, he wrote many more checks, totalling a little more than $25,000. He wrote these as willingly as he had written the first.

The 1925 Giants were an artistic success, but an expensive one. They finished fourth in the twenty-team league, with an 8-4 record, but they came up to the final game with Mara some $40,000 in the hole. He desperately needed a big attraction, and he got it.

Mara tried to sign Red Grange, but found George Halas had got there first. Halas had already reached an agreement with Grange and his manager, C. C. Pyle. Mara arranged a game in the Polo Grounds with the Grange-Pyle-Halas combination, and came back to New York to order 70,000 tickets printed for the contest.

He sold almost all of them immediately. The game is usually listed as having drawn 65,000 fans, but with the gate crashers counted, almost 80,000 were on hand. The Giants' share of the profits was nearly $60,000, wiping out Mara's indebtedness and leaving him with a tidy profit for the season.

The Bears won, 19-7, and Grange contributed a touchdown on the runback of an intercepted pass. The fans, who had come to see Grange run, were satisfied. Despite the defeat, so was Mara.

On the basis of Grange's remarkable drawing power, Pyle leased Yankee Stadium for the following year, violating Giant territorial rights, and tried to muscle his way into the

151

NFL. He was turned down by unanimous vote, so he organized his own league. It lasted only one year, but it was more grief for the Giants, who had to compete with clubs in Brooklyn and in Yankee Stadium.

Pyle's league raided the Giants for their head coach, Bob Folwell, and for one of their top players, Century Milstead, an All-American tackle from Yale. Giant attendance dropped off, but the outlaw league's teams took a horrendous beating at the box office and the league went out of existence at the end of the season.

Dr. March, who was still running the club, had installed Joe Alexander, another All-American from the 1925 team, as coach. Alexander, who played center and studied medicine, found his multiple duties too exacting. After the 1926 season, the head coaching job was turned over to another player, halfback Earl Potteiger from Ursinus.

A big and capable rookie on the 1926 club was Steve Owen, who came to the Giants from Phillips University and the Kansas City Cowboys. The 1926 club again won eight and lost four but dropped to seventh. In 1927, with Owen, Milstead, who had returned after the demise of the outlaw league, Cal Hubbard, Red Badgro, Al Nesser and Indian Joe Guyon from Carlisle, among others, the Giants won their first NFL championship, losing only one and tying one game in twelve.

It was not a spectacular team, but it was the prototype of the great Giant defensive teams of the years to come. It shut out the opposition in eleven games. The key victory for the championship was scored over a good Chicago Bear team led by Grange and Paddy Driscoll. The Giants won by the then-startling stratagem of passing on fourth down from deep in their own territory, catching the Bears completely by surprise and making a long gain which set up the winning touchdown.

After the vicious, bruising game, Owen, the massive Giant tackle, slumped to the ground. "It was the roughest football game I ever played," Owen said later. "I played sixty minutes at tackle opposite Jim McMillen. When it was over, we just sat there. We were too tired to move."

Three of the old Giants who made up the nucleus of some great teams were Ken Strong (left), coach Steve Owen (center) and center Mel Hein. Strong was great kicker, Hein an all-time, all-pro at center.

Strong exercises his specialty against the Chicago Bears as he kicks an extra point. Ken returned to help Giants in 1963, when he coached Don Chandler in place-kicking after retirement of Summerall.

The Giant defense collapsed in 1928 and the club slipped from first to sixth, winning only four games and losing seven and giving up touchdowns with alarming frequency. Mara, never one to accept this kind of adversity with equanimity, felt the club needed a spark and decided that Benny Friedman, Michigan's superb passer, was the catalyst the team required.

Unfortunately, Friedman played with Detroit. Mara attempted several times to buy him, but Detroit would not sell. So Mara bought the entire club, including the coach.

He paid Friedman what was to remain for a long time the highest regular salary in pro football — $10,000 per season. Friedman and the other Detroit players, including Steve Owen's brother Bill, sent the Giants rocketing toward the top of the league, but not quite all the way. Although the 1929 club won twelve, lost one and tied one, the Green Bay Packers won the championship with a 12-0-1 record.

Red Cagle, the great Army star, joined the Giants in 1930. He and Friedman, who had proved eminently worth his big salary in 1929, led the Giants to another winning season. The club won thirteen and lost four, but lost first place by four percentage points to the pesky Packers, who won ten, lost three and tied one.

The Giants were not as successful at the box office. Occasional games drew good crowds, especially when the Bears played in the Polo Grounds, but the overall attendance was poor. The depression and the strong hold college football had on New York combined to make Sundays lean days at the box office.

The biggest crowd the Giants drew in 1930 was for a charity game for the benefit of the New York City unemployment fund.

This game, played in the Polo Grounds on December 14, 1930, matched the Giants with a Notre Dame All-Star team coached by Knute Rockne. The Notre Dame club included the Four Horsemen, plus many other notables of recent Irish teams, including Adam Walsh, who had been center and captain of the team which had included the Four Horsemen.

153

The 55,000 fans who responded to the magic of the Notre Dame name contributed a gate which returned $115,000 to the unemployment fund. The game was not as satisfying. Rockne, making one of his very few errors in judgment, told the Irish just before game time: "The Giants are big, but slow. Score two or three quick touchdowns on passes, then play defense. Don't get hurt."

By halftime, the Irish not only had not scored any touchdowns but they had not gained a yard against the "big, slow Giants." The score was 14-0. It might have swelled in the second half had not the Giants mercifully called off the dogs and sent in their third team, which scored one more touchdown for a 21-0 victory.

There's a tale that Johnny Law, a 170-pound Notre Dame guard, took one look at the massive Giant team as it lined up for the kickoff and trotted over to an official. "Pardon me," he said. "How much time is there left to play?"

The Giants skidded in 1931 to fifth with a 6-6-1 record. Steve Owen began his long tenure as head coach toward the end of the year when Leroy Andrew, who had come to the club in the Detroit purchase, resigned.

Owen took over temporarily but he remained in the job for twenty-two years and brought the Giants eight division and two world championships.

Owen graduated from Phillips University at Enid, Okla., in 1922 and for three years after that played on small-town pro teams in the Midwest. In 1924, he joined a team

The 1927 Giant football team which won eleven games and lost only one. posed for this picture in the Polo Grounds with Governor Al Smith, who was to be the Democratic candidate for president in 1928. Smith, without

known as the Kansas City Cowboys, which lost a 9-3 game to the Giants in 1925. Owen impressed the Giants so much that he was invited to accompany the club on a barnstorming tour of the South. The next year, the Giants bought his contract from the Cowboys for $500, one of the best bargains in Giant history.

Owen was a superb defensive coach, the originator of the umbrella defense which stopped the Cleveland Browns cold. He also set up effective defenses against players like Don Hutson, Sam Baugh and Hugh McElhenny. Although he was primarily known for his defenses, he was an ingenious and imaginative offensive coach as well, the inventor of the A formation and the swing T, both of which generated explosive football.

In Steve's first four years as the Giant coach, the club reached the championship game three times. In 1933, the first year that the league was split into divisions, Owen led the Giants to the championship of the East with an 11-3 record. Mel Hein had joined the club at center, the ends were Badgro and Ray Flaherty, and Ken Strong, a Giant immortal, was one of the backs. Harry Newman had taken over from Friedman at quarterback.

The Bears won that first championship game, 23-21. The 1934 game between the two clubs was the famous sneaker game won by the Giants in the second half with the help of canvas tennis shoes. In the 1934 championship game a shy rookie, Ed Danowski, came into his own. He got in the game only because Newman was injured and unable

he derby which was to be his trademark, stands in the center of the picture, wearing a felt hat and a triped suit. Standing next to him, bare-headed and wearing an overcoat is the Giant owner, Timothy Mara.

Tuffy Leemans, one of the brightest of all Giant stars, drives into the line against the Brooklyn Dodgers. Leemans was the first in the long line of fine players discovered by Wellington (Duke) Mara.

to play. He intercepted a pass, passed for one touchdown and scored one himself in the Giants' 30-13 victory.

The Giants repeated as Eastern champions in 1935, but lost to the Detroit Lions, 26-7, in the championship game. It was the year that John Dell Isola emerged as one of the great Giant linemen.

Dell Isola got his baptism of fire against Bronko Nagurski when he replaced an injured Giant middle guard in a game against the Bears. On the first play, Nagurski slanted into the middle through a wide hole and Dell Isola, anxious to see for himself how tough the fabled Bronko was, hit him head-on.

"It was the hardest tackle I ever made," Dell Isola recalled later. "We went down and I remember saying to myself, 'I guess that will show you, Nagurski.' Then I heard the official say, 'Second and two!' "

Many old Giant stars retired after the 1935 season and the club won only five games in 1936. Wellington Mara, who with his brother Jack had become active in the Giant operation, that year gave an early indication that he would become a near-genius in judging football talent.

"I'm going to Washington, D.C.," Wellington (called the Duke for obvious reasons) told his father.

"Why?" old Tim asked.

"On business."

"What business?"

"I want to sign Tuffy Leemans," Wellington said.

"Who's he?"

"You'll see," Wellington said.

Leemans, who had played at George Washington from 1932 through 1935, had been overlooked by most pro scouts. He was the leading ground gainer in the NFL his rookie year and he became one of the best ball-carriers in Giant history.

156

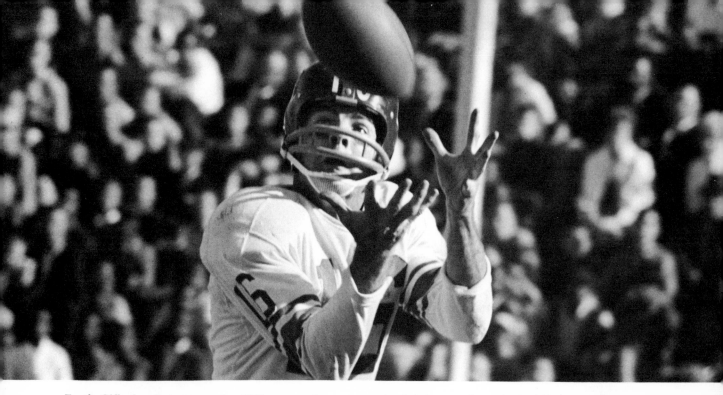

Frank Gifford, who sat out the 1961 season after a severe head injury at the end of 1960, returned in 1962, learned the unfamiliar flanker back position quickly, helped the club to a division title.

A crop of strong rookies helped beef up the Giants for 1937. They included Ward Cuff of Marquette and Hank Soar of Providence, backs, and a handful of superb ends: Will Walls of Texas Christian, Jim Lee Howell of Arkansas, Jim Poole and Charlie Gelatka, both of Mississippi. Rookie linemen Tarzan White, Orville Tuttle, Ken Lunday, Ed Widseth and Ox Parry all made the club.

Owen devised the A formation and the Giants moved up to second place in the East. They went all the way in 1938, then beat Green Bay, 23-17, before 48,120 in the Polo Grounds. Owen later called the 1938 squad the finest group he ever coached.

They won the Eastern championship again in 1939, but this time, playing Green Bay in Milwaukee, they fell before the redoubtable Cecil Isbell-to-Don Hutson passing combination. Hutson did not catch a touchdown pass that afternoon, but he set up two with great catches and was a constant menace that disrupted the Giant defenses.

Complacency caught up with the Giants in 1940 and the same group of stars who had performed so well for the three years managed to lose four, win six and tie one game, finishing third in the East.

Another bumper crop of rookies gave the 1941 club a lift. They included Len Eshmont of Fordham, Frank Reagan of Pennsylvania, George Franck of Minnesota, Marion Pugh of Texas A&M, all great backs, and a handful of good linemen.

The Giants had clinched the Eastern title by December 7 of that year, when they played the Brooklyn Dodgers in the Polo Grounds. The news of the attack on Pearl Harbor came at the half. The Giants were trailing, 14-7. The Dodgers went on to win, 21-7, but no one paid much attention.

Two weeks later, the Giants met the magnificent Chicago Bears for the championship. Even a club as talented as the 1941 Giants was no match for the Bears and the Chicago team won, 37-9. Most of the Giants were gone by the time 1942 rolled around. Service calls decimated the club as they did most clubs in pro football.

The Giants struggled through the war years with better success than many other

Emlen Tunnell wandered into the Giant office and convinced Wel Mara he could make the club. He went on to set league defensive records, lead the Giant defense for years. He returns punt here.

Jack Stroud, the powerful Giant blocking guard, leads Alex Webster into hole in Cowboy line as the strong Webster

clubs. They dropped off in 1942, but came back to tie Washington for the Eastern Division title in 1943, losing in a playoff. In 1944, they won the division championship again as Cuff and Soar returned from the wars and Hein commuted from a college coaching job. Tuffy Leemans coached the backs and played. Arnie Herber, who had been let go by the Packers, provided a still-accurate passing arm and Bill Paschal, a youngster from Georgia Tech, put running power in the A formation.

Although Herber completed a touchdown pass against his old team, the Giants lost the championship game to the Packers, 14-7. The 1945 season was another bad one, with some of the veterans slowing down and some of the younger players called into service. The Giants won only three games. It was with considerable relief that Owen found many of his key players returning from the wars as the 1946 season opened.

Among the Giants on hand for 1946 were Frank Filchock, who had come from the Washington Redskins, and Merl Hapes, a halfback who had joined the club from Mississippi in 1942, and had just returned from service.

The team won seven, lost three and tied one and won the Eastern title, but it was given a severe shock just before the championship game with the Chicago Bears.

Mayor William O'Dwyer of New York called Tim Mara on the Saturday before the game.

"You'd better come down to City Hall," he said.

Jack and Wellington Mara and Steve Owen hurried there to find police questioning Filchock and Hapes. The players had been seen in the company of a notorious gambler, Alvin Paris. Paris was charged with offering Hapes a bribe to throw the cham-

cuts back out of the grip of a tackler. Webster is a fine runner on cut-back plays and he is a powerful blocker, as well.

More than 20 years of experience in pro football is embodied in this picture of two Giant quarter-backs, veterans Charlie Conerly (left) and Y. A. Tittle, both of whom have keyed Giant championships.

pionship game. Hapes had refused but had not reported the bribe offer; Filchock, while he had known of the offer, was not involved. Both were cleared of criminal action.

League Commissioner Bert Bell was not so lenient. The mere fact that neither had taken a bribe meant nothing to Bell; they had not reported the bribe attempt, either. Bell banished Hapes from pro football at once, allowed Filchock to play in the championship game the next day, but suspended him immediately thereafter.

The action was a shock to the team. The news was broken to the squad by the Reverend Benedict Dudley, the unofficial team chaplain, the next morning.

"This game of yours always has been played in the sunlight," Father Dudley said to the players. "Because of this incident, today's game will be played in the shadows—the shadows of doubt. It's up to you to restore the faith of the fans in pro football."

The Giants tried mightily. Filchock, playing like a madman, threw two touchdown passes, exhausted himself with his fierce effort. But Sid Luckman, the Bear magician, won the game by scoring the go-ahead touchdown on a bootleg play that surprised everyone in the stadium, including George Halas, who considered Luckman too valuable a piece of property to risk on running plays.

Following that game, the Giants moved into a bleak and discouraging period. The All-American Conference had put two teams in the New York area and once again the Giants were up to their pocketbooks in fierce competition for players, dates and spectators. Unfortunately, the club hit the skids at the same time. The veterans who had held up through the 1946 season went over the hill and the cost of bidding for young players coming up was almost prohibitive.

In 1947, the club won only two games. The addition of Paul Governali, acquired in a trade with the Boston Yanks in mid-season, helped a little but not nearly enough.

The 1948 season was not much better; the Giants won four, lost eight, and finished third. But championship seeds were sown in 1948. In the Giant training camp that year were Charlie Conerly of Mississippi, obtained from the Washington Redskins, Bill Swiacki and Bruce Gehrke, two exceptional ends from Columbia, and Tony Minisi, a back from Pennsylvania.

An unheralded back from Iowa walked into the Giant office that year and informed

160

Wellington Mara that he was a football player and could make the Giants. Well, who has a sixth sense in the judgment of football players, studied the cocky youngster for a moment and was convinced. The player was Emlen Tunnell, who became just about the best defensive back in Giant history.

Al DeRogatis of Duke, Bill Austin of Oregon State and Jon Baker of California bolstered the line in 1949, when the club broke even, 6-6. Then the All-America Conference died and the Giants got the biggest bonus of experienced players since Mara had bought the Detroit club in 1928.

From the New York Yankees came Arnie Weinmeister, a massive tackle who ranked with the best, plus three great defensive backs—Otto Schnellbacher, Tom Landry and Harmon Rowe. Guard John Mastrangelo was another ex-Yankee who helped. From other dissolved AAC teams came still more help.

Fullback Eddie Price was drafted from Tulane, and from Texas came another good rookie, halfback Randy Clay. It added up to a tremendously powerful team. At the same time, the Cleveland Browns also received significant help as their former associates in the AAC disbanded.

The Giants turned out to be the only club that could beat the Browns. Owen, devising his famous umbrella defense specifically to handcuff Otto Graham, succeeded. In their first game, the Giants blanked the Browns, 6-0, the first shutout in Brown history. The Giants won the second game, 17-13, but Cleveland finally won the big one, an 8-3 victory in the playoff for the division title.

The umbrella defense was an extension of the plan Owen had used in defending against Sammy Baugh. Knowing that Baugh could unload the football in the wink of an eye, Owen never tried to rush the great Redskin passer, as most clubs did. Instead, he spent most of his defensive personnel on blanket coverage of Baugh's receivers. He did the same thing to Graham.

The umbrella was a 6-1-4 arrangement, but the defensive ends often dropped off into the flat to cover short receivers, setting up a forerunner to the modern 4-3-4 defense. The deep semicircle of six players set up when the ends dropped off produced a formation like an umbrella, hence the name.

That playoff loss to the Browns in 1950 sounded an ominous note. The Giants did not win another division title until 1956; the Browns won six straight Eastern championships. The Giants always had good luck against the Browns, but the Cleveland machine always managed to win enough games against the rest of the division to take the championship.

Owen, who had been with the Giants so long that he seemed a fixture, was let go in 1953 after a miserable season had been capped by a 42-14 thumping by the Browns.

Owen had let the tide of football flow by him. The game had changed radically in the twenty-odd years since he had joined the Giants, but Steve had not changed with it.

It was an intensely emotional moment when T. J. Mara and his two sons called in Steve and told him they thought it best to make a coaching change. They offered to retain Steve as head of personnel recruiting as long as he lived, but the hurt Owen stalked out.

He was replaced by big, puppy-friendly Jim Lee Howell, who brought a new concept of coaching to the Giants. Jim Lee surrounded himself with capable assistants and delegated to them complete authority. The system was an immediate success.

His assistants were Vince Lombardi, the tough, intelligent offensive specialist acquired from West Point; Tom Landry, who was a playing defensive coach for the first two years; Ed Kolman, a massive perfectionist who had played tackle for the Chicago Bears with distinction, and Bill Swiacki, who had retired from football but returned to work with the Giant ends.

A measure of the competence of this staff is that Lombardi, as coach at Green Bay, won general acclaim as one of the top coaches in the game, as did Landry when he went on to coach the Dallas Cowboys. Kolman remained with the Giants. Swiacki was replaced later by another ex-Bear, Ken Kavanaugh.

The draft of 1954 produced fullback Bobby Epps, Dick Nolan, a fine defensive back, and Don Heinrich, who became part of one of the most effective quarterback tandems in the league with Charlie Conerly. Wellington Mara and Howell demonstrated their acumen as traders that year, coming up with Bill Svoboda, Bob Schnelker, Herb Rich, Ray Collins and Barney Poole—players who would take key parts in the rehabilitation of the Giants.

They also discovered a great pair of free agents—Cliff Livingston and Ken MacAfee —and picked Ben Agajanian, the elderly place-kicking expert, from the discard heap.

Among the leftovers from the 1953 squad were more jewels: Rosey Brown, Frank Gifford, Ray Wietecha, Conerly and Kyle Rote. The 1954 Giants—rookies, tradees, holdovers, free agents—surged to a 7-5 record and third place in the East.

More pieces fell in place in 1955. Jim Patton, Rosey Grier and Mel Triplett were added in the draft. Alex Webster was lured back to the United States from Canada. And the Wellington Mara-Howell trading combine came up with two more plums— Walt Yowarsky from the Detroit Lions and Harland Svare, a bright, tough linebacker from the Los Angeles Rams.

When Allie Sherman took over as head coach of the Giants in 1961, some fans doubted that he could fill Jim Lee Howell's shoes. He proved to be one of the brightest coaches in professional football.

Football is not all glory. Frank Gifford is being carried from the field after a serious head jury which kept him out of football for a year. He returned to play wonderfully well in 19

The club started slowly, as Landry sorted out his defensive troops and Lombardi juggled the offense, sending Rote out to the flank and putting Webster into the running back spot. Triplett took over at fullback. While the settling-down process was going on, the Giants lost five of their first seven games. With everything in place and jelled, they won six of their last seven.

The addition of a power play using single-wing double-team blocking improved the running game late in the season. It was an integral part of the crunching New York ground game in the years to come.

Another exceptional flock of draftees and another bit of shrewd trading strengthened the team more in 1956. Up from the colleges came Sam Huff, Jim Katcavage and Gerald Huth. In the trading mart, Wellington Mara slickered Dick Modzelewski, the square, immovable tackle, away from Pittsburgh and defenders Ed Hughes, a halfback, and Andy Robustelli, an end, from the Los Angeles Rams. Don Chandler was another draft choice from Florida. His punting kept Giant opponents at arm's length for years.

The 1956 team won the Eastern Division championship, then crushed the Chicago Bears, 47-7, on a freezing afternoon in Yankee Stadium. This was the beginning of a perennial domination of the East by the Giants. Only twice in the next six years did they fail to win the Eastern title and they finished second and third in the non-title years.

They finished second in 1957, with a 7-5 season. The addition of Pat Summerall, again through one of Wellington's extraordinary trades, plugged a hole in the secondary and gave the team one of the league's best place kickers. The Giants won in the East again in 1958, beating Cleveland in a division playoff.

Much of the success of the 1958 team was attributed to an extraordinarily sticky

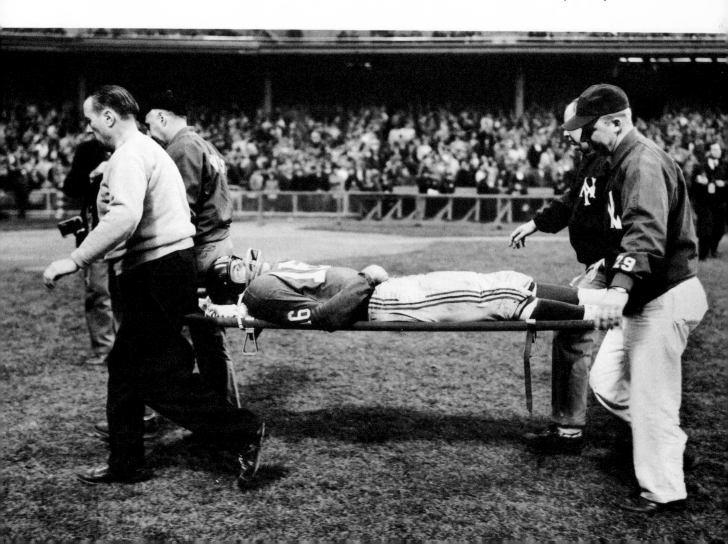

defense, led by Huff, Robustelli, Svare, Modzewleski, Grier and the tight-knit crew of defensive backs.

At one point, in the middle of the season, the offense bogged down and the Giants won three games in a row without scoring a touchdown.

"It got pretty bad," Kyle Rote admitted later. "I remember once going out on the field to take over on offense after the defense had scored on the Cardinals. Robustelli was coming off and he stopped to pat me on the back. 'See if you can hold them,' he said."

The club lost the championship to Baltimore in the most dramatic of all championship games—the sudden death playoff in Yankee Stadium.

In 1959, Lombardi left the staff to take over at Green Bay. He was replaced by Al

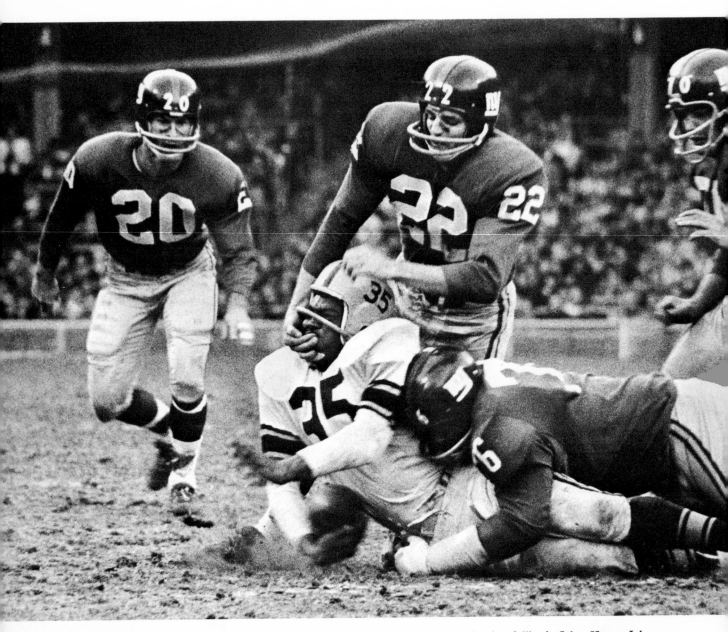

A sticky defense has long been the trade mark of the Giants, as Steeler fullback John Henry Johnson discovers here, with Roosevelt Grier (76) and Dick Lynch (22) trying earnestly to pull his head off.

Sherman, who had been backfield coach under Steve Owen from 1949 through 1953, had gone to Canada for three years as a head coach, then returned to the Giants as a personnel scout in 1957.

Sherman is a quiet, intelligent man who ranks at the very top of his profession. He took over the Giant offense in 1959 and did a remarkable job, blending daring innovations with sound football strategy to produce one of the most exciting attacks in Giant history.

The 1959 Giants, thundering through the Eastern Division race with a scoring average of nearly twenty-four points a game, won ten games and lost but two. En route to the championship, they demolished the Browns, 48-7, in an awesome display of power. Charlie Conerly, nearing forty, was a near-perfect quarterback. Always underrated as a passer, the greying, lean old man led the NFL in passing and, Sunday after Sunday, ignored the punishing slings and arrows of outraged defenses to direct the Giants quietly, almost stoically, to the championship.

Then the Giants faced the Colts again, this time in Baltimore. Tom Landry, the defensive coach, had developed a meticulous defense, based on a calculated risk.

"We wanted to cover Lennie Moore with one man," Landry said. "Then we could cut off the rest—Raymond Berry, Jim Mutscheller, Alan Ameche. We figured Moore would score twice, and we were willing to concede that. We thought we could score more than that."

Landry's estimate proved to be almost exactly right. Moore scored one touchdown and set up another. But the Baltimore defense scored, too, and that upset the calculations.

The Colts won their second league championship in a row, 31-16.

The 1960 Giants tailed off slightly. The Philadelphia Eagles, with Norman Van Brocklin engineering miracles almost every Sunday, won the championship. The Giants, hindered by injuries, finished third. At the end of the season, although he was under no pressure and had done an outstanding job as a head coach, Jim Lee Howell stepped down. The pressure of coaching had told on him; he became the Giants' chief talent scout and Al Sherman replaced him.

Eyebrows were raised when Sherman was named head coach. He was young, for one thing. For another, many Giant fans yearned for the return of Lombardi, who had begun to build an empire in Wisconsin.

But Sherman stilled the voices of his detractors. He set about building the Giants back into championship stature without fanfare, but with skill.

Two more big trades helped. The Giants got Y. A. Tittle to help Conerly at quarterback and acquired Del Shofner from the Rams. Tittle fitted into the Giant offense as though machined for the part. Shofner, who had had a poor season with the Rams the year before, caught sixty-eight passes and scored eleven touchdowns. Even without the services of Frank Gifford, who had been badly injured in a 1960 game against the Eagles and stayed out of football in 1961, the Giants won the division championship. Much of the credit went to Sherman, who had ignored his critics, produced a fine football team and was selected as coach of the year.

The Giant team retained the dedicated, cohesive team spirit which marked the club under previous coaches. The defensive unit, which was captained by Robustelli, had a hard-bitten spirit of its own. Modzewleski, the square, rugged tackle, had his hand ripped open in a game against the Browns and showed the gaping wound to Sam Huff.

Huff glanced down at it.

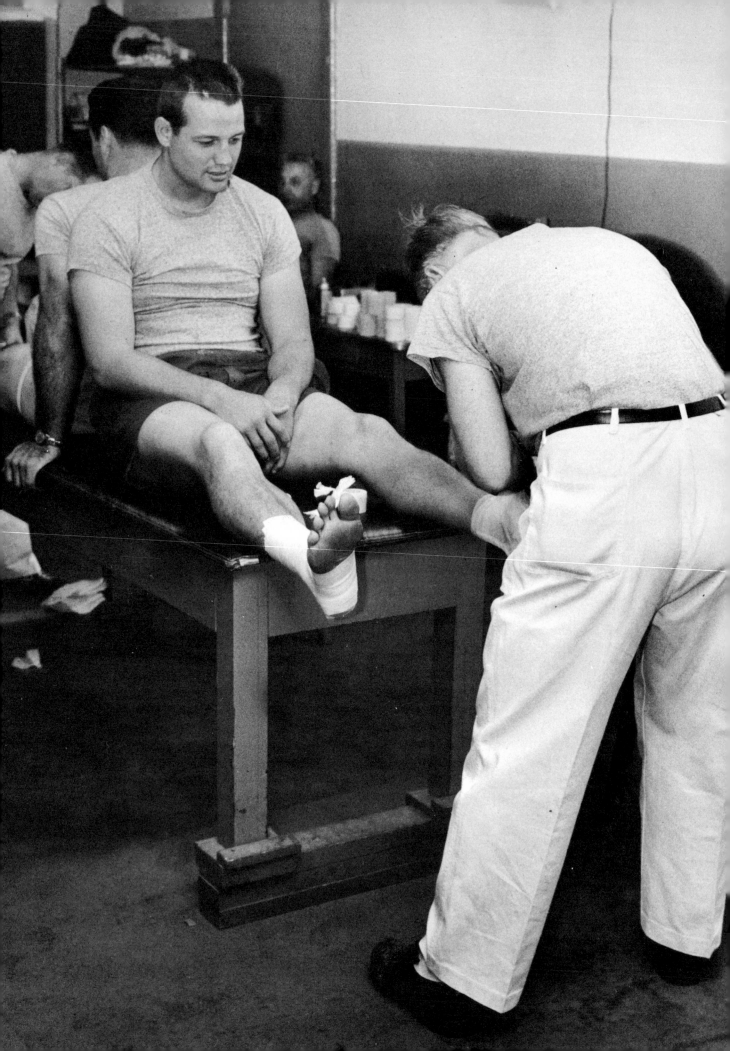

"It's not too bad," he said. "Shove it together and keep knocking."

Modzewleski did.

The **Giants hit** a smoking-hot Green Bay team in Green Bay in the championship game and lost, 37-0, but at the season's finish, it was clear that the club had 1) a truly top-flight coach, and 2) another group of players capable of winning championships.

Conerly retired after the 1961 season. He had played thirteen years for the Giants and had taken boos and cheers alike with the same calm patience. As his last season neared its end, he looked exhausted and drawn in the dressing rooms after the games.

"It takes too long to recover," he said once. "I used to feel pretty good again by Tuesday. Then it was Wednesday and later, Thursday. Now it's Saturday before I get over it. That's the years."

Landry had gone to Dallas and Svare back to Los Angeles. Ralph Guglielmi was obtained from St. Louis as a backstop for Tittle. There were some new faces, but not many.

Tittle, in his fifteenth year as a pro, had a magnificent season. Gifford, coming back, was moved out to a flanker back post. As soon as he acclimated himself to the new position, he became a more than adequate replacement for Rote, who had retired to become backfield coach. The ageless Webster was a thumping, dependable halfback still and Phil King, now in his fourth season, became a powerful, hard-blocking fullback.

Joe Walton, another player Wellington Mara had obtained in a trade, took over one end post and Shofner continued his heroics at the other. Sherman, even more poised and sure of himself, continued to direct the club with the aplomb of a champion.

The Giants again won the Eastern championship and met Green Bay for the second year in a row for the championship, this time in Yankee Stadium on a bitterly cold day and on a frozen field. A high, gusty wind destroyed one of the Giants' best weapons— the long pass from Tittle to Shofner. The Giant defense supposedly grown old in service, led by Sam Huff, Rosey Grier and Robustelli, played with the fury of young men, but the Giants lost a heartbreaking game, 16-7.

One key to dazzling air attack of the Giants is receiving of speedy Del Shofner, long pass catcher.

167

Hard-running Ted Dean is one of the best young fullbacks in the league. His surprisingly quick development in 1960 added the rushing strength the club needed to win the division and league titles.

# THE PHILADELPHIA EAGLES

$\mathbb{B}$ERT BELL, the late commissioner of the National Football League, was a many-faceted man. At one time or another, he was an enthusiastic playboy, a good halfback, a talented raconteur. His career in pro football, before he became the commissioner, included experience as owner, business manager, ticket seller, publicity man, equipment manager, trainer and head coach—all at the same time.

That was when Bert was the first owner of the Philadelphia Eagles. In 1933, he and Lud Wray, a former University of Pennsylvania teammate, bought the franchise of the Frankford Yellow Jackets in northeast Philadelphia for $2500. Because this was the era of the New Deal and the National Recovery Act, Bell changed the name of the club to the Philadelphia "Eagles" in honor of the NRA symbol—the blue eagle.

The Eagles were the first team to play on Sunday in Philadelphia. The old blue laws were repealed in their first year, one of the reasons Bell was anxious to buy the franchise. The other was a deep and abiding affection for football.

The years immediately following were not especially propitious for the beginning of a pro football team. In his first three seasons, during which Wray was the head coach, Bell and his associates lost almost $80,000. The club won eleven games during that time.

First big drawing card for the Philadelphia Eagles was tiny Davey O'Brien, who had just set a league record in the the last game of his career when this picture was taken. He had completed 33 forward passes.

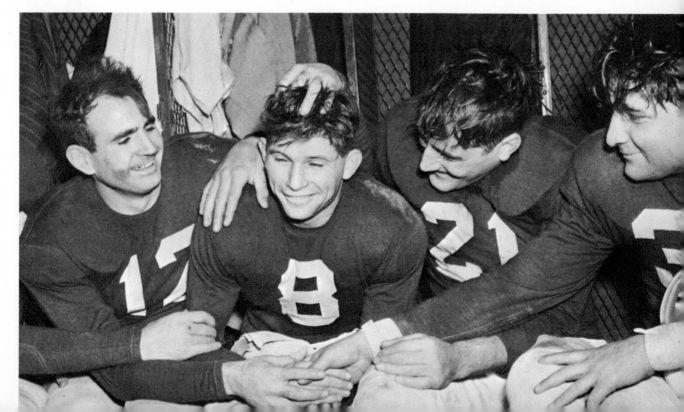

With no draft then, the solvent teams simply outbid their poor relation in Philadelphia.

So, in 1935, Bell proposed a player draft, and it was adopted on May 19, to go into effect for the 1936 season. The Eagles, having finished last, had first pick in 1936 and selected Jay Berwanger of Chicago, who never got around to playing professional football. By now, Bell's associates in the club had slowly dropped away. In 1936, he acquired sole ownership for $4000, disposed of Wray as head coach and took over the coaching chores himself.

The team had been strengthened by the addition of a big, strong fullback from Temple, Dave Smukler, and the acquisition, by trade, of veteran end Bill Hewitt of the Bears. Both were fine football players, but the Eagles had little to go with them. Bell's first venture as a head coach left something to be desired. The club won one game and lost eleven.

The next year, Bell doubled his coaching efficiency with two victories, a not inconsiderable feat considering the fact that coaching was only one of his chores. Frequently he hawked tickets on the streets of Philadelphia, although he found few buyers. Only a man of his iron determination would have persisted in the face of failure on the field and at the box office, but Bert had determination to spare.

He had been a notable bon vivant before his marriage. A small, dapper man, he was a familiar figure on Broadway and in the night clubs of Philadelphia. He gave it all up over night. He was courting the girl he later married. As they sat at a table in a crowded club, she watched him quietly a moment, then spoke.

"I'll never be able to take you seriously, Bert," she said. "Not as long as you spend

Steve Van Buren, a big, slashing runner, led the Eagles to their first world championship behind blocking like this. Van Buren was particularly adept at swinging wide, then slanting in for long gains.

your evenings drinking and night-clubbing."

Bell was halfway through a drink. He put the drink down unfinished. "That," he said, dramatically, "is the last drink I take as long as I live." And it was.

He had his best year as a coach in 1938, winning five and losing six. But the crowds still were thin. The addition of Davey O'Brien, the tiny All-American back from TCU, helped in 1939, but not too much. In 1939, playing a game against Brooklyn, Bell and the Eagles probably hit the all-time low in attendance.

The game was played in a downpour. Bell had suggested to Brooklyn club owner Dan Topping that they call the game off, or postpone it. But Topping had brought a friend with him from New York. He wanted his friend to see the game and insisted that it be played. Topping and his companion watched from an automobile parked along the sideline. The rest of the spectators fitted comfortably into the press box. The few fans who had bought tickets took refuge there from the storm.

O'Brien, an accurate passer and unbelievably durable for one so small, had his best day in a losing cause and away from home. Against the Chicago Bears, little David threw thirty-six passes and completed twenty-one. He was so impressive that even the normally impassive Bears applauded his efforts.

The next year, his last, O'Brien again saved his heroics for a game out of Philadelphia. This one matched him with his even more famous predecessor at TCU, Sammy Baugh. O'Brien, passing on virtually every play, set league records by throwing sixty passes and completing thirty-six, with no interceptions. He won his personal duel with Baugh but the Eagles, as usual, lost, 13-7.

Norman Van Brocklin (11), a pudgy, glue-footed quarterback with one of football's best arms and sharpest minds, passed to Tommy McDonald (25) for the big gains to lead the Eagles to the 1960 title.

These are the 1950 Eagles before they lost to Cleveland. The backs, left to right, Ziegler, Thompson, Myer

As O'Brien gave up pro football after the 1940 season, Bell gave up the Eagles, in a fairly complicated deal. He sold half the franchise to Art Rooney, who had sold his Pittsburgh franchise to Alexis Thompson of New York. Before the teams took the field in 1941, Rooney and Bell swapped Thompson their Philadelphia franchise for his Pittsburgh club.

Thompson, whose money came from steel, was a devil-may-care sportsman whose hobbies included bobsledding, soccer and lacrosse. By the time he bought the Steelers and swapped them for the Eagles, he had broken his leg twice—once at soccer and once at lacrosse—and injured himself more or less seriously several times on bobsled runs.

cott. In the line are Pihos, Kilroy, Maronic, Bednarik, Patton, Sears, Ferrante. Injured Van Buren is missing.

He promptly broke his leg again as soon as the Eagles went to training camp, this time in playing touch football with some of the players.

Thompson hired Greasy Neale to coach the Eagles. Neale's pro background extended back into the early twenties and late teens, when he had played with the Canton Bulldogs, among other teams, while still coaching at West Virginia Wesleyan. Thompson hired him away from Yale, where Greasy was serving as backfield coach.

Neale brought the T formation to the Eagles. He had been a single-wing coach, but the Chicago Bears sold him on the T. He borrowed films of the Bears' 73-0 walloping of the Redskins and went over them time and again, charting the plays, until he had the

173

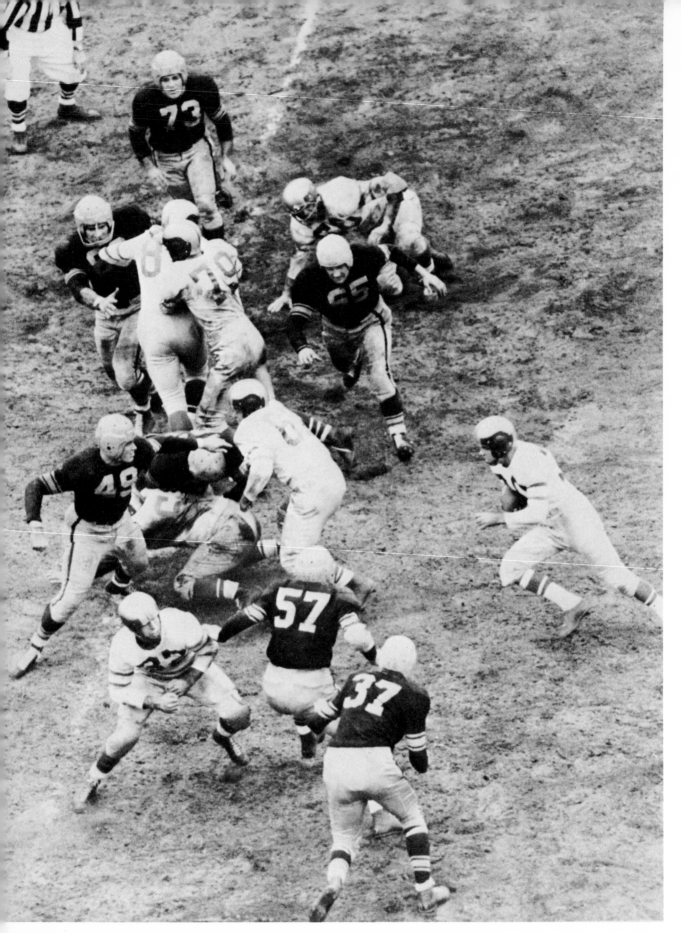

Fox-fast Bosh Prichard gains five yards against the Pittsburgh Steelers for the 1949 Philadelphia championship team. He might have gone farther had not Steeler Frank Sinkovitz (57) slipped block.

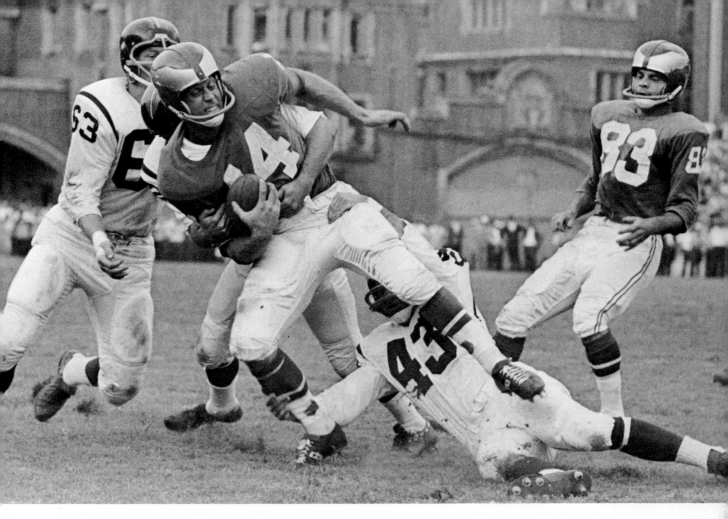

Strong factor in the Eagle air attack is Pete Retzlaff, a powerfully built end with exceptional hands. Bobby Walston (83), the other Eagle end and leading scorer, watches here as Retzlaff fights for gain.

full Bear repertoire at his command.

"I stole the whole Bear system," he admitted cheerfully. "I figured any offense that could score that much was good enough for me."

In Greasy's first season—1941—the Eagles acquired a one-eyed quarterback from the University of Tulsa, Tommy Thompson. He came to Neale as a tailback in the single wing but Neale, intent on his new T, transformed Thompson into a T quarterback, a role he filled to perfection.

Neale's T was no panacea for the Eagles' troubles and even Thompson's growing artistry as a T quarterback was not enough to overcome a serious shortage of manpower. In 1941, the Eagles won two, lost eight and tied one. The next year, with the services depleting the team even more, they won two and lost nine. For the 1943 season, as a wartime measure, the Eagles and the Steelers merged.

The hybrid team was called the "Steagles," presumably a less misleading name than "Eagers." Neale and Walt Kiesling, the Pittsburgh coach, put their heads together as a joint board of strategy and proved that two heads, especially when they are directing the fortunes of two teams combined into one, are definitely better than one. The Steagles did better than either the Steelers or the Eagles had done in 1942. They won five, lost four and tied one.

Their moment of joint glory over, the clubs separated again after the 1943 season.

The Eagles, bolstered by the advent of players like Vic Lindskog and Bruno Banducci, two tremendous linemen from the West Coast, and the return from service of a jack rabbit fullback, Jack Banta, and a sound end, Jack Ferrante, who had not attended college, were ready to move. Their first draft choice for the 1944 season was the square-jawed, husky thunder runner from Louisiana State, Steve Van Buren.

With Van Buren slashing for long yardage on the ground, the Eagles led the league in rushing, won seven games, lost one and tied two, but finished second to the New York Giants, a team they had defeated, 24-17, and tied, 21-21.

Tommy Thompson came back in 1945 and Van Buren continued to run brilliantly, leading the league again in rushing and in scoring, but the club finished second again, this time a game behind the Washington Redskins.

An injury to Van Buren slowed him during 1946, although he still managed to finish third in rushing as the Eagles, for the third year in a row, finished second. By now, Neale and Thompson were set to make capital of their T. Bosh Pritchard, Joe Muha and Russ Craft settled into backfield spots to take some of the load off Van Buren, and in 1947 a big, powerful fullback from Indiana, Pete Pihos, joined the club. Neale made him an end and put in a play called "the Pihos screen," a short pass behind the line which

Sonny Jurgensen, who learned his trade sitting on the bench watching Norm Van Brocklin, takes over as the number one quarterback. Giant Sam Huff (70) comes in as Jurgensen prepares to loose the ball.

wreaked havoc among defenses in the next few years.

Neale, who had picked up the T from Bear movies, now operated it in his own inimitable fashion. Often he jotted down the offense on whatever was at hand when an idea occurred to him. One season, an ex-Eagle said recently, most of the Eagle offense came from the back of a brown paper sack on which Greasy recorded his ideas.

However he came by the ideas and by whatever method he recorded them, he made the Eagles into an awesome football team for the next three years. His defense, which depended on linebackers to hold up the offensive ends and a trio of monsters in the middle of the line to discourage a ground attack, worked beautifully. The Eagles won the 1947 Eastern championship by defeating Pittsburgh, 21-0, in a playoff but, on an icy field, they lost the championship game to the Chicago Cardinals, 28-21.

Part of the blame for this defeat may be ascribed to Hugh L. (Shorty) Ray, the league's supervisor of officials. The Eagles, because of the frozen field, had filed their cleats to points. The Cardinals, understandably apprehensive, protested that the sharpened cleats were lethal weapons and illegal. The official on the field inspected the shoes and approved them. Ray sent word from the press box that the shoes were illegal and the Eagles had to go back to regulation cleats.

Thompson passed brilliantly, but Van Buren, without sneakers and deprived of traction by the banning of his special shoes, gained only twenty-six yards in eighteen carries. The Cardinals, shod in sneakers, broke away for four long scoring runs to win the game.

The 1948 team, with Thompson leading the league in passing and Van Buren in running, waltzed to the Eastern title, despite a series of injuries in the closing weeks. Everyone was healthy for the championship game, played in a blizzard. Hours before the game, Bert Bell, by then commissioner, asked the players if they wanted to go ahead or to postpone. They voted to play and over 35,000 spectators peered through the swirling snow as the Eagles beat the Cardinals, 7-0.

A year later, when the Eagles played the Los Angeles Rams in a cloudburst in the Coliseum in Los Angeles, frantic Ram officials called Bell, who had remained in Philadelphia, to ask permission for a postponement. Inexplicably, Bell, giving as his reason radio commitments, refused to let the game be postponed. Ram fans, accustomed to sunshine and not nearly so hardy as the Philadelphians, stayed away from the game.

Ironically, Eagle owner Lex Thompson did not see his club win a championship. He had spent freely and lost heavily in building a championship team, but he was in a New York hospital, where he had been operated on for appendicitis, when the Eagles beat the Cardinals. Soon after, he sold the team to a syndicate organized by James P. Clark, owner of a trucking company. Clark and his 100 stockholders paid $250,000 for the franchise on January 15, 1949.

The 1949 Eagles were a powerful team. The big line was anchored by a massive middle guard named Mario Gianelli, who was flanked by Bucko Kilroy and Piggy Barnes. Rookie Chuck Bednarik joined the team from Pennsylvania. Thompson, Pritchard, Craft, Pihos, and a powerful offensive line were at their peak.

A year later, many of them had passed the peak and Neale's defense had been solved. But in 1949, this was one of the wonder teams. They won eleven games and lost only one, and scored 378 points to their opponents' 134. One of their victories was a 38-14 trouncing of the Rams, who had won six straight when they met the Eagles.

This game was played in Philadelphia. Ed Pauley, one of the Ram owners, had brought a trainload of friends from Washington to see his team end a longstanding Eagle

Top scorer and one of the top receivers on the modern Eagles was Bobby Walston, lining up a field goal attempt. Although he was not large, Walston was still a sure and very crisp blocker.

jinx, but at half-time the score was 28-0 in favor of the Eagles.

Among Pauley's friends was General Mark Clark. Pauley, feeling drastic measures were needed, induced Clark to accompany him to the Ram dressing room, where coach Joe Stydahar was trying desperately to devise a defense for Van Buren and Bosh Pritchard, a small but blazing fast Eagle halfback who always murdered the Rams. Pauley interrupted Joe's exegesis of offense and defense and introduced Clark, who gave the team a brief but impassioned pep talk, pointing out the rigors of war, citing the crossing of the Rapido River, and reminding the men that a team that won't be beat can't be beat.

The Rams kicked off to begin the second half. It was a long kickoff and Russ Craft took it three yards deep in the Eagle end zone and returned it all the way for a touchdown.

Vitamin Smith, sitting morosely on the Ram bench next to Stydahar, watched stonily as Craft skittered through the Ram tacklers until he crossed the goal line. Then he turned to the Ram coach.

"Joe," he said, "why don't you go ask the General what we do now?"

The drenching rain which made the Coliseum field a shallow lake precluded any long kickoff returns in the championship game, but it did not hamper Van Buren. Carrying the ball on a play which began as a sweep, then suddenly turned into an off-tackle slant as he cut back, the big Eagle back ran for 196 yards, far more than the entire Ram team managed to gain.

Strangely enough, Van Buren did not score. The two Eagle touchdowns in the 14-0 victory came on a 31-yard pass from Thompson to Pete Pihos and on a blocked punt. Ed Skladany, a Philadelphia end, paddled through the muck to knock the kick down, then recovered it in the end zone.

This game marked the crest of the Eagle wave of supremacy. The following year the Cleveland Browns joined the NFL just as the Eagles began to decay. The Browns underscored the beginning of the end by walloping Philadelphia in the first game the two teams played, then going on to win the Eastern championship. Neale was released in 1951 and the team began a long rebuilding process which was not to reach fruition for nearly ten years. The 1950 team won six and lost six and Bo McMillin replaced Neale in February of 1951.

McMillin's tour as coach was tragically short. He was a dying man when he took the job and, by the second game of the season, he was too sick to go on. He died the following March. Wayne Millner, who had been a more than competent end for the Eagles, took over. The Eagles drifted gently down the standings for the next few years. Good rookies helped now and then. In 1951, a black-browed, drawling youngster joined the club and was named rookie of the year. He was Bobby Walston, a talented end and a fine place-kicker. But he was not enough; the team finished fifth, with four victories and eight losses.

Another of McMillin's assistants succeeded Millner in 1952. Jim Trimble took over just before the league season started. The Eagles got Bobby Thomason, a handsome, articulate and accurate passer from the Rams, to help Adrian Burk at quarterback. Bud Grant was in his second year at end, Wayne Robinson, a rookie center from Minnesota, helped the line, along with Lum Snyder, a big tackle from Georgia Tech. Norman (Wild Man) Willey, a ferocious defensive end from Marshall College, was just growing up in his third year and Frank Wydo, a rookie tackle, was already mature.

Trimble depended on his defense for most of the seven games the 1952 team won. The offense was only adequate, waiting for a truly great quarterback.

It looked as if the club had two great passers the next season. Burk and Thomason, sharing the quarterbacking, combined to gain 3089 yards passing and the aging Pihos, still a formidable runner and an ingenious receiver, led the league in receiving. He caught sixty-three passes and scored ten touchdowns as the Eagles finished second to Cleveland. Clark retired as president of the club and was succeeded by Frank McNamee, which had no effect on the operation of the team. Vincent McNally was the general manager.

The Eagle ends, Walston and Pihos, keyed the club for the next few years. Walston

Classic finish to a classically run pass pattern by the Eagles' Tommy McDonald finds the ba

led the league in scoring, Pihos in receiving, and Trimble managed second place finishes in 1953 and 1954, during the hey day of the Browns. The club slipped in 1955. Pihos was still a marvelous receiver, but cracks appeared elsewhere and the team posted a 4-7-1 record, even though Pihos led the league in receiving.

That was the end for Trimble. He was succeeded by Hugh Devore, whose first team won three, lost eight and tied one. The Eagles had touched bottom, but they had a gleam of hope the next season, signing thick-wristed, red-haired, happy-go-lucky Sonny Jurgensen

clearing the frantic finger tips of New York's Erich Barnes as McDonald goes into the end zone.

This impromptu one-arm handstand ended Chuck Bednarik's unfamiliar role as ball carrier against the Cleveland Browns. Bednarik is one of the most **durable** and most versatile of all of the Eagles.

from Duke as a rookie quarterback. Sonny had a strong day against the Browns, beating them by 17-7, but the team won four and lost eight and the upswing of the pendulum seemed distant.

The next year the foundation was poured for another championship team. Devore was fired and the club hired silver-haired, quiet and tolerant Buck Shaw as head coach. Shaw had been a good coach for the San Francisco Forty-Niners. The Eagles also obtained Norman Van Brocklin from the Los Angeles Rams in a trade. Van Brocklin and Sid Gillman, the Ram head coach, had been at odds for some time. Pete Retzlaff, a big, muscular end, had matured in two years with the team. Tom Brookshier, who became one of the best corner backs in football, had reached his peak. Clarence Peaks of Michigan State added running strength to the team and a small, alert and incredibly elusive flanker back, Tommy McDonald, had had a year to develop moves as a pass receiver.

Retzlaff tied for the league lead in pass-catching that year, but the team was still jelling. It takes more than one year for a group of strangers to become a cohesive, effective pro football unit. They won only two games, lost nine and tied one, but Shaw, a patient man, was not worried.

The next year, with Van Brocklin hitting McDonald and Retzlaff and a stumpy, enthusiastic halfback named Billy Barnes running and blocking, the Eagles moved up to second. On October 11 in Franklin Field, while the Eagles were playing the Pittsburgh Steelers, a former owner of both clubs and the commissioner of the league, Bert Bell, died. He died as he probably would have chosen—in the closing minutes of an exciting game played before a sellout crowd.

The Eagles won the championship in 1960. It was the last year of his career for Van Brocklin. Chuck Bednarik, an amazingly agile and durable man in his twelfth season in the league, played both offensive center and middle linebacker on this team.

Tommy McDonald was the best deep receiver in the league and Retzlaff could catch passes anywhere. Peaks, Barnes and Ted Dean, a big rookie from Wichita, ran better than expected and the whole team, inspired by the driving personality and unflagging will to win of Van Brocklin, surprised themselves, the league and the experts.

Cleveland beat them with almost contemptuous ease in their opening game, but the Eagles came back under the scalding leadership of the Dutchman to win nine in a row. They beat the New York Giants twice and they won the Eastern Division championship and faced Green Bay in the title game in Philadelphia as the underdogs.

Van Brocklin, in his last regular game as a pro, picked apart the Green Bay defense with cool competence and the Eagle defense played inspired football. The game ended with Bednarik stopping the last Packer drive on the Philadelphia nine-yard line and the Eagles ahead, 17-13.

After that climactic year, Shaw and Van Brocklin retired. Van Brocklin was under the impression that he would be named head coach on Shaw's retirement, but if such an agreement had been made, the Eagle excutives either forgot it or chose to ignore it. Nick Skorich, a short, stocky and likeable man raised in the hard-blocking tradition of Jock Sutherland, was named head coach. Van Brocklin, fuming, accepted the head coaching job with the newly-born Minnesota Vikings and did a superb job.

Jurgensen, who had sat and watched and learned while Van Brocklin ran the Eagles for three years, took over as quarterback in 1961. He looked the very model of Van Brocklin, with the same chubby body, the same insouciance, the same flair for picking the right play. In his first year at the controls, he set two league records: 235 pass completions for 3723 yards. The Eagles finished second.

Unfortunately, Jurgensen suffered a serious shoulder separation in the second-place game in Miami against Detroit and started slowly in 1962. The team was racked with other injuries and before it could recover its poise, it slipped badly. The Eagles finished last; the pendulum was swinging down and the swing of the pendulum takes time.

Bill Dudley (left), sparked the Pittsburgh single wing attack under the severe regime of Dr. Jock Sutherland. Here he chats with another famous All-American before game — Michigan's Tom Harmon.

# THE PITTSBURGH STEELERS

ARTHUR ROONEY, a mild, generous and patient man, acquired the Pittsburgh Steelers because of his strong faith in long shots. None of these long shots had anything to do with football; they were of the race track variety.

Rooney came from an Irish family and was the oldest of six children. Most of his relatives in the small town of Coulterville, Pa., were steel workers. His father owned an inn in the town and later moved it to Pittsburgh, where the Rooney saloon, near the old ball park, was a rendezvous for the sports world.

Art was a fine athlete in his youth. He was a good football player, was offered contracts by two major league baseball teams and might have been a champion had he turned professional as a boxer. From the time he was born, his principal interest in life was sports; after his competitive years, he became an inveterate horse follower.

It was his predilection for the races which led to his purchase of a pro football franchise for Pittsburgh.

Rooney had dabbled in many sports. He had been manager and a player on a minor league baseball team and a fight manager. In 1932, with a fighter named Buck Crouse, he went to New York. He had some $300 with him; he took the money with him to the Empire City race track and, in the course of a Saturday afternoon, parlayed the $300 into $21,000.

He took his $21,000 and his good luck with him to Joe Madden's saloon to celebrate. During the celebration, Madden convinced him that he should not quit while his luck was running strong, so the two of them went to Saratoga.

Rooney's Saratoga sweep is history now, although he does not talk about it much. He began by betting $2000 on an 8-to-1 horse named Quel Jeu. Quel Jeu came in to begin Art's incredible streak of luck.

Rooney won five bets, all on long shots. The last one was another 8-to-1 horse. This one came in with $10,000 of Rooney's money on its nose and it boosted Art's take for the day to $256,000.

So, in 1933, when Joe Carr, the president of the NFL, offered Rooney a Pittsburgh franchise for $2500, Art had the money for the fee, plus operating expenses for a long time. He bought the Steeler franchise as casually as Tim Mara had bought the Giants. Not until several years later did Rooney become deeply interested in the team.

Carr had wanted a franchise in Pittsburgh because the blue laws were ended in 1933. Rooney's first game was scheduled to take place the Sunday after repeal.

The vote was held on a Tuesday but the City Council had to ratify the repeal before it became effective. Unfortunately, they did not get around to it by Sunday, so the op-

A tragic picture of a great athlete — Big Daddy Lipscomb, one of the best defensive tackles in the history of pro football, gazes out on the field from the Pittsburgh sideline. He died after 1962 season.

ponents of repeal, on Sunday, sought out the Pittsburgh chief of police to get him to stop the game with the New York Giants.

They looked high and low, but couldn't find him. Meanwhile, the Steelers had started their game. By the time the blue noses had located the chief of police, the game was over and the Steelers had begun their NFL career with a loss. The chief of police, of course, was out of reach because he was a spectator at the game.

Coach of the first Steeler team — which was called the Pirates, not the Steelers — was Jap Douds, who came to Rooney from Washington and Jefferson. His club won only two games and lost six, with two ties. Douds was replaced in 1934 by a Pitt graduate named Luby Dimeolo, who did even worse than Douds. His club won two and lost ten.

With no draft as a basis for building a team, Rooney and his coaches found it difficult, in the early years, to compete with the established pro clubs in the battle for talent. Joe Bach took over from Dimeolo and enjoyed some success as the club slowly accumulated a core of good football players. Under Bach, the Steelers came close, in 1936, finishing one game behind Boston for the Eastern Division championship. Their record that season was 6-6.

A measure of the deficiency of the Pittsburgh talent during the pre-World War II years is that not a single Steeler made the all-league team from 1933 until 1942, when Bullet Bill Dudley was selected.

Bach left for greener pastures after the 1963 season and Rooney hired Johnny Blood as a playing coach. Blood, while not the most successful Steeler coach, was certainly the most exciting.

He began by giving his players a perfect example of how he wanted them to perform: he took the opening kickoff of the first game of his first season 100 yards for a touchdown.

The rest of the club, however, was not talented enough to emulate Blood. He was an unusual coach. Far from being a disciplinarian, he was more apt than his players to miss

This is Bill Dudley trundling along on one of his spectacular runs for the Steelers. Dudley, who did not have really good speed, was one of the most elusive backs who ever carried a football.

Byron (Whizzer) White led the league in ground gaining during his brief career in pro football, both with the Steelers and with Detroit. The former Rhodes scholar is now a Supreme Court Justice.

The powerful stride of rangy John Henry Johnson, Pittsburgh fullback, is clearly shown in this fine action picture. Eagle tackle Charlie Bradshaw (71) is drawing bead for a block on Giant Jim Katcavage.

practice. He enjoyed life and did not let football interfere with pleasure. For a time, his own ability as a player helped, but Blood was past his peak and beginning to slow down.

Under Johnny's carefree stewardship, the Steelers won four and lost seven in 1937, but they dropped off to 2-9 the next year and 1-9-1 in 1939, Blood's final season.

Walter Kiesling succeeded Blood, but the fortunes of the Steelers remained at low ebb. In the war years, the club combined first with Philadelphia, in 1943, and then with the Chicago Cardinals, in 1944, but even with the addition of fresh blood from the other teams, Pittsburgh could not win a division championship. Indeed, when the Steelers finished their thirtieth year in pro football, they still had not won a division championship.

This was by no means due to parsimony on the part of Rooney. Not long ago, the league prepared an operations manual, charting the costs of the various teams, for the benefit of new teams just going into business. One item under expenses was for advances and loans to players. For most teams, this amounted to a few thousand dollars. For the Steelers and the generous Mr. Rooney, the figure was nearly $80,000.

After the war the Steelers began to perk up. Rooney, long an admirer of iron-fisted disciplinarian Jock Sutherland when Jock coached great teams at the University of Pittsburgh, finally persuaded Dr. Sutherland to take over the Steelers. This was in 1946. Sutherland took a team which had won two games and lost eight in 1945 and broke even in 1946.

Star of the 1946 team was a rather small, not particularly fast, back from the University of Virginia, Bill Dudley. Dudley was the second super-player to grace the Pittsburgh roster. In 1938, for one year, Byron (Whizzer) White played for the Steelers before accepting a Rhodes scholarship. White is now a justice of the United States Supreme Court.

Dudley was the tailback in Sutherland's unsubtle, power-animated single-wing forma-

Here John Henry Johnson demonstrates another ability rare in so big a man — the ability to cut sharply at full speed without losing momentum or balance. Johnson's running implemented Steeler passes.

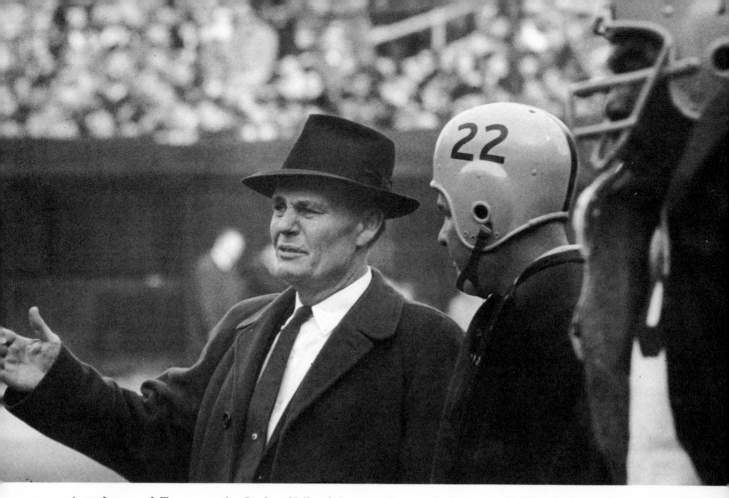

A conference of Texans on the Steeler sideline brings together coach Raymond (Buddy) Parker and quarterback Bobby Layne. Note Layne's helmet; he is one of only two players who do not use face bars.

tion. Jock was a relentless taskmaster. At one point in his first year with the Steelers, the players, who thought that Sutherland was unnecessarily harsh, revolted and Sutherland had to make concessions to them.

Dudley led the league in rushing and the club in pass defense; he picked off ten enemy passes in 1946 for a club record. He also punted, place-kicked and passed.

He was a wonderful runner to watch. Not blessed with exceptional speed, he had perfect control and a deceptive change of pace. He could change direction at top speed without losing momentum.

But the tailback spot in Sutherland's bruising single-wing attack was a punishing position. Dudley, who did not take to Sutherland's drillmaster tactics any more happily than any of the rest of the players, asked that he be traded in 1947. He went to the Detroit Lions.

Steve Lach provided most of the punch for the 1947 Steeler team, which set the high water mark in Steeler history by finishing in a tie with the Philadelphia Eagles for the Eastern Division championship. This was a team built entirely on offense. Although the club had the best record in Steeler history with eight victories and four defeats, it actually gave up more points than it scored. In the playoff game with the Eagles for the division championship, the Steelers were shut out, 21-0.

Sutherland was forced to give up the Steeler job before the 1948 season because of poor health; he died in 1948. He had contributed much to the Steelers. During his regime, the team was sold out for every home game because of the magic of his name and his

191

popularity in Pittsburgh.

On the theory that what the Steelers needed was more of the Sutherland influence, Rooney hired young John Michelosen, who had played under Jock at Pittsburgh and had been an assistant to Sutherland. Michelosen retained the hard-hitting single wing throughout his four-year tenure; the rest of the league had long since shifted to the T.

Recruiting became difficult for the Steelers since there was a dearth of single-wing players in college football, and Michelosen's single wing, while it was rugged and rough, was not exciting to watch. Nor was it overly productive of victories. From 1948, when he took over, to 1951, his last season, Michelosen had only one better than .500 season, in 1949, when the Steelers' 6-5-1 record put them in second.

Continuing pressure from fans, plus the difficulty to find single-wing players, forced Rooney to replace Michelosen with Joe Bach, serving his second term as coach, in 1952.

Buddy Dial reaches for pass from Layne. Dial, who came to the Eagles from the New York Giants, has been one of the most effective receivers in the league, blessed with exceptional speed, moves.

Steelers' Tom (The Bomb) Tracey heads for trouble as he tries to crack the Giant line. Waiting for him are Andy Robustelli (81) and Dick Modzewleski (77). On one hand is Giants' Roosevelt Grier.

Bach installed the T formation. To operate it, he had a fine passer from Tulsa named Jimmy Finks, who had come to the team in 1949. The impetus of the T and an excellent season for Finks as a passer brought the Steelers their highest-scoring season in 1952, when they tallied 300 points. The opposition nearly matched that total, however, and the club finished fourth, with a 5-7 record. Finks and Bach scored less but won more in 1953, when the club broke even at 6-6.

Walter Kiesling replaced Bach in 1953. The Steelers enjoyed three so-so years under Kiesling before Rooney opened a new era for the Steelers by hiring Buddy Parker, who had quit the Lions as coach in 1957.

Parker, a moody, intelligent Texan, treats his players like adults, but demands a full performance for an adequate wage. He is a genius at what might be called the re-habilitation of football players. Many of the men he acquired in the next few years for the Steelers had been misfits or unhappy on the teams they left. Under Parker, they became sound and happy football players. In his first year with the Steelers, Parker fashioned a .500 season, with six wins and six losses. In 1958, after the club had played two league games, Parker obtained Bobby Layne from Detroit, where Layne was not particularly happy splitting the quarterbacking with Tobin Rote. Layne and Parker had won three world championships with the Lions. They went together hand in glove and Layne, a fierce competitor with a tremendous desire to win, was what Pittsburgh needed.

The mediocre years in Pittsburgh had produced a losing habit. Layne, bawling at the team in his high-pitched Texas drawl, shook them out of the lethargy of defeat and convinced them they could win if they wanted to badly enough.

Layne and Parker lifted the club to third place in 1958, with one of the best records in club history: 7-4-1. Parker, searching desperately for mature talent to give the Steelers an immediate lift, traded away draft choices freely to obtain seasoned players. He operated on his theory from the day he took over the Steeler job. Only injuries have kept the Steelers from the top in the last few years. Parker's trades have been good ones.

He acquired, besides Layne, players of the caliber of Big Daddy Lipscomb (from the Colts); Buzz Nutter (from the Colts); Dan James (from the Forty-Niners); Mike

Sandusky (from the Forty-Niners); Buddy Dial (from the Giants); Charlies Bradshaw (from the Rams); Preston Carpenter (from the Browns); Ed Brown (from the Bears); Tom Tracy (from the Lions); John Henry Johnson (from Detroit); Lou Michaels and George Stugar (both from the Rams); and Johnny Sample (from the Colts).

Layne roomed with Ernie Stautner, who had put in almost as many years in the pro grid wars as Bobby had. Stautner, an all-pro defensive tackle, entered the league in 1950, two years after Layne.

With his trades and with the leadership of Layne, Parker did much to improve the Steelers. This has been a consistently unlucky team, its chances to move often ruined by injuries. Unlike many teams, the Steelers do not usually have a deep bench. It has been a good year when Buddy has had twenty excellent players. Most of the time, there has been a solid nucleus of some sixteen or seventeen. Thus, injuries to a few key players destroy the Steelers' chances quickly.

A staunch defense has always been one of the strong points of Pittsburgh teams, principally because of players such as Lou Michaels (79), shown here putting pressure on Y. A. Tittle on passing play.

A case in point was the 1960 season, when the Steelers, confident with Layne at the throttle and equipped with good football players, seemed ready to move. Layne's chief targets were Jimmy Orr and Goose McLairen at the ends. Both were injured in the final game of the exhibition season.

Layne injured his throwing hand early in the season. John Henry Johnson, who carried the brunt of the running attack, suffered a leg injury; then two starting linebackers, Rudy Hayes and Mike Henry, were hurt. The best blocking guard on the club, Mike Sandusky, was knocked out, too.

This run of bad luck ended whatever hopes the Steelers had had for the season. The team which should have been in contention for the division championship finished at 5-6-1 and in fifth place.

The following year was almost as bad. Layne was injured, again in the final exhibition game, suffering a deep bruise on the side.

He tried to play anyway but aggravated the injury and was placed on the disabled list. Without his leadership, the Steelers stumbled to a 6-8 season.

The 1962 Steelers, hampered early by injuries, rallied sharply toward the close and finished second to the New York Giants, playing the Detroit Lions a vicious, hard-fought game in Miami in the second-place playoff before losing.

In Pittsburgh, there is, in good years and bad, a hard core of some 15,000 fans who go out to watch the Steelers play. For thirty years they were frustrated. So was Art Rooney. But the grey-haired, bushy-browed Rooney still has unflagging good humor despite the long years and pocketfuls of money spent chasing the championship.

Not long ago, at a league meeting, a newsman watched him chatting with the other owners.

"There's a man who is the finest living example of something Leo Durocher once said," he said. "Leo said, 'Nice guys finish last.' That's Art."

The choice of some experts as the greatest college football player of the last fifty years, Ernie Nevers proved to be as good a pro. His scoring record for one game, set against the Bears, still stands.

# THE ST. LOUIS CARDINALS

THE St. Louis Cardinals are the oldest club in point of continuous operation. They began playing in Chicago twenty-three years before the Chicago Bears arrived and it is a mark of the peculiar predilection for misfortune of this club that it was the Bears, not the Cardinals, who captured the imagination of the Chicago football fans.

When the club started in 1898, on Chicago's South Side, where it was to remain for sixty-two years, it was the brain child of Chris and Pat O'Brien and it was known, to a narrow circle of friends and spectators, as the Morgan Athletic Club.

When the team moved its playing site to Normal Field, still on the South Side, the name was changed to the Normals. Some ten years later, O'Brien found a bargain in faded University of Chicago jerseys and changed the name again, to the Cardinals, much to the unhappiness of Amos Alonzo Stagg, then coach at Chicago and a bitter enemy of pro football.

The Cardinals lived a hand-to-mouth existence then, as did most athletic club teams, but in 1920 O'Brien acted to stabilize his team.

First, he secured the services of Paddy Driscoll, a brilliant player at Northwestern and at Great Lakes Navy, for $300 per game. Second, he challenged the Chicago Tigers, a rival pro club, to play a game for the exclusive right to the Chicago territory. For one year, then, until Halas showed up, O'Brien had the only game in town; Driscoll had run forty yards for the touchdown which beat the Tigers, 6-3.

Driscoll, who is now an assistant coach for Halas with the Bears, was a thorn in George's side in the first few years the Bears were in Chicago. The rivalry between the two Chicago teams, then as now, was fierce. In 1920, when Halas' team was still in Decatur, the clubs split two games and in 1921, when the Bears won the league championship, they played a scoreless tie.

By now, Halas wanted Driscoll so desperately that he offered the Cardinal halfback a one-third interest in the Bears, with Halas and Sternaman. Driscoll was, of course, willing, but the league president, Joe Carr, would not agree to the deal.

It was not until 1926 that Halas was able to get his hands on Paddy. Meantime, Driscoll had set a league record with four scoring drop-kicks against Columbus and had negated Red Grange's debut with the Bears by angling twenty-two of twenty-five punts away from the Galloping Ghost. That was in 1925, the year the Cardinals claimed the championship after hastily scheduling two late games to fatten their percentage of wins after Pottsville had ostensibly won the title.

Grange was responsible for Driscoll's leaving the Cardinals to go to the Bears. In 1926, he and C. C. Pyle, his ebullient manager, started their own league, which had a team in

Mud does not seem to have slowed Charlie Trippi, brilliant Cardinal halfback, on this run against Washington in a 1947 game. Trippi, who hailed from Georgia, was part of Cards' million dollar backfield.

Chicago called the Bulls. The first time the two leagues met head-on in scheduling, Grange, playing with the New York Yankees against the Bulls, drew 20,100 spectators; the Bears and the Cardinals drew only 12,000.

O'Brien was badly in need of money and the Bears were a better drawing card than the Cardinals, even then. The league felt that Halas needed a star to match Grange, and Driscoll filled the bill.

So O'Brien, to relieve his fiscal discomfort and to help the league, sold Driscoll to Halas for a sum variously reported to be from $3500 to $10,000. It was a particularly unselfish act on O'Brien's part since the new league had offered him a sizable amount of money to jump the National League and bring Discroll with him to the new league.

The money he obtained for Driscoll was only a stopgap, though. Without Paddy, the Cardinal gate dropped even lower and in 1929 O'Brien accepted an offer of $25,000 for the club from a Chicago doctor named David Jones, who immediately secured a superstar to replace Driscoll.

That was Ernie Nevers, the All-American fullback from Stanford. Pop Warner, who coached both Nevers and Thorpe, picked Ernie as the greatest player of all time over the big Indian not so much on his physical ability as on his temperament.

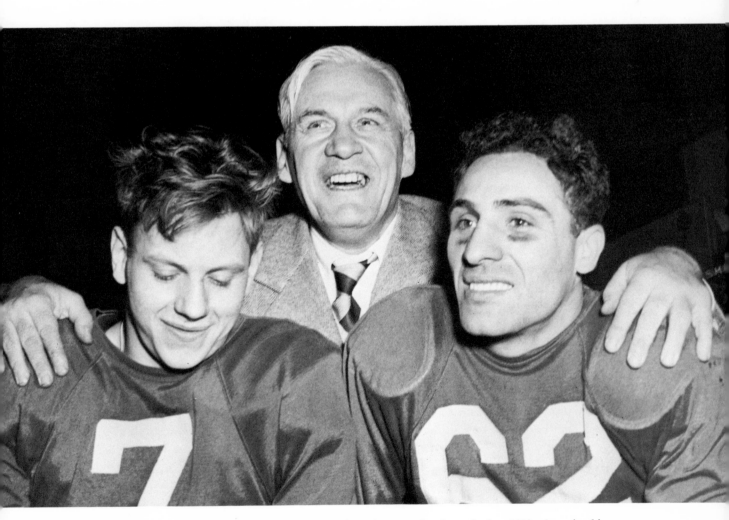

Half the million dollar backfield plus Coach Jimmy Conzelman exult after winning 1947 championship from Eagles, 28-21. Elmer Angsman (left) and Trippi (right) each scored twice on long runs for win.

Marshall Goldberg (99) was best known for his running ability during his days with the Cardinals, but he was a tough, hard-tackling defender as well. Here he tackles Bears' Don Kindt in playoff game.

Nevers coached and played on the 1929 Cardinal team, which finished fourth with a 6-6-1 record. On Thanksgiving Day of 1929, Nevers scored six touchdowns and kicked four extra points, establishing a one-game scoring record never equalled. Even with Nevers, the Cardinals did not move up, either in standings or attendance. Ernie stayed with the club through the 1931 season, during which he played every minute of nineteen games and the Cardinals crept over the .500 mark with five wins and four losses.

By 1933, after four years during which he had never seen his team finish higher than fourth, Dr. Jones was in a receptive mood when he was made what seemed to be a casual offer during dinner one evening on the yacht of Charles W. Bidwill. Bidwill, a multi-millionaire sportsman and business man, had bailed out Halas earlier in the year by arranging a $5000 bank loan for him. Now, expansive over after dinner brandy, he asked Dr. Jones if he would like to sell the Cardinals.

Bidwill was then owner of a racing stable, president of the Chicago Stadium Operating Co. and of a printing company and active in turf associations. He was a friendly man,

One of the most violent blockers, as well as one of the most shocking runners in Cardinal history, was fullback Pat Harder, here being ankle tackled by Philadephia defensive halfback Russ Craft.

deeply interested in sports, and enjoyed the company of owners and athletes in football, baseball and racing.

Jones did not ponder long over Bidwill's question.

"You can have the club for $50,000," he said. Within a week, Bidwill owned the Cardinals.

From 1933 to 1946, the Cardinals never rose above fourth; in six of the thirteen years, they finished last in their division. Bidwill, a Bear fan before he became a Card fan, accepted adversity philosophically. Once, when the Bears needed a victory over the down-trodden Cardinals to avoid a playoff for a division title, Bidwill inadvertently showed that he remained, at heart, a Bear fan at that time.

The Bears squeaked by the Cardinals and Bidwill, sweating profusely, shook his head at Jimmy Conzelman, his head coach.

"That," said Charlie, "was too close for comfort."

Conzelman left the Cards in 1943 after three years as head coach, and returned in

1946, just in time to lead the club during the three years of its greatest glory.

During his absence, the club had played the 1944 season as a joint venture with the Pittsburgh Steelers, the combined team being known as the Card-Pitts. It was a wartime measure and it had no effect on the Cardinals, who had lost ten straight games in 1943 and proceeded, after the merger, to lose ten more in 1944.

**John David Crow** (44, with ball) could truthfully be called a pro's player. Among other players in the league, he

They were under Phil Handler at the time. In 1945, they won one game, completing a horrendous three years in which the club had won one and lost twenty-nine games.

By the time Conzelman had come back to coach in 1946, however, a deep reservoir of top draft choices, selected in the barren years, awaited him.

Marshall Goldberg, who had come to the team as an All-American from Pittsburgh

is regarded as one of the three or four best backs in the game. Injuries have hampered him during his career.

in 1938, had just reached his peak. Paul Christman of Missouri was out of the Navy and ready for his second season of pro football. He was an accurate, intelligent quarterback. His targets were a pair of superb ends from the southwest: Billy Dewell of Southern Methodist and Mal Kutner of the University of Texas. Elmer Angsman, a stumpy, hard-running halfback from Notre Dame and Pat Harder, a big, hard-blocking fullback from Wisconsin, reported in 1946, too. In the line was one of the finest tackles ever to play in the league — Stan Mauldin of Texas.

The Cardinals finished fourth in 1946 with a 6-5 record. In 1947, they acquired an All-American back from Georgia who was as elusive as a waterbug. His name was Charley Trippi and he was all the Cardinals needed to win their first title since 1925.

The backfield of Angsman, Harder, Trippi and Christman was known as the "million-dollar" backfield, since Bidwill claimed he would not take that for the quartet.

Bidwill, who had spent generously to accumulate this team, hoped to see it win the championship, just as he had long wanted to win the Kentucky Derby with one of his horses. But the Cardinals are a star-crossed team. Bidwill died suddenly in 1947 of pneumonia and was never to see the club he had so expensively assembled win the title.

Not long after Bidwill's sudden death, Cardinal halfback Jeff Burkett was killed in an airplane crash. The third tragedy to hit the Cardinals occurred after the first game of the 1948 season when Mauldin, the giant tackle from Texas, dropped dead of a heart attack in the dressing room.

Dick Huffman, a three-year all-pro tackle with the Rams and one of the strongest men ever to play football, called Mauldin the best tackle he had ever played against.

"He was so quick it was hard to reach him," Huffman said. "And he was the only tackle I ever played against I wasn't always sure I could handle physically."

Once Greasy Neale, who coached the Philadelphia Eagles in the game which ended in Mauldin's death, spent an hour showing his team movies of Mauldin in action, so they could appreciate perfect tackle play.

Mauldin's death was totally unexpected; like all pro players, he had passed a rigorous physical examination before reporting to camp. But he took himself out of the Eagle game, complaining of exhaustion. Later, coming out of the shower in the dressing room, he complained of dizziness, collapsed and died.

Despite this succession of tragedies, the 1947-49 Cardinals played brilliantly. It was a team reminiscent of the modern Packers — able to slash away for long gains on the ground or take to the air with equal facility. And it was a tough, hard-bitten club.

Early in his career, Trippi demonstrated his right to be a member of the football version of the Cardinal Gas House Gang. Harrassed, battered and generally abused over the course of a long afternoon by the Bears' small but very rough end, Ed Sprinkle, Trippi bided his time until the last play of the game, when a penalty would do no harm to the Cardinal cause.

On the last play, Sprinkle was knocked to his knees as he came across the line of scrimmage. Trippi calmly walked over to him, measured him as he was getting to his feet, then dropped Sprinkle with a beautiful right cross to the chin and walked sedately off the field.

"It was worth the $100 fine," he said later.

Few opponents took liberties with this Cardinal club. Pat Harder, the rock-hard fullback, later drilled home a lesson to another end in the league: an injury to one Cardinal was an injury to all.

Sonny Randle (88) is one of the fastest ends in the league and, during recent seasons, has learned good moves. He plucks ball away from Dallas' diving Don Bishop for a considerable gain for Cards.

The end, coming in hard to try to block an extra-point try, had roughed Jim Hardy, a quarterback the Cardinals obtained from the Rams. Later in the game, again with time running out, Harder asked the Cardinal quarterback to call a play which would assign him to block the end.

The big end barrelled in hard, took a swing at Harder, then dropped like a pole-axed steer as Harder's forearm smashed into his face. It was after this incident that, for the only time in the history of the league, a coach asked an opposing team to pay the hospital bills for one of its injured players.

Oddly enough, the end, who was to spend weeks in the hospital, was penalized for unnecessary roughness on the play. The official had seen him swing but had not seen Harder's counter-punch.

In 1947, with Christman passing for over 2000 yards and seventeen touchdowns and with the backs running wild, the Cardinals won nine and lost three, edging the Bears out of the Western Division title.

The championship game, against the Philadelphia Eagles, was played on a frozen field in Comiskey Park before 30,759 fans. Neale had installed an eight-man line on defense against the Eagles but the Cardinals, firing Angsman and Trippi past the first rank of the defense on quick-openers, found it easy to handle.

Trippi popped through the bulky Eagles for forty-four yards and a touchdown on a quick-opener in the first quarter and added a seventy-yard punt return for another touchdown in third.

Angsman, ideally suited for the quick-opening plays with his jet-fast start, scored twice, both times on seventy-yard runs, in the second and fourth quarters. When it was all over, the Cardinals had their first uncontested league championship with a 28-21 victory.

The 1948 Cardinals, despite the tragic loss of Mauldin, put together the best season in the club's history. The superb backfield had returned intact and the club played with the asurance and flair of champions. They won eleven games and lost only one — to the Chicago Bears. In the Eastern Division, the Eagles also repeated, so the 1948 championship game was played in Shibe Park on December 19.

Incredibly, 36,309 fans turned out to watch this game, played in the worst snow storm Philadelphia could remember in fifty years. The sidelines disappeared and so did the yard markers. The wind howled and snapped at players and fans and swirling snow all but hid the game from the stands.

The Eagles won, 7-0, after recovering a fumble on the seventeen-yard line of the Cardinals but the game, of course, was no true test of football skill. True to their luck, the Cardinals ended their brief tenure at stage center on an unpleasant note, losing the championship under the worst conditions in league history.

Conzelman retired again after the 1948 season and the team of Phil Handler and Buddy Parker coached the club in 1949, finishing third with a 6-5-1 record. Walter Wolfner, who was made managing director of the club after his marriage to Bidwill's widow, hired Curly Lambeau for the 1950 and 1951 seasons, but the decline of the club continued and Lambeau was let go after the 1951 season.

Joe Kuharich was head coach in 1952, a season notable chiefly for the first-round draft choice of Ollie Matson, who was to be one of the best backs in Cardinal and league history. However, Matson was not enough to bring the club out of its doldrums and the 1952 club won four and lost eight, prompting Kuharich to move on.

For the next five years, the Cardinals were under the direction of former Bears as

Anxious face of quarterback Charlie Johnson reflects the problems of a young signal caller as he listens to instructions and advice from the coaches in the press box. Johnson, from New Mexico, had taken over at quarterback

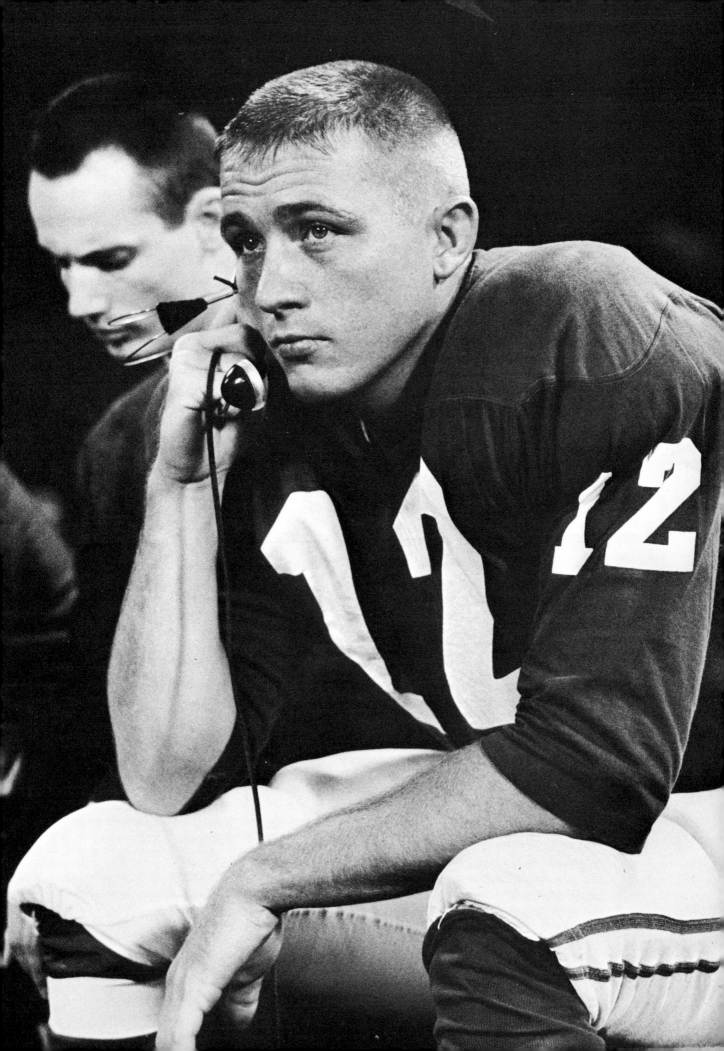

Among the better recent players for the Cardinals is versatile Bobby Joe Conrad, of Texas A&M, who has gone high among a crowd of defenders to come down with this hook pass for short yardage.

head coaches — Joe Stydahar in 1953 and 1954 and Ray Richards in 1955-6-7. Matson blossomed as a super-star, but one star was not enough and the club's best record in the five-year span was 7-5 in 1956.

In 1958, Wolfner turned to Canada for a head coach and got Frank (Pop) Ivy, who installed a new, double-wing T offense and began rebuilding the club slowly. He acquired Bobby Joe Conrad in a deal with the Giants and drafted the top back in the nation, John David Crow, in 1958. The Cardinal backfield of Crow, Matson and Conrad approximated that of the 1947 Cardinals.

In 1959, in a sweeping move to add overall strength, Wolfner and Ivy negotiated an eleven-for-one deal with the Los Angeles Rams for Matson. Only two of the players obtained for Matson are still with the Cardinals; again, typical of Cardinal luck, both were lost to the club for long periods after the trade due to injury. Defensive tackle Frank Fuller broke his left leg in 1960 and missed five games; offensive tackle Ken Panfil missed most of the 1961 season with a dislocated kneecap.

It was an exceptionally unlucky year in 1961, even for the Cardinals. Ivy had acquired Sam (The Rifle) Etcheverry, Canada's best passing quarterback, to solve a problem in air offense. Etcheverry showed up with a sore shoulder and was not effective. John David Crow, who had taken Matson's place as the best running back on the team, broke his leg before the season started. He came back in time to carry the ball only forty-five times after setting a club record for ground-gaining the year before.

The club had moved to St. Louis in 1960 and found a reasonably warm welcome. It finished 6-5-1 that year, then 7-7 in 1961, despite the disastrous run of injuries.

Ivy resigned with two games to play in 1961 and assistants Chuck Drulis, Ray Prochaska and Ray Willsey finished the season.

Tragedy hit again early in 1962, when Mrs. Violet Wolfner, widow of Charles Bidwill, died suddenly in Miami, leaving the Cardinals to her two sons, Charles Bidwill, Jr. and William Bidwill.

The Bidwills, in effect, traded coaches with the Houston Oilers of the American Football League as the 1962 season opened, getting quiet, soft-spoken defensive specialist Wally Lemm in exchange for Ivy.

The development of young Charlie Johnson at quarterback and the return, in full good health, of John David Crow at halfback produced a better-than-average season for the Cardinals in 1962. For a team so consistently beset with disaster, it seemed that luck must, some day, change.

One of the early stars of the San Francisco Forty-Niners was oak-legged halfback Johnny Stryzkalski, shown breaking free from the grasp of tackler Chuck Fenenbock, of the new defunct Los Angeles Dons.

# THE SAN FRANCISCO
# FORTY-NINERS

THE San Francisco Forty-Niners were the dearest possession of a warm-hearted, hard-headed, soft-spoken, generous man named Tony Morabito. And they were the death of him.

Tony was the son of an Italian immigrant who built up a good business in ship's services on the San Francisco waterfront, only to see most of it waste away. When Tony graduated from Santa Clara University in hard times, he was fortunate to get a job as a truck driver. His own initiative, drive and personality carried him from the seat of a truck to a desk as the owner of a lumber-carrying trucking concern which spread-eagled the Pacific Northwest.

Raised in an area that bred Joe DiMaggio and other great baseball players, Tony nevertheless was a rabid football fan, principally of Santa Clara. Because a Santa Clara fullback named Nello Falaschi became a pro star, he transferred some of his interest from college to pro football. By 1941, he had become enough of a pro *aficionado* to approach the NFL with a request for a franchise. He was turned down on two counts: travel to the West Coast was too expensive and the San Francisco area, with five major college teams, had more football than it could handle.

Tony offered to guarantee to put a team in operation within three months after the end of World War II; he was still turned down by the NFL. When he heard from a San Francisco sports editor that Arch Ward of the *Chicago Tribune* was organizing the All America Conference, Tony was eager to join.

He attended the first meeting of the prospective franchise owners of the new conference in June, 1944. The San Francisco Forty-Niners were charter members of the league.

"I expect to lose money," Tony said, frankly. "It will take time before pro football catches on in San Francisco. But I think this is a great sports town and I'm willing to gamble."

He had two partners in the Forty-Niners when the club began operation in 1946. They were his partners in Lumber Terminals, his trucking concern — Allen E. Sorrell and E. J. Turre. Tony's younger brother, Vic, had a small interest in the Forty-Niners.

Two years and a quarter of a million dollars later, Tony bought out Sorrell and Turre. He and Vic became the principal owners, with Tony holding three-fourths of the stock and Vic one-fourth.

Tony had gone to his alma mater for a coach. Silver-haired Buck Shaw had produced exciting and successful football teams for Santa Clara, including Sugar Bowl champions in 1936 and 1937. Persuading Buck to take the head coaching job of the Forty-Niners was a big step toward insuring the confidence of the public in professional football.

Tony took more insurance by signing another Bay Area hero as his quarterback. Frankie Albert had been the prototype of the T quarterback under Clark Shaughnessy at Stanford. When he signed with Morabito, he gave the club an exciting name immediately.

Tony spent lavishly in the first year and the 1946 Forty-Niner squad was studded with established pros. Norm Standlee, Albert's backfield running mate from the 1940 Stanford team which made history by coming from an all-losing to an all-winning season in one year, signed with Morabito after a brilliant rookie year with the Chicago Bears in 1941. Other NFL players who suddenly appeared on the San Francisco roster that first year included Bruno Banducci, a guard from Stanford and the Philadelphia Eagles; Len Eshmont, a halfback from Fordham and the New York Giants; Parker Hall, a halfback from Mississippi and the world champion Cleveland Rams; and Bob Tichenal, an end from San Jose State and the Washington Redskins.

It was one of the best teams in the new conference. However, the Forty-Niners were

Left-handed Frankie Albert, a small, resourceful and courageous quarterback, was very good at doing what he is doing here. He has evaded tackler, poses threat to defenders of either a run or a pass.

started out on a long career as a bridesmaid when they and the Cleveland Browns were placed in the Western Division of the conference. Had the Forty-Niners not been in the same division with the Browns for the first three years of the AAC, they undoubtedly would have played the Browns each year for the championship. They finished second to the Browns in 1946, '47 and '48. In the fourth year, when the AAC dropped the divisional groupings, the Forty-Niners finished second to the Browns, then lost the championship game to them.

During the early years, Morabito was involved in two controversies. In 1947, he tried to sign West Point's Touchdown Twins — Glenn Davis and Doc Blanchard. Each had ninety days' furlough coming; Morabito reasoned that if they would take it during football season, they could play with the Forty-Niners. A storm of unfavorable editorial comment moved Army officials to announce that the players would not be granted furlough time in order to participate in a business venture for personal profit.

Later, the independent colleges in the Bay Area, most of which played on Sunday to

Tall, raw-boned Gordy Soltau was doubly valuable — as a place kicker and as a receiver. Here he catches touchdown pass from then San Francisco quarterback Y. A. Tittle, being tackled at upper left.

avoid conflicts wtih such big Pacific Coast Conference schools as Stanford and California, charged that the Forty-Niners were hurting them by scheduling Sunday games. Morabito, through his attorney, Marshall Leahy, pointed out that the Forty-Niners and college games were in conflict only three times during the season. He said that the colleges' attendance had begun to fall off long before the arrival of the Forty-Niners, principally because the big coast schools would not play the independents. In a battle for dates in Kezar Stadium, Tony won.

Although Shaw, with his generous helping of NFL veterans, had finished second to the Browns in 1946 and 1947, it seemed evident after the 1947 season that the Forty-Niners needed a youth movement. The 1947 team won eight, lost four and tied two. When the 1948 squad reported to training camp, only twenty veterans were on hand.

By the time Shaw reduced the team to the final thirty-three, the rookies outnumbered the veterans, seventeen to sixteen. It is doubtful that any team, beginning with a nucleus of veterans, ever kept as many rookies as the 1948 Forty-Niners. But the 1948 rookie crop was not only big; its quality was exceptional.

Among the youngsters were Hal Shoener, a mild-mannered wild man from Iowa, who played defensive end; Verl Lillywhite, a bruising runner from Southern Cal; Jim Cason, a talented all-around player who was ambidextrous and could play on offense or defense; Bill Johnson, a tough offensive center from Tyler Junior College in Texas; and another junior college product from Compton, in Calif., Joe Perry. In the next fifteen years, Perry was not only one of the best runners in pro football, but certainly the most durable heavy-duty back in the game.

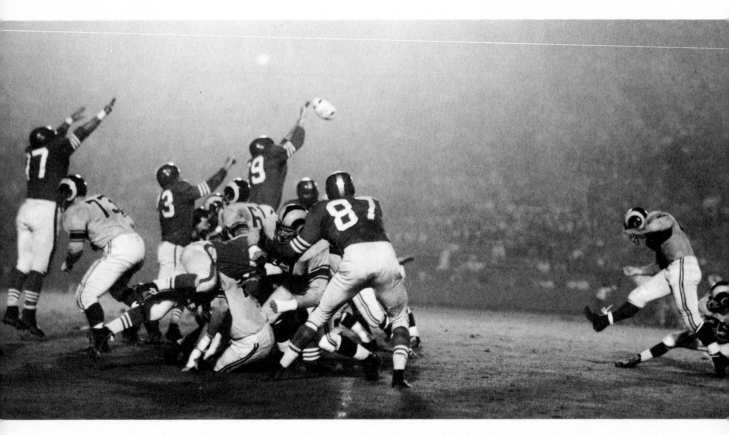

Rare picture of a field goal actually being blocked shows Bob St. Clair, giant San Francisco tackle, climbing high out of the ruck in the middle of the line of scrimmage to bat ball out of the air.

Perry, who came to the Forty-Niners at 200 pounds and who had been timed in the 100-yard dash at 9.6 seconds, gave a clear indication of what he would do in the years to come the first time he carried the ball in a league game. On a quick opener against the Buffalo Bills, Perry, a jet-fast starter, popped through a narrow hole in the Buffalo line, got by the linebackers before they saw him, and went on for fifty-eight yards and a touchdown.

Perry, Lillywhite and Johnny (Strike) Stryzkalski gave the 1948 Forty-Niners a fearsome ground attack to complement Albert's passing to ends like Alwyn Beals, who caught fourteen of Frankie's twenty-nine touchdown passes.

The Forty-Niners lost only two games, both to Cleveland. The Browns did not lose any games and finished first in the Western Division. The 1948 Forty-Niners rank with the finest scoring teams in the game; they racked up 495 points. The team gained a fantastic 3663 yards on the ground and 5767 overall and scored sixty-five touchdowns, or an average of nearly five per game. Home attendance jumped, but this was the winter of near-disaster elsewhere in the All-America Conference and the Forty-Niners' travel costs, not offset by adequate revenue in the cities they visited, resulted in another losing season financially.

In 1949 Tony and his brother bought out the other two partners. To consummate this deal and to insure capital for operating the team during 1949, Tony had to mortgage his home and borrow $100,000 from a bank. It was a courageous affirmation of his faith in the future of professional football in San Francisco.

It was particularly courageous in face of the fact that the AAC had sued for peace with the NFL, and failed to get it only because of the intransigence of the Baltimore Colts. The league was clearly on its last legs.

Tony did not let his financial difficulties affect his generosity toward his players. Frankie Albert's 1949 contract was for $20,000, a record for that era. Frankie was worth it.

The Forty-Niners, with high expectations, started the 1949 season as if they would shake the second-place jinx. They won five of their first six games. The fifth victory was over the Cleveland Browns at Kezar Stadium in an explosive demonstration of scoring power, 56-28. The Browns were not beaten as badly again until the Detroit Lions flattened them in the 1957 NFL championship game.

The next week the Forty-Niners rolled on, burying Buffalo, 51-7. But in the Buffalo rout disaster struck. Strykalski broke his leg and was out for the year and Eddie Carr, a key back, suffered a knee injury which ended his career. With much of the running attack wiped out by the two injuries, the Forty-Niners lost to the New York Yankees on the following Sunday as the Yankee defense ganged up on Perry.

The Forty-Niners again wound up second. In this, its last year of existence, the All-America Conference had devised a playoff for the championship, with the second and third teams meeting each other and playing the winner of a game between the first and fourth teams for the championship. The Yankees finished third and the Forty-Niners beat them, 17-7.

There was a near player rebellion when the team asked for a share of the money for the game. This died a-borning when Morabito threatened to forfeit the game if the strike was carried out.

Cleveland exercised its usual mastery over the Forty-Niners in the championship game, 21-7. This game was a record for anti climaxes. Before it was played, the AAC had surrendered to the NFL. Few people cared about the outcome of the Cleveland-San Francisco game and few came to watch it. The game was played in sprawling Cleveland Municipal Stadium; only 22,550 fans were sprinkled about the stands.

Survivors of the AAC were the Browns, the Forty-Niners and the Colts. Bert Bell, the far-seeing commissioner of the NFL, treated the newcomers to the NFL as fairly as he did the long-time members of the league. Both conferences had held their drafts. A less fair commissioner might have ruled that the NFL draft would take precedence, but Bell held that a new draft was in order.

The Los Angeles Rams had drafted a big tackle from Minnesota, Leo Nomellini, in the original NFL draft. In the interim between that draft and the NFL-AAC merger, they had heard that Nomellini was inclined to dog it occasionally. When the second draft was ordered, the Rams skipped Nomellini and took a fullback named Ralph Pasquariello. The Forty-Niners drafted Nomellini and Leo the Lion became one of the top defensive tackles in the game year after year. Pasquariello played only briefly with the Rams.

Bay Area fans, titillated by the chance to see their team against the heralded clubs of the NFL, bought season tickets in record numbers for the 1950 season. This proved to be, at best, a mixed blessing.

Morabito, supremely confident of his team's ability to play on a par with NFL clubs, told the players before their first exhibition game with the Washington Redskins: "Score a hundred points. Then take a deep breath and score another hundred."

What with the addition of Nomellini and other fine rookies like Don Campora, Ray Collins and Jack Nix in the line, and Don Burke, Jimmy Powers and Emil Sitko in the backfield, Morabito seemed to have good reason for his confidence. Several sports writers in Cleveland, Baltimore and San Francisco agreed with him.

The Redskins did not. They thumped the Forty-Niners, 31-21, before more than 50,000 fans. The following Sunday the Philadelphia Eagles handed the Forty-Niners another warning that they had moved up in class. The NFL champion Eagles, playing without their star running back, Steve Van Buren, came to Kezar Stadium and drubbed San Francisco, 28-10.

The only club the Forty-Niners could beat during the exhibition season was a familiar patsy from the AAC — the Baltimore Colts. They went on to a dreary 3-9 season in their first excursion into the National Football League. Only Cleveland, which won the title, upheld the honor of the AAC.

The Forty-Niners, who led a life of frustration in the conference in which they had begun, found life no more beguiling in the NFL. Shaw, whose only nemesis had been Paul Brown, found a multiplicity of Paul Browns facing him, with the same knowledge of the game and the same plethora of skilled players.

He helped the team in 1951 by acquiring Y. A. Tittle from the defunct Colts. Lou Spadia, the San Francisco business maanger, won Tittle on the flip of a coin with the Green Bay Packers, who also had a 3-9 record in 1950. A strong set of draftees sent the Forty-Niners into the 1951 season sure they would prove equal to NFL clubs. Their confidence was justified.

The bountiful crop of rookies included Billy Wilson, a deft end; Pete Schabarum; Bill Jessup; Nick Feher; Joe Arenas; and a violent, if small, linebacker, Hardy Brown.

But the luck of the Forty-Niners was unchanged. Albert hurt his shoulder in the first league game, before Tittle had had time to adjust to Shaw's offense. Tittle was not used to the personnel, either; he was still getting around late on handoffs to Perry, who started so fast that the quarterback had to make a special effort to get the ball to him on quick dives into the line.

The club lost two games, then rallied to run the Los Angeles Rams out of Kezar

The narrow lanes available for pass completions are shown in this picture as John Brodie sights through mass of players to find receiver with defenders closing in on him from front and rear.

Stadium, 44-17. Shaw put in a special defense to handle the lightning-quick Ram runners and receivers, replacing big, slow-footed linebackers with defensive backs. It worked in San Francisco. A week later, playing the Rams in Los Angeles, Shaw found that the Rams had prepared the riposte. When the Forty-Niner coach put in light but fast linebackers, the Rams countered by putting all three of their fullbacks in the game at the same time. The Ram bull elephant backfield ran over the light San Francisco linebackers. When Shaw put in the big linebackers, the Rams removed the fullbacks and replaced them with their racehorses. The Rams won, 23-16.

It has always been difficult for a team to win with more than one quarterback. Dissension hit the Forty-Niners, with Tittle and Albert factions in the stands and on the field. The team still retained an outside chance for a division championship in the last game of the season, against the Lions. The Rams would have to lose to Green Bay and the Forty-Niners beat the Lions. They did beat the Lions in the last few minutes, but the Rams ran wild over the Packers and the Forty-Niners, as usual, finished just out of the money.

Two more talented rookies joined the Forty-Niners in 1952. One, Hugh McElhenny, was as accomplished a ball-carrier as ever played football. The other, tackle Bob Toneff, was adept at clearing the way for men of McElhenny's ability.

The 1952 Forty-Niners began nobly and turned toward mediocrity on one play. The careers of a great back and of a great coach turned on the same play.

The Forty-Niners won five games in a row, including a resounding 40-16 victory over the Chicago Bears in Chicago. They returned to San Francisco from a road trip with the city jubilant. Their sixth game of the season was a return match with the Bears. A few nagging injuries had slowed the club, but in midseason they seemed, at last, on their way to a championship.

The injuries hampered them somewhat, but in the fourth quarter they led the Bears, 17-10, before a happy full house at Kezar Stadium. With fourth down and two yards to go on the San Francisco thirty-two yard line, Albert dropped back to punt. A reasonably good punt would put the ball somewhere in the vicinity of the Bear twenty or thirty-yard line, where the San Francisco defense, which had held Chicago in check, could be expected to keep the road to victory sealed off.

Albert thought he saw daylight between a Bear tackle and end. Instead of punting, he ran. The hole he had seen closed abruptly as Ed Sprinkle, the small but tough Bear defensive end, snapped shut the trap. Sprinkle knew that Albert liked to run from punt formation; he had left the gap open to tempt the Forty-Niner quarterback.

Albert missed the first down and the Bears took over deep in San Francisco territory and moved to the tying touchdown quickly. With only a minute to go in the game, George Blanda lofted a forty-eight-yard field goal through the sea gulls which gather in the late evening at Kezar and the Bears won, 20-17.

Although Shaw defended Albert after the game, the incident widened a rupture. It did not help when the Forty-Niners collapsed in the stretch, losing four of their last six games and finishing third.

Albert, embittered by the tension between him and Shaw after the Bear loss, retired at the end of the season. Shaw lasted two more years. Tittle, bald as an egg and calm as a cucumber, took over as quarterback in 1953.

The Forty-Niners caught fire in the 1953 opener. The blaze was set off by a wild-swinging free-for-all initiated by a scuffle between Charley Powell and the Philadelphia Eagles' end, Bobby Walston. The battling lasted almost twenty minutes; the Forty-Niners went on to win the game, and a fiery team spirit was born.

The club seemed to develop cohesion from this gang warfare. It stood them in good stead the rest of the year. Tittle was a magnificent quarterback; had he not suffered a serious injury against Detroit in the third game, this might have been the year for the Forty-Niners.

Driving into the Detroit end zone in the third period, Tittle was hit high and hard. His cheekbone was broken in three places and the Forty-Niners lost, 24-21.

With a defensive back, Jimmy Powers, filling in at quarterback, the Forty-Niners won the next game, but Powers could not keep up in this return match with Detroit and the Forty-Niners lost. Tittle came back, his face protected by a cage of iron, but it was too late. The Lions won the division championship with a 10-2 record; the Forty-Niners were 9-3.

Tittle suffered a hand injury in 1954 and again the Forty-Niners fell short. By now there was considerable grumbling about Shaw, although he had done as well as any man could have, considering the injuries. After the team finished third in 1954, Morabito resorted to the time-honored remedy for a losing team. He fired Shaw.

He replaced Buck with Red Strader, who had coached the New York Yankees. Morabito had once accused Strader, when he was the Yankee coach, of sneaking a scout into the Forty-Niner practice before a Yankee game.

**Gordy Soltau,** the fine San Francisco end, demonstrates another of his skills by kicking a field goal against the Los Angeles Rams in 1956 game, the second of the day. Kick was away barely in time.

A noble experiment by San Francisco coach Red Hickey was the shotgun offense, the formation the club is in in this picture. Offense gave quarterback host of targets, but no protection in backfield.

Strader instituted a regime radically different from Shaw's. Shaw had been a quiet, easy-going man; the Forty-Niner camp was known, among players, as a country club. It began to look more like a concentration camp under Strader. The older players did not take to this happily.

"He treats us like kids," one of the old-timers said. "I expect to be tucked in every night."

McElhenny suffered a foot injury in the exhibition season and never was up to par. This, plus the disaffection of the players, resulted in one of the Forty-Niners' worst seasons (4-8) and the departure of Strader.

Morabito shocked the fans and sports writers by naming Frankie Albert, who had had almost no coaching experience, as the new head coach. It was a desperate move and not a particularly successful one.

Albert, who had been the archtype of the gambler as a quarterback, was far more conservative as a coach. He was prone to send in plays to Tittle, who did not take to

220

direction from an ex-teammate very happily. Many times, when the San Francisco fans were yelling "Go! Go! Go!" on fourth down and short yardage at midfield, Frankie, who would have run automatically had he been quarterback, swung his leg on the sideline as an order to punt.

He started slowly, with a 5-6-1 season, then took the Forty-Niners to their most successful season in the NFL. This was in 1957, when the club, with the help of an acrobatic end named R. C. Owens, who could jump six feet straight up, tied the Detroit Lions for the Western Division championship.

The playoff game was in Kezar Stadium. Early in the third quarter it seemed absolutely certain that the San Francisco team had finally won at least a division championship.

This team had been shocked in October by the death of Tony Morabito at a game in Kezar Stadium against the Chicago Bears. Morabito had had a heart attack before this; his doctor had advised him to give up pro football, but he had refused. He died just before the half. The team, trailing, had been informed of his death and had come back to win. They had played inspired football the rest of the season.

In the third quarter of the playoff game, they led the Lions, 27-7. It seemed inevitable and ironic that they would win a championship in the year of Morabito's death. But the Detroit team, after stopping the Forty-Niners with a field goal when they had first and goal on the Detroit nine-yard line, rallied for a 31-27 victory and the division title.

Albert lasted one more year, a year in which the Forty-Niners finished fourth with a 6-6 record. Albert had gone to John Brodie as his No. 1 quarterback, benching Tittle. He was criticized for this, although the decision to go with Brodie had been a majority decision of the coaches. Albert tried to resign four games before the end of the season. He did just before the final game.

Red Hickey, who had been an assistant, replaced Albert. He had played with the Los Angeles Rams and been an assistant on that ball club before coming to the Forty-Niners.

Hickey is a tough, intelligent and demanding coach. Once, in discussing the qualifications of an offensive end (Red played that position), Hickey ignored speed, hands and moves.

"You have to have a willing disregard of the consequences," Hickey said, blue eyes cold. "You can't hear footsteps."

He demanded complete effort from the Forty-Niners. Hickey's philosophy was simple: one hundred percent desire all the time.

He once said to a friend, "It's a simple deal. You sign a contract. You get all the money the contract says; you give all the effort you can. That's what you're selling."

Hickey kept the Forty-Niners over the break-even point for four straight seasons. He initiated the shotgun offense which for a time had rivals desperately searching for a defense. He traded Tittle to the Giants because the tailback in the shotgun must be able to run and Y. A., by the time Hickey developed this offense, was no longer a runner.

Hickey was criticized for this but he stubbornly refused to bow to the critics. His teams have been well-conditioned, intelligent and hard to beat.

# THE WASHINGTON REDSKINS

GEORGE PRESTON MARSHALL, the ebullient owner of the Washington Redskins, was confined to a hospital bed following a serious operation in the early fall of 1962. For a man imbued with the restless energy which drives Marshall, the confinement was onerous, especially since his Redskins had begun their pre-season football schedule.

By special dispensation, he had a television set installed in his room so that he could watch the club against the Philadelphia Eagles. This was a night game, played after visiting hours, but Marshall also obtained permission for Dick McCann, who had been his general manager, to keep him company.

Marshall's doctor had agreed to all of this reluctantly and only upon Marshall's promise to remain calm. But midway through the third quarter, the Eagle ground attack began to rip the Redskin line and Marshall grew increasingly upset. Finally, when an Eagle back broke through a gap left by an errant linebacker, Marshall slammed his fist down on the bedside table, upsetting a glass, and roared, "Look at that bum!"

A nurse hurried in.

"May I help you, Mr. Marshall?" she asked.

"Not," Marshall replied bitterly, "unless you can play linebacker."

A man who might easily have been successful as a producer, politician or actor and was successful as a businessman and publisher, Marshall has spent most of his life obsessed with professional football. Since he purchased the Boston team in 1932, he has devoted most of his bubbling energy to altering the face of pro football to his showman's idea of what it should be.

The Redskins have, during recent years, been something less than a success on the field; the show put on at half-time by the Redskins has always been one of the most spectacular in the league.

Marshall came into pro football indirectly, through a basketball team he organized to promote his business, the Palace Laundry. This team was entered in the old National Basketball League and Marshall met George Halas as a result. By 1932 Halas and Joe Carr, the NFL president, had sold Marshall on pro football; with three partners (Vincent Bendix, Jay O'Brien and M. Dorland Doyle) he purchased the Boston franchise for $30,000.

Because the team played at Braves Field, Marshall called them the Braves; in 1933, after losing $46,000 in his first season, Marshall moved to Fenway Park, changed the name of the club to the Redskins and took over his three partners' interests.

To carry out the Indian theme, Marshall hired Lone Star Dietz, a full-blooded Indian, to coach the club and Dietz did a good job. He did not manage to win a division

George Preston Marshall, the ebullient owner of the Washington Redskins, peers happily from box in the new stadium his club now inhabits in the nation's capital. Marshall is one of the game's top showmen, smartest owners.

championship but he once out-foxed George Halas.

Halas, in Boston to play the Redskins, had been the first man to recognize the worth of movies in the evaluation of players and for scouting. On this occasion, he had assembled the Bears in a conference room of their hotel to go over the pictures of their first Redskin game.

He imposed maximum security on the meeting, with guards on the doors to make sure no strangers gained admittance, then settled back to point out the errors of omission and commission in the first game the Bears had played against the Redskins. It was a detailed and careful exegisis and when the lights went up at its conclusion, Dietz, who had sneaked in under the nose of the guards, arose from a front row seat.

"Thanks, George," he said blandly. "That was very helpful."

It was not, however, until Marshall hired Ray Flaherty as his head coach that the team won its first Eastern championship, an accomplishment Bostonians accepted with typical Boston reserve. This was in 1936; confronted with dwindling attendance even in the face of the championship, Marshall decided to move the club to Washington. And, considerable charm to sign Baugh, who preferred a career in baseball. It also took quite

Redskin tackle Wee Willie Wilkin, one of the game's immortals, stopped the Chicago Bears' Bill Osmanski on this play, but the Bears were not often stopped in this game, the 1940 73-0 massacre.

When Sammy Baugh (left) completed this pass against the New York Giants in a 1937 game, he had set a new league record for completions in one season — 81, a mark which means nothing in modern game.

a neutral site since the Redskins were playing the Green Bay Packers.

The Redskins had a powerful running game with Cliff Battles, Ernie Pinckert, Pug Rentner and Riley Smith, but they did not have an accurate passer to throw to ends Charlie Malone and Wayne Millner.

Marshall's decision to move the game out of Boston was vindicated by the crowd of nearly 30,000 which watched the Packers win, 21-6. The Redskins' chances disappeared early in the game when Battles was severely injured.

In Washington, Marshall's showman's instincts flowered. He organized the Redskin Band and started providing the spectacular half-time shows which were the first in pro football. It was Marshall who suggested the league be divided into two divisions, with a championship playoff. With Halas, he changed the passing rule to allow the ball to be thrown from anywhere behind the line of scrimmage and had the goal posts moved back to the goal line.

During these years, Marshall had been interested in politics as well as pro football. He was a delegate to the Democratic convention in 1932 and 1936, a good friend of Jim Farley and an intimate of Jimmy Walker. By 1937, he had decided to devote most of his energies to football and the operation of the Palace Laundry and he gave up his political affiliations.

In 1937, he hired Sam Adrian Baugh, a tough, whip-thin Texan with the most accurate passing arm in football. Most experts considered Sammy too frail for pro ball, but he played for Marshall for sixteen years, a record for longevity. It took all of Marshall's considerable charm to sign Baugh, who preferred a career in baseball. It also took quite a lot of his considerable money.

Among Baugh's many talents was punting. He was one of the longest and one of the most accurate punters in league history, as well as one of the best passers and one of the sturdiest of all backs.

Sammy Baugh leads interference for Cliff Battles (20) on this play against the New York Giants in 1937. Battles broke loose for 76 yards as the Redskins drubbed the Giants, 49-14, on their way to a division title.

Baugh arrived in Washington teetering precariously in high-heel boots and wearing the inevitable ten-gallon hat. What no one but Baugh and Marshall knew at the time was that Baugh had never worn high-heel boots and a cowboy hat; it was at Marshall's instigation that he bought these especially for the occasion.

Baugh's amazingly accurate passes, combined with the running talent already on hand, took the Redskins to the Eastern Division championship in 1937. They won the championship by demolishing the Giants, 49-14, as 10,000 Washington fans accompanied the team to New York.

Baugh, given superb protection by his teammates, completed eleven of fifteen passes. Twice he threw key blocks to clear the route for long touchdown runs by Battles. And Turk Edwards, a giant tackle, wiped out the interior of the Giant line with stupendous blocks whenever the Redskins needed short yardage.

Sammy was just as effective in the championship game against the Bears. Although the weather was frigid and the field in Chicago frozen, he threw three long touchdown passes as the Redskins defeated Chicago, 28-21.

The Redskins seemed poised to repeat in 1938, but it proved to be a year of misfortune. First, Baugh suffered a shoulder separation against the Eagles so severe that one surgeon thought he would never play again. But the supposedly fragile Baugh was back in action in a matter of weeks, only to be hurt again. The club still finished second to the New York Giants, with a 6-3-2 record.

In 1938, Marshall began a still-continuing feud with Shirley Povich, the fine Washington sports columnist. Returning from Chicago after a game with the Bears, Povich was pondering a column when Marshall dropped in to tell him the Redskins' share of the gate was the biggest check for a visiting team in Chicago history. Later, Povich says, he sought out some Redskin players for column material and discovered that Marshall had moved the club from the Pullman section to the day coaches at Pittsburgh to avoid paying Pullman prices all the way to Washington. This provided Povich with a column; Marshall called him a fifth columnist and has disliked him heartily since.

Baugh missed a couple of games through injury in 1939, but a strong draft which included halfbacks Dick Todd and Wilbur Moore carried the club to another second-place finish, a game behind the Giants again. Todd and Baugh became inseparable; Todd was a Texan, too, having played with Texas A&M. Dick McCann, a small, wry man who was the Redskin publicity man at the time, once told a broadcaster who had

Baugh was wearing a newly acquired and unfamiliar ten-gallon hat when he greeted George Preston Marshall on his arrival in Washington to talk terms with the owner of the Redskins back in 1937.

Another Texan who played a large part in the success of the Redskins was Dick Todd of Texas A&M, who was a brilliant running back and a perfect foil for the aerial darts of best friend Baugh.

asked to interview Baugh, "He will be there, Todd willing."

A healthy Baugh led the club to the Eastern Division title in 1940. En route, they defeated the Chicago Bears, 7-3, two weeks before the season's end. They met the Bears again in the championship game. That, of course, was the game in which the Bears rolled up a 73-0 score on the Redskins. In the final two games of the season, the Washington club had suffered key injuries.

Under the impact of this defeat, Marshall's infallible instinct for promotion seemed to falter for a moment. In the middle of the fourth period, with the Redskins trailing by over sixty points, he had the public address announcer say: "Don't forget to make your season ticket applications for next year as soon as possible."

The announcement was greeted with a storm of boos, but Marshall, as usual, was right; the Redskin season ticket sale for 1941 was bigger than ever.

It was not until 1942 that Marshall and the Redskins avenged the 73-0 beating. This was Flaherty's last season as Redskin coach before going into the Navy and he used a simple but effective device to inspire the team before the championship game with the Bears.

The Bears, at the peak of their power, had not lost a league game during 1942; they were, of course, heavy favorites to beat the Redskins.

Flaherty, eschewing any pep talk, simply wrote, in large figures, "73-0" on the blackboard in the Washington dressing room. The team suited up grimly with the silent message staring them in the face. Then they went out and whipped the Bears, 14-6, as Baugh passed to Wilbur Moore for one touchdown and Andy Farkas ran for another.

They played the Bears for the championship again in 1943, Dutch Bergman's first and only year as head coach. Baugh was injured early in the game and the Bears, with more of their personnel surviving the World War II draft than the Redskins, won by 41-21.

Bergman and Marshall never enjoyed the rapport George had felt with Dietz or Flaherty. "Football to him is show business," Bergman said later. Once, he recalls, he

The Redskins' determination to revenge themselves for the 73-0 title game drubbing by the Bears in 1940 shows in this 1942 championship game picture of Andy Farkas diving over Bear line in 14-6 win.

wanted to sequester the team at a country club in New York before a Giant game so they would not be distracted by the lures of Manhattan.

"How much will it cost?" asked Marshall.

"About $3000," Bergman answered.

"Are we going to win?" Marshall asked.

"Yes," Bergman said. Marshall okayed the trip.

Marshall, who has always been generous in his help to coaches on the technical aspects of football, impressed Bergman with his keen analyses of Redskin games, until Dutch learned that Marshall made a practice of studying the game movies beforehand. Marshall does indeed have an imposing knowledge of strategy and tactics, however. He is not loath to admit this, although, during Bergman's regime, he refused responsibility for coaching after at least one game.

Quiet, capable and immensely likeable Bill McPeak, head coach, goes over a play on the sidelines with the new Sammy Baugh, Redskin quarterback Norm Snead, who survived hard rookie year to star.

The Eagles had just thumped the Redskins and a youngster, waiting outside the Redskin dressing room, stopped Marshall to ask for his autograph.

"Are you the head coach?" he asked.

"Not today," Marshall said.

Bergman was succeeded by Turk Edwards, who, with the help of Clark Shaughnessy, installed the T formation. Baugh, who had spent his whole football life as a tailback, regarded the new formation at first with suspicion. Later, when he had learned the intricacies of T formation quarterback, he liked it.

"I could play in a white tie and tails in this formation," he said.

The Redskins dropped to third in 1944 while Baugh was mastering the T, but led the East again in 1945, with Sammy back in top form. The 1945 championship game was against the Cleveland Rams. This was the game the Redskins lost, 15-14, when a Baugh pass from behind the Redskin goal line hit the goal posts for an automatic safety.

Baugh continued to play brilliantly until he retired after the 1952 season. He set a host of passing records which were not approached until Bobby Layne, another Texas quarterback, threatened both his passing and longevity marks.

Baugh's last season—1952—was the rookie year of another Redskin quarterback who was almost the opposite, physically, of Baugh. This was Eddie LeBaron, a tiny (5-7) ball-handling magician from the College of the Pacific. LeBaron, like Baugh before him, was to prove a much tougher man than he looked.

"Sam helped me a lot," LeBaron said later. "He spent time with me, not on the technical aspects of playing quarterback, but on the right attitude and on strategy and tactics. We were built so differently that we couldn't do the things the same way physically. But he taught me an awful lot, anyway."

Despite the development of LeBaron and the play of men like Vic Janowicz, Bones Taylor, Don Bosseler, Gene Brito, Ed Sutton, Bert Zagers and others, the Redskins were not able to win another division championship. Taylor was one of the finest receivers in football during his career, which spanned the end of Baugh's career and the beginning of LeBaron's.

During the long dry spell, the Redskins maintained their hold on the Washington fans. Marshall's "Midfield Matinees" remained the best half-time show in football and the club was still exciting to watch. LeBaron charmed Washington fans; he was backed by Jack Scarbath and Al Dorow but LeBaron himself was the key to much of the Redskin attack.

The Redskins were blessed with spectacular runners, as well, in Charlie Justice, Rob Goode, a giant fullback from Texas A&M, Billy Wells, Janowicz, Bosseler and Johnny Olszewski, among others.

During this period Marshall was criticized for not drafting Negro football players. He defended himself by saying that if the proper Negro player were available, he would draft him. Strong pressure put on him by various groups solidified his resentment. It was not until the 1962 season that the Redskins used a Negro player.

Marshall had picked a Negro as his first choice in the draft: All-America Ernie Davis of Syracuse, who had taken up at that school where Jim Brown left off. Before the 1962 season, Marshall traded the rights to Davis to the Cleveland Browns for Bobby Mitchell, another Negro back who was one of the most exciting runners in football.

Marshall's first draft choice in 1961 had been a handsome, beetle-browed youngster from Wake Forest College named Norman Snead, Physically, Snead seemed almost a

Wilbur Moore, one of the early stars on the Washington team, was a quick and resourceful pass defender. He has gone high in the air to hook a hand on the head of a Card-Pitt end in 1944 contest.

replica of Baugh. He was tall, raw-boned and quiet. During the 1961 season, he proved that he had Baugh's courage and skill as well.

The 1961 Redskin team won one game, lost twelve and tied one. This was the first season as head coach for Bill McPeak, a soft-spoken, patient man who worked tirelessly with Snead.

Snead took a fearful battering operating behind the porous Redskin line.

"I had to spend a good deal of time just cheering him up," McPeak said. "He would

The new home of the Redskins and stage for Marshall's super-spectacles at the half-time is the 50,000 seat D.C

come in after a bad game and sit dejectedly before his locker, staring into space. Then the next day we'd spend a few hours going over the film of the game and I would point out to him all the good things he had done and he would perk up again. He never showed any effect of the shellacking he was taking; he stayed in there and threw. He got three years of experience crammed into one season in 1961."

The pressure-cooker rookie year made Snead into a poised, accurate and fearless quarterback. With Mitchell added to his corps of receivers in 1962 to pose a deep threat

**Stadium.** It is a double-decked structure, with no posts to obstruct the view of the fans and ample parking.

The new look of the Redskins is symbolized by Bobby Mitchell, first Negro to play on the team and one of the brightest stars of the 1962 team. Mitchell is great receiver, superbly evasive ball carrier.

with the already strong short receiving of Fred Dugan and Bill Anderson, Snead became one of the most formidable passers in the league.

McPeak had shored up the Redskin offensive line, too. Snead now had time to look a little before he threw. Mitchell, converted to a flanker back, was a thorn in the side of early opponents and the Redskins amazed the league by leading until mid-season.

McPeak, the fifth coach in the last decade for the Redskins, instilled in the team faith in their ability to win. The addition of Billy Barnes, Bob Freeman and Bob Pellegrini, who had learned to develop a belief in winning under Norman Van Brocklin on the Eagles, helped build the morale, too.

But this was not yet a championship team and the surge of the New York Giants ended the Redskin hopes.

The Redskins began playing in the new 50,000-seat District of Columbia stadium in 1961; in 1962, the club set a new team home attendance record. Marshall recovered slowly from his operation during the season. By the time the league owners had their annual meeting in Miami in January of 1963, he was up and around, however, and showing some of his old fire.

Earlier in the year, someone had asked him if it were true that there was a new, milder Marshall.

"I'm not any different than I ever was," he answered testily. "People say 'Marshall's not as wild as he used to be.' Well, hell, Marshall was never wild."

When C. Leo De Orsey, Marshall's attorney and financial adviser, arranged the thirty-year lease on the new D.C. stadium, Marshall asked him, "Did you get an option to renew?"

"Why?" asked De Orsey, "I won't be here."

"I will," Marshall said.

At the meeting in January, he appeared drawn and tired, but indomitable. Someone asked him how he felt and Marshall said, "Don't worry about me. I'll be back. I always have."

He was silent a moment, the strong hawk face thoughtful.

"I'm only interested in one thing," he said. "Getting the Redskins back to what they were — winners."

# CHRONOLOGY

1895—First professional football game, Latrobe, Pa., (12), sponsored by Y.M.C.A., vs. Jeannette, Pa., (0), at Latrobe. (Aug. 31.)

1902—First night football game, Philadelphia Athletics, (39), vs. Kanaweola A. C., (0), at Elmira, N. Y. (Nov. 21.)

Connie Mack organized Philadelphia Athletics with Rube Waddell in lineup, and claimed professional football championship of the United States after defeating Pittsburgh, with Christy Mathewson at fullback, 12 to 6. (Nov. 26.)

First indoor football game, Syracuse with Glenn Warner at guard, (6), vs. Philadelphia Nationals, (0), in Madison Square Garden. Attendance, 3,000. (Dec. 28.)

1905—Charles (Cy) Rigler organized Massillon Tigers with Charlie Moran in lineup.

Organization of Canton Bulldogs.

1920—Formation of the American Professional Football Association at Canton, O., with following membership: Canton Bulldogs, Cleveland Indians, Dayton Triangles, Akron Professionals, Massillon Tigers, Rochester (N. Y.), Rock Island (Ill.), Muncie (Ind.), Staley's of Decatur (Ill.), Chicago Cardinals and Hammond (Ind.). (Sept. 17.)

Jim Thorpe (Canton) elected president; Stan Cofall (Massillon) vice-president; A. F. Ranney (Akron) secretary and treasurer.

Membership set at $100.

First pro player deal took place. Bob Nash purchased from Akron by Buffalo for $300.

1921—American Professional Football Association reorganized at Akron, O. Joe F. Carr (Columbus) elected president; M. O'Brien (Decatur) vice-president; and Carl L. Storck (Dayton) secretary and treasurer. (April 30.)

J. E. Clair of Acme Packing Company granted franchise for Green Bay, Wis. (Aug. 27.)

1922—Franchise of George Halas for Staley A. C. (Decatur, Ill.) transferred to Chicago and

team renamed Chicago Bears. (Jan. 28.)

J. E. Clair turned Green Bay franchise back to league following discussion over alleged use of ineligible players. (Jan. 28.)

Professional football gets first eight column newspaper headline. ("Stagg Says Conference Will Break Professional Football Menace.") Chicago *Herald and Examiner* of Jan. 30.

Earl Lambeau granted franchise for Green Bay, Wis. (June 24.)

Name of American Professional Football Association changed to National Football League. (June 24.)

1924—Frankford Yellow Jackets (Philadelphia) awarded franchise.

1925—Timothy J. Mara and Will Gibson granted franchise for New York for $2,500. (Aug. 1.)

Jimmy Conzelman granted franchise for Detroit. (Aug. 1.)

Red Grange signed with Chicago Bears. (Nov. 22.)

1926—Adoption of rule making all players ineligible for National League competition until their college classes have graduated. (Feb. 6.)

Adoption of maximum (18) and minimum (15) player limit. (Feb. 7.)

Edward Butler granted franchise for Brooklyn, N. Y. (July 10.)

Milwaukee fined $500 for using four high school boys against Chicago Cardinals and A. L. McGurk ordered to dispose of franchise within 90 days. (July 10.)

1927—National League reorganized with withdrawal of Brooklyn, Detroit and nine other clubs. (July 27.)

Brooklyn franchise transferred to C. C. Pyle for New York Yankees eleven with Red Grange.

1928—Detroit's application for re-instatement approved; Cleveland withdrew. (Aug. 12.)

Duluth and Buffalo franchises dropped.

1929—Sale of Chicago Cardinal franchise by Chris

O'Brien to Dr. David J. Jones. (July 27.)

C. C. Pyle surrendered Brooklyn franchise; Stapleton A. C. of Staten Island, N. Y., awarded Brooklyn franchise. (July 27.)

Boston syndicate awarded Pottsville franchise. (July 28.)

Adoption of rule to employ fourth official, a field judge. (July 28.)

Chicago Cardinals become first professional team to go to an out-of-town training camp (Coldwater, Mich.). (Aug. 21.)

1930—Player limit increased to maximum of 20 and minimum of 16. (Jan. 25.)

Harold Griffen awarded franchise for Portsmouth, O. (July 12.)

Detroit franchise declared inactive. (July 12.)

William B. Dwyer and John Depler purchase Dayton franchise from Carl L. Storck for Brooklyn, N. Y. (July 12.)

New York Giants raised $115,163 for New York Unemployment fund by beating Notre Dame All-Stars, 21 to 0. (Dec. 14.)

1931—Chicago Bears, Green Bay and Portsmouth fined $1,000 each for having players on their rosters whose college classes had not been graduated. (July 11.)

1932—Inactive Boston franchise transferred to new syndicate composed of George P. Marshall, Vincent Bendix, Jay O'Brien and M. Dorland Doyle. (July 9.)

Chicago Bears defeated Portsmouth Spartans (9 to 0) for championship indoors in Chicago Stadium. (Dec. 18.)

1933—Clipping penalty increased to 25 yards. (Feb. 25.)

Goal posts returned to goal line. (Feb. 25.)

Forward passing legalized from any spot behind line of scrimmage. (Feb. 25.)

The first World Championship game between the divisional winners was played in Chicago. It drew 17,866 paid admissions, a gross gate of $23,441.90 and a net of $14,606.92. The winning Chicago Bears player's share amounted to $210.34 and the losing New York Giants player's share $140.22. Each team received 25 shares. Bears 23, New York 21. (Dec. 17.)

Membership fee raised to $10,000. (July 8.)

A resolution by George P. Marshall setting up a divisional system and a championship playoff adopted. (July 8.)

A. J. Rooney and A. McCool awarded franchise for Pittsburgh. (July 8.)

Frankford Yellow Jackets franchise declared forfeited and awarded to Bert Bell and Lud

Wray of Philadelphia. (July 9.)

William B. Dwyer and John Depler transferred Brooklyn franchise to Chris Cagle and John (Shipwreck) Kelly. (July 9.)

Chicago Cardinal franchise sold to Charles Bidwill by Dr. David J. Jones. (Oct. 24.)

1934—G. A. Richards purchased Portsmouth franchise and moved team to Detroit. (June 30.)

Chris Cagle and John (Shipwreck) Kelly transferred Brooklyn franchise to Daniel R. Topping. (June 30.)

Chicago Bears held to scoreless tie by Collegians in first annual Chicago All-Star game. (Aug. 31.)

Franchise of Cincinnati transferred to St. Louis. (Nov. 5.)

Player waiver rule adopted. Proposed by George P. Marshall. (Dec. 10.)

1935—Player limit increased to 24 men. (Sept. 4.)

Selection of players proposed by Bert Bell, Philadelphia Eagles, and adopted. (May 19.)

1936—Jay Berwanger, University of Chicago halfback, first player selected in first National League draft. Chosen by Philadelphia. (Feb. 8.)

Player limit increased to 25 men. (Feb. 9.)

1937—Homer Marshman granted franchise for Cleveland. (Feb. 12.) Boston franchise transferred to Washington. (Feb. 13.)

1938—Player limit increased to 30 men. (Feb. 19.)

1939—Kickoff out-of-bounds ruled receiving team's ball on its 45-yard line. (Feb. 11.)

Joe F. Carr, National League president since 1921, died at Columbus, O. (May 20.)

Carl L. Storck named president of National League. (May 25.)

1940—Detroit Lions fined $5,000 for tampering with Bulldog Turner, Hardin-Simmons center, drafted by Chicago Bears. (Feb. 2.)

Fred L. Mandel, Jr., purchased Detroit Lions and franchise from G. A. Richards. (Feb. 10.)

Membership fee raised to $50,000. (April 12.)

Player limit increased to 33 maximum and 22 minimum. (April 12.)

Clipping penalty reduced to 15 yards. (April 12.)

All distance penalties enforced from spot on field of play limited to half the distance to the goal. (April 12.)

Dennis J. Shea elected treasurer of League. (April 12.)

Alexis Thompson of New York purchased Pittsburgh Steeler franchise from Arthur. J. Rooney, who purchased half interest in Philadelphia Eagles. (Dec. 9.)

1941—Elmer F. Layden, head coach and athletic director at the University of Notre Dame, named commissioner of professional football for five years. (March 1.)

Carl L. Storck resigned as president-secretary. (April 5.)

Elmer F. Layden elected president for five years. (April 5.)

Philadelphia franchise and club transferred to Pittsburgh and Pittsburgh franchise and club transferred to Philadelphia. (April 5.)

Umpire made official timer of League games. (April 6.)

Cleveland franchise transferred from Homer Marshman and associates to Daniel F. Reeves and Frederick Levy, Jr. (June 1.)

1942—National Football League raised $680,384.07 for War Relief charities.

1943—Cleveland Rams, with co-owners Maj. Fred Levy and Lt. Dan Reeves in service, granted permission to suspend operations for one season. (April 6.)

Free-substitution rule adopted for duration. (April 7.)

Maj. Fred Levy transferred his stock in Cleveland Rams to Lt. Dan Reeves. (April 16.)

Philadelphia Eagles and Pittsburgh Steelers granted permission to merge under name of Phil-Pitt Eagles. (June 19.)

Ted Collins granted franchise for Boston, to become active in season of 1944 or as soon thereafter as league deems advisable. (June 20.)

Adoption of a ten-game schedule. (June 20.)

Player limit reduced to 28 men for one year. (Aug. 25.)

Philadelphia Eagles and Pittsburgh Steelers merger automatically dissolved on last day of season. (Dec. 5.)

1944—Boston Yanks granted permission to activate franchise in season of 1944. (April 19.)

Cleveland Rams granted permission to resume operations in season of 1944. (April 19.)

Player limit of 28 reaffirmed for one year. (April 20.)

Free substitutions adopted for another year. (April 20.)

Adoption of rule assessing five-yard penalty for kick-offs out of bounds, obligating kicking team to re-kick after each offense. (April 20.)

Coaching from bench legalized. (April 20.)

Dennis J. Shea re-elected treasurer of National League for three years. (April 20.)

Chicago Cardinals and Pittsburgh Steelers

requested by league to merge for one year under the name of Card-Pitt. (April 21.)

Card-Pitt merger dissolved automatically on last day of season. (Dec. 3.)

1945—Striking an opponent with forearm or elbow (flying elbow blocks) barred. (April 9.)

Inbounds spot changed from 15 to 20 yards in from side lines, one year only. (April 9.)

Free-substitution rule renewed for one year. (April 9.)

Wearing of socks in league games made mandatory. (April 9.)

Defensive team permitted to advance with muffed snap from center. (April 9.)

Rule regarding attempts to consume or conserve time at the end of the second and fourth periods extended to include first and third periods also. (April 9.)

Brooklyn Tigers and Boston Yanks merged for one year under name of The Yanks. (April 10.)

Committee named to confer with colleges on all matters pertaining to eligibility of players. (April 11.)

1945—By V-J day (Aug. 14), the National League's service roster for World War II, limited to men who had participated in league games, totaled 638 men, 355 of whom were commissioned, 69 were decorated and 21 had lost their lives.

Pre-war player limit of 33 men restored. (Sept. 15.)

Dan Topping announced he was abandoning Brooklyn franchise to enter a new league. (Dec. 6.)

National League, in special executive session at Cleveland, ratified action of Commissioner Layden in which Brooklyn's franchise was declared forfeited and all players on its active and reserve lists were assigned to Boston Yanks. (Dec. 17.)

1946—Adoption of rule limiting National League to ten teams. (Jan. 11.)

Elmer F. Layden resigned as commissioner of professional football and president of the National League. (Jan. 11.)

Bert Bell of Philadelphia, co-owner of Pittsburgh Steelers, named to succeed Layden and given three-year contract. (Jan. 11.)

Toss of coin for choice ordered before teams leave field at conclusion of pre-game warm-ups. (Jan. 11.)

Substitutions limited to no more than three men at one time. (Jan. 11.)

Receiving team permitted to run punts and

unsuccessful field goal attempts out from behind goal line. (Jan. 11.)

Forward passes made incomplete automatically upon striking either team's goal post. (Jan. 11.)

Cleveland Ram franchise and club transferred to Los Angeles, Cal. (Jan. 12.)

National League entered into three-year major-minor league agreement with American Association (later renamed American league), Dixie league and Pacific Coast league. (Jan. 13.)

The world championship game between the Chicago Bears and the New York Giants in the Polo Grounds drew an attendance of 58,346 and gross receipts, $282,955.25, highest in league history. Each Bear player received $1,975.82 and each Giant player $1,295.57, a new high for players. (Dec. 15.)

All attendance records for National Football League broken: 1,732,135 (average per game 31,493) total 55 games. Adding non-championship games and world championship game, a total of 2,346,724 spectators witnessed N. F. L. games. All figures are for paid admissions. Money raised for charity in non-championship games, in excess of $500,000.

1947—Bert Bell's contract as Commissioner of the National Football League renewed for five years. (Jan. 1.)

An amendment to the constitution imposing a major penalty for anyone not reporting the offer of a bribe, an attempt to fix a game or any other infraction of the rules having to do with gambling. (Jan. 1.)

During a forward pass if spot of a pass violation is behind A's goal line the usual penalty is enforced from previous spot. (Jan. 24.)

During a forward pass if spot of a pass violation by A is behind B's goal line, during fourth down, it is a touchback if the usual enforcement leaves the ball inside B's 20. (Jan. 24.)

If pass interference by A, behind B's goal line, during fourth down and previous spot was inside B's 5, it is a touchback. (Jan. 24.)

When a scrimmage or return kick crosses receivers' goal line from impetus of kick, it is a touchback. (Jan. 24.)

Field judge may use whistle to assist Referee or other officials in declaring ball dead. (Jan. 24.)

A fifth official, with primary duties as prescribed, is to be used on the field. He is known as Back Judge. (Jan. 24.)

Sudden death method of deciding tie game in divisional playoff or championship game adopted. (Jan. 24.)

Charles W. Bidwill, owner of the Chicago Cardinals, died after brief illness. (April 19.)

Revised use of observers by Hugh L. Ray, National Football League Technical Adviser, resulted in 162.1 plays per game, an all-time record. It also resulted in the breaking of the all-time record of total yards per game. The total amounted to 542.4 yards per game.

The all-time record for attendance at professional football games was established in 1947 when 2,448,848 spectators saw the games as follows: Regular season (60 games) 1,837,-437; non-championship games 580,682; world's championship game 30,759. Average attendance for regular season games was 30,624.

1948—A clarification of the clipping rule, permission to use an artificial tee at the kickoff, and the equipping of all officials with whistles were among the important items passed by the Rules Committee and approved at the annual meeting. (Jan. 14.)

Player limit increased to 35 for the entire season. In 1947 it was 35 for first three games and 34 for remainder of season.

A syndicate headed by D. Lyle Fife purchased the Detroit franchise from Fred L. Mandel, Jr. (Jan. 15.)

Hugh L. Ray, Technical Advisor, announced that an all-time high in plays per game had been reached in 1947 with 165.5. He also reported that the all-time record of total yards per game had been broken. The new mark is now 643.3. The league teams came within four plays of reaching 10,000 for the 1947 season.

Constitution, under schedule meetings, amended to read as follows: As long as Mr. Bell is Commissioner, the Commissioner shall draft a schedule and present it to the membership at the annual meeting each year. (Jan. 16.)

Dr. John B. "Jock" Sutherland, Coach of the Pittsburgh Steelers, died after an operation. (April 11.)

1949—A syndicate headed by James P. Clark purchased the franchise of the Philadelphia Eagles from Lex Thompson. (Jan. 15.) Bert Bell, as commissioner-president, and Dennis J. Shea, as vice-president and treasurer, appointed for ten-year terms. (Jan. 20.)

Player limit of 32 adopted. In 1948 the limit was 35 for the entire season. (January 20.)

For one year only the league adopted the free substitution rule. (Jan. 20.)

Unanimous consent of the league given for the cancellation of the Boston franchise and a new franchise awarded to Ted Collins in New York City under the name of the New York Bulldogs. (Jan. 21.)

Hugh L. Ray, Technical Advisor, in his statistical review of the 1948 season, announced that 29 new league records were established during the season. For the third successive year the number of plays per game established a record, 174.5, as compared with 165.5 for 1947. Total yards from scrimmage per game also was broken with 659 in 1948 to 643.3 a year ago. The league teams broke the all-time record for plays with 10,451, compared to 9,996.

Bert Bell, Commissioner of the National Football League, and J. Arthur Friedlund, representing the All-America Conference, announced a merger of the two leagues. Baltimore, Cleveland and San Francisco joined the ten teams in the National Football League. (Dec. 9.)

1950—The free substitution rule was readopted for an indefinite term. (Jan. 23.)

Player limit of 32 retained. A minimum of 25 players must be dressed for a championship game. (Jan. 23.)

A backward pass going out of bounds between the goal lines shall belong to the team last in possession. (Jan. 23.)

Any team may option any number of players above the 25 minimum and within the player limit. (Jan. 23.)

Upon the advice of counsel and unanimous consent of member clubs the Commissioner announced that the league would use the name National Football League, divided into American and National Conferences. The American Conference includes Chicago Cardinals, Cleveland, New York Giants, Philadelphia, Pittsburgh and Washington. The National Conference includes Baltimore, Chicago Bears, Detroit, Green Bay, Los Angeles, New York Yanks and San Francisco. (March 3.)

Carl L. Storck, secretary-treasurer of the National Football League from 1921 until 1939 and president from 1939 until 1941, died in Dayton, Ohio. (March 13.)

A new all-time record for attendance during the regular playing season was established. A total of 1,977,556 spectators witnessed the 78

games. Two playoff games drew 106,896. The championship game was attended by 29,751.

1951—The first Pro Bowl game played under the auspices of the Los Angeles Publishers' Association was won by the American Conference All-Stars over the National Conference All-Stars 28 to 27 before 53,676 spectators. George P. Marshall, of Washington, fostered the adoption of the game by the league. (Jan. 14.)

Abraham Watner returned Baltimore franchise to league and was voted $50,000 for Colt players. (Jan. 18.)

Player limit of 33 voted. A minimum of 25 players must be dressed for a championship game. (Jan. 18.)

No tackle, guard or center may become eligible for a forward pass. Adopted for one year. (Jan. 18.)

Chris O'Brien, one of the founders of the NFL in 1920 and original owner of Chicago Cardinals, died. (June 3.)

Frank J. Jonet, pioneer in professional football and active with Green Bay since its inception, died at age 69. (August 17.)

Gross receipts including television and radio for the championship game between Los Angeles and Cleveland amounted to $328,052.33, highest in league history. Attendance in the Coliseum was 57,522. Each Ram player received $2,108.44 and each Brown player $1,483.12, the highest in league history. During the regular season the attendance was 1,913,019 for 72 games.

1952—The tackle eligible rule was made permanent. (Jan. 18.)

On pass interference on the part of the offense, the penalty shall be fifteen yards from the previous spot and not loss of down. (Jan. 18.)

The assets and franchise of the New York Yanks were purchased by the National Football League. (Jan. 19.)

A new franchise was awarded the Dallas Texans after they purchased the assets of the New York Yanks from the National Football League. (Jan. 24.)

Alvin "Bo" McMillin, who coached Detroit and Philadelphia, died after an illness of several months. (March 31.)

All attendance records for the regular playing season were broken. A total of 2,052,126 spectators witnessed the 72 games, an average of 28,502 for each game. The playoff game between Detroit and Los Angeles drew 46,573 and the championship game between Cleveland and Detroit drew 50,934. The gross receipts including radio and television of the championship game amounted to $314,318.50. Each Detroit player received $2,274.77 and each Cleveland player $1,712.49, a new high for players' shares for a championship game. (Dec. 28.)

1953—Modification of the rule player requirement after substitution. The elimination of the penalty on a player returning to the game at any time except after disqualification. (Jan. 23.)

Elimination of the "dead ball" plays rule, except (1) 30 second delay; (2) official not in position at snap. (Jan. 23.)

A new franchise was awarded to Baltimore. (Jan. 23.)

Permanent Conferences, Eastern and Western, were established. (Jan. 24.)

James Thorpe, famous Indian athlete, brilliant professional football player and first president of the American Professional Football Association (1920), which was renamed the National Football League in 1922, died on March 28 in Lomita, California.

Arthur B. McBride, first owner of the Cleveland Browns, sold the club franchise to a syndicate headed by Dave R. Jones. (June 10.)

All paid attendance records for a regular season championship game broken in the Los Angeles Coliseum where the Los Angeles Rams and the Detroit Lions played before 78,240 spectators. (Nov. 1.)

Judge Allan K. Grim, of the United States District Court for the Eastern District of Pennsylvania, has rendered his decision on the antitrust case which was brought by the government against the National Football League and its members. The primary effect of the decision was to uphold the restrictions on telecasts into the home territory of a club on the day that such club was playing at home. (Nov. 12.)

For the second year in succession attendance records for the regular playing season were broken. The 72 games drew 2,164,585 spectators, an increase of 5.2 percent over the previous high, 1952. The gross receipts of the championship game, including radio and television, $358,693, were greater than for any previous game. Each Detroit player received $2,424.10, a new high for a winning player's share. Each Cleveland player received $1,654.26. A total of 134 live TV outlets carried the championship game to millions of viewers in every part of the country. (Dec. 27.)

1954—Commissioner-President Bert Bell was given a new twelve-year appointment. (Jan. 29.)

An offensive team ruled to have the right to request a dry ball when the field is perceptibly wet or slippery. The clock will not be stopped. (Jan. 29.)

For the second successive year all paid attendance records broken for a regular season championship game in the Los Angeles Coliseum where the Los Angeles Rams and the San Francisco Forty-Niners played before 78,945 spectators. (Oct. 3.)

Paid attendance records for the regular season were shattered for the third year in a row when 2,190,571 spectators witnessed the 72 games, an increase of 1.1 percent. Another record was broken in the championship game when each Cleveland player's winning share amounted to $2,478.57. Detroit players each received $1,585.63. The championship game was carried by 187 live TV outlets to an estimated 30 millions in all sections of the country. (Dec. 26.)

1955—Joseph A. Donoghue elected assistant treasurer. (Jan. 27.)

If a player touches ground with any part of his body, except his hands or feet, while in the grasp of opponent and irrespective of grasp being broken, ball is declared dead immediately. (Jan. 28.)

Interpretation of false start calls for penalty for any movement by an interior lineman after he has taken three point stance on the scrimmage line. (Jan. 28.)

Any two players on Chicago *Tribune* All-Star squad may be carried over and above the 33 active players for the first two games of the regular season. (Jan. 29.)

Los Angeles defeated New York 23 to 17 in first sudden death game played in Portland, Oregon, in pre-season. (Aug. 28.)

The year-by-year climb in paid attendance during the regular season continued for the fourth straight year with 2,521,836 spectators witnessing the 72 games, an increase over the previous high of 15.1 percent. The championship game was witnessed by the greatest crowd in the history of the playoffs, 85,693, in the Coliseum in Los Angeles. A new mark was established for player's share in the championship game with the Cleveland player's winning share amounting to $3,508.21 and the losing Los Angeles player's share to $2,316.26. Over 30,000,0000 witnessed the championship game over 159 live TV stations.

1956—Dennis J. Shea, treasurer since 1940 and asso-

244

ciated with the league since 1932, retired on pension. (Jan. 16.)

When an interior lineman takes a three point stance and moves after taking that stance, he must be ruled offside or illegally in motion. (Jan. 16.)

The ball is dead when any part of a ball carrier, other than his hands or feet touches the ground after he has made contact with the defense. (Jan. 16.)

Austin H. Gunsel elected treasurer of the league. (Jan. 16.)

George S. Hallas, whose career as a coach and executive of the Chicago Bears spanned 36 years, an organizer of the league and veteran of World Wars I and II, retired as head coach of the Bears. (Feb. 2.)

Hugh L. "Shorty" Ray, technical advisor of the National Football League from 1938 to 1952, author of rules, friend of officials and players, died in his 72nd year. (Sept. 16.)

For the fifth year in succession the league attendance record was shattered. The paid attendance for 1956 was 2,551,623, an increase of 1.17 percent over the previous high. The gross receipts for the championship game, $517,385.00, established a new record. For the second year in a row the record for the player's share in the championship game was broken. The winning New York Giants player's share rose to $3,779.19 and the losing Chicago Bears player's share to $2,485.16.

1957—On all requested time-outs the referee shall not sound his whistle for play to start prior to sixty seconds of elapsed time. (Feb. 1.)

Commissioner Bell and officials of member clubs paid tribute to George P. Marshall for his twenty-five years' service to the National Football League. (Feb. 1.)

A player under contract may not be asked to, and/or report to, training camp for practice prior to nine weeks prior to the first league game except for championship team preparing for the Chicago *Tribune* All-Star game in accordance with the contract. (Feb. 2.)

No club may at any time have under contract more than 60 players. This number shall be reduced to 43 active players by the day after Labor Day. This number shall be further reduced to 38 two weeks prior to opening game of season and to 35 players by Tuesday prior to the first league game. There shall be no injured reserve list. (Feb. 2.)

Waivers may not be recalled on the same player more than once in any one year by the same club. (Feb. 2.)

Anthony J. Morabito, president and co-owner of the San Francisco Forty-Niners, died. (Oct. 27.)

All paid attendance records for regular season game shattered in Los Angeles Coliseum where Los Angeles Rams and San Francisco Forty-Niners played before 88,312 spectators. (Nov. 10.)

All paid attendance records for one day—six championship games—broken with total of 291,541 spectators who watched games in Chicago (Bears), Cleveland, Los Angeles, New York, Philadelphia and Washington. (Nov. 10.)

League paid attendance soared for the sixth season in succession as 2,836,318 spectators attended the 72 regular season games. The increase was a spectacular 11.17 percent. The gross receipts of the championship game reached a new high of $593,967.50. The player's share in the championship game was broken for the third consecutive year. The winning Detroit Lions each received $4,295.41 and the losing Cleveland Browns each $2,750.30.

1958—Emil R. Fischer, former president and long associated with Green Bay Packers, died. (Jan. 2.)

The Back Judge was designated as the official timer of the game. (Jan. 29.)

On all requested time-outs the Referee shall not signify that the ball will be put in play prior to one minute and thirty (30) seconds of elapsed time. (Jan. 29.)

The bonus pick, started in 1947, eliminated. (Jan. 29.)

Dennis J. Shea, league treasurer from 1940 until his retirement in 1956, died. (Feb. 7.)

Alexander (Al) Ennis, associated with the league since 1941 and member of the league staff, died. (Feb. 8.)

Russell W. Bogda, president of Green Bay Packers, died. (Feb. 22.)

For the second year in succession the paid attendance record for a regular season game was broken in the Los Angeles Coliseum where the Los Angeles Rams and the Chicago Bears drew 90,833 spectators. (Nov. 2.)

The one-day paid attendance record for six championship games broken for the second time in as many years when 328,865 spectators witnessed games in Chicago (Bears), Cleveland, Los Angeles, New York, Philadelphia and Washington. (Nov. 9.)

Paid attendance for the 72 regular season games went over the three million mark for the first time in the history of the league. The record-breaking attendance for the seventh season in a row was 3,006,124, a 5.98 percent increase over 1957. The gross receipts for the championship game rose to a new record of $698,646. For the fourth year in succession the record for the player's share in the championship game was broken. The winning Baltimore Colts each received $4,718.77 and the losing New York Giants each $3,111.33.

Baltimore defeated New York 23 to 17 in the first use of the sudden death method of deciding a championship game. The Colts scored a touchdown after 8 minutes, 15 seconds of overtime play. (Dec. 28.)

1959—For the first time since 1933 no changes were made in the playing rules. (Jan. 22.)

The annual selection meeting shall be held prior to the end of the season. Twenty selections shall be made by each club. This is a reduction of ten from previous selection meetings. (Jan. 23.)

Timothy J. Mara, founder of the New York Giants Football Club, whose contributions to professional football from 1925 on had much to do with the success enjoyed by the National Football League, died. (Feb. 17.)

Player limit raised to 36 for 1959, subsequently increased to 38 for 1960 and decreased to 36 for 1961. (Sept. 17.)

Bert Bell, Commissioner of the National Football League since 1946, died after a heart attack suffered in Franklin Field during the last two minutes of the Philadelphia Eagles-Pittsburgh Steelers game. Aged 65. (Oct. 11.)

Austin H. Gunsel, league treasurer, was named President in the office of the Commissioner until the annual meeting in January, 1960. (Oct. 14.)

William F. Hilgenberg, member of the board of Baltimore Colts, died. (Dec. 2.)

For the eighth season in succession the league attendance record was broken with 3,140,409 paid spectators attending 72 championship games, an increase of 4.46 percent over the record-breaking total of 1958. The players' pool in the championship game between Baltimore and New York reached a new high with $389,020.21 for distribution. Each Colt received $4,674.44 and each Giant $3,083.27. The individual player's share was not a new record because of the larger number of shares voted by each club.

1960—Pete Rozelle, general manager of the Los Angeles Rams, named Commissioner for three-year term. (Jan. 26.)

The minimum guarantee for the visiting team raised to thirty thousand ($30,000). (Jan. 25.) Dallas awarded a franchise for the 1960 season and Minneapolis-St. Paul for 1961. (Jan. 28.) Dallas subsequently took the name Cowboys and played each team in the league, although listed in the Western Conference standings. Minnapolis-St. Paul named the Minnesota Vikings.

Transfer of the franchise and club of the Chicago Cardinals to St. Louis approved. (March 13.)

Andrew R. Turnbull, 75, first president and founder of Green Bay Packers, died. (Oct. 17.) For the third season in succession league attendance passed the three million mark with 3,128,296 paid admissions for the 78 games. A record for gross receipts for a championship game was set in Franklin Field, Philadelphia. Including television and radio, the gross receipts for the game between Philadelphia and Green Bay totalled $747,876. A record for the winning player's share was set when each Philadelphia player received $5,116.55.

1961—Detroit defeated Cleveland 17-16 in inaugural Playoff Bowl between second place teams in each conference. Nationally televised game was played in Orange Bowl at Miami and League's share of proceeds went to Bert Bell NFL Player Benefit Plan for group medical, life insurance and retirement benefits. (Jan. 7.)

Arthur B. Modell of New York headed group that purchased Cleveland Browns and took over as Chairman of the board. (March 22.) Commissioner signed two-year contract awarding NBC radio and TV rights to the world championship game for $615,000 annually. (April 5.) Club owners later voted $300,000 yearly off top of championship game TV-radio rights directly into Bert Bell Player Benefit Plan.

Dallas assigned to Eastern Conference and Minnesota joined Western as home-and-home, 98-game schedule announced. (April 12.)

League entered into first single network television agreement and immediately petitioned Federal Judge Allan K. Grim (see 1953) for approval. (April 26). Judge Grim voided contract which was two-year agreement with Columbia Broadcasting System (July 20) and subsequently denied NFL petition to go ahead for 1961 season only. (July 28). League forced to return to individual team TV contracts but carried fight to Congress. A bill legalizing single network TV contracts by professional sports leagues was introduced by Rep. Emanual Celler and passed the House (Sept. 18) and Senate (Sept. 21). It was signed into law by President Kennedy (Sept. 30), and League was thus free to negotiate single network contracts in the future.

Canton, Ohio, where League was formed in 1920, selected as site for Professional Football Hall of Fame. (April 27.)

A one-day paid attendance record for League set when seven games (in Baltimore, Cleveland, Dallas, Los Angeles, New York, Philadelphia and San Francisco) drew 332,621 fans. (Nov. 5.)

Season attendance hit a new high when 3,986,159 paid to see the 98 regularly scheduled games. It was the fourth straight year of better than three million attendance.

The first million dollar gate in the history of professional football was achieved when the Green Bay Packers defeated the New York Giants 37-0 in Green Bay. The game was attended by 39,029 fans. Gross receipts, including radio and TV, were $1,013,792. Members of the winning team received $5,194.44 each; the losers $3,339.99 each. Both figures were record shares.

1962—Commissioner Rozelle re-elected for new five-year term. (Jan. 8.)

First rule change in four years made it illegal to grab face mask of any player. Previously, grabbing of face mask of all players, except ball carrier, was illegal. (Jan. 9.)

League again entered into single network agreement with Columbia Broadcasting System, received $4,650,000 annually in two-year contract covering 1962 and 1963 seasons. Agreement made possible by federal law, insured continuation of unique NFL plan of road TV back to league cities. (Jan. 10.)

Mrs. Violet Bidwill Wolfner, principal owner and chairman of the board of the St. Louis Cardinals, died in Miami. (Jan. 29.)

Dick McCann, for more than 16 years the general manager of the Washington Redskins, was appointed director of the Professional Football Hall of Fame. (April 3.)

James P. Clark, chairman of the board of the Eagles, died in Philadelphia. (April 17.)

NFL completely vindicated of all charges in civil antitrust case decided by U.S. District Judge Roszel Thomsen sitting in Baltimore federal court. American Football League had charged monopoly and conspiracy on part of NFL in areas of expansion, television and player signings. Case lasted two and one-half years, trial two months. Judgment in favor of NFL included court costs. (May 21.)

Retirement phase of Bert Bell NFL Player Benefit Plan finalized at meeting in New York City. Plan calls for payments at age 65 for players with five years' active service starting in 1959. Owners also raised minimum group life insurance for players from $5,000 to $10,000. (May 24.)

NFL owners voted to reduce halftime intermission in 1962 regular season games from 20 minutes to 15 to further tighten elapsed time. In 1961, from kickoff to final gun, 98 games averaged 2 hours, 35 minutes. (May 24.)

Thirty-five pre-season dates, including the first double-header in league history, drew 1,070,725 fans, first time the total attendance in pre-season had topped the million mark. Regular season attendance also set a record when 4,003,421, paid to see the 98 league games. It was the first time the four million mark had been achieved and represented nearly twice as many paid admissions as the league had drawn in 1952.

Daniel F. Reeves purchased his partners' stock in the Los Angeles Rams and became majority owner. (Dec. 27.)

A federal judge in New York City upheld the legality of the National Football League's TV blackout within a 75-mile radius of home games and denied an injunction sought by persons who requested the world championship game be televised in the New York City area. (Dec. 28.)

The world championship game, played at Yankee Stadium in New York City, produced record gross receipts of $1,243,110. A crowd of 64,892 paid to see the Green Bay Packers win their second straight title, 16-7, over the New York Giants. The Packers received record winning shares of $5,888.57 apiece. The Giants received $4,166.85, also a record. (Dec. 30.)

1963—Edwin (Ted) Etherington, president of the American Stock Exchange, agreed to serve on the board of trustees of the NFL Player Benefit Plan. (Jan. 29.)

# STATISTICS

**MOST YARDS RUSHING, LIFETIME**
1. Joe Perry, San Francisco, Baltimore, 1950-62: 8280
2. Jim Brown, Cleveland, 1957-62: 7459
3. Steve Van Buren, Philadelphia, 1944-51: 5860

**MOST PASSES ATTEMPTED, LIFETIME**
1. Bobby Layne, Chicago Bears, New York Bulldogs, Detroit Lions, Pittsburgh Steelers, 1948-62: 3700
2. Y. A. Tittle, Baltimore, San Francisco, New York, 1950-62: 3169
3. Sammy Baugh, Washington, 1937-52: 3016

**MOST PASSES COMPLETED, LIFETIME**
1. Bobby Layne: 1814
2. Y. A. Tittle, 1750
3. Sammy Baugh, Washington, 1937-52: 1709

**MOST YARDS GAINED PASSING, LIFETIME**
1. Bobby Layne: 26,768
2. Norman Van Brocklin, Los Angeles Rams, Philadelphia Eagles, 1949-60: 23,611
3. Y. A. Tittle: 23,396

**MOST TOUCHDOWN PASSES, LIFETIME**
1. Bobby Layne: 196
2. Sammy Baugh: 186
3. Norman Van Brocklin: 173; and Charles Conerly, New York Giants, 1948-61: 173

**PASSING EFFICIENCY, LIFETIME**
1. Milt Plum, Cleveland, Detroit, 1957-62: 57.2
2. Sammy Baugh: 56.7
3. Bart Starr, Green Bay, 1956-62: 56.6

**MOST PASSES CAUGHT, LIFETIME**
1. Don Hutson, Green Bay, 1935-45: 488
2. Bill Howton, Green Bay, Cleveland, Dallas, 1952-63: 470
3. Raymond Berry, Baltimore, 1955-62: 419

**MOST TOUCHDOWN PASSES CAUGHT, LIFETIME**
1. Don Hutson: 101
2. Pete Pihos, Philadelphia, 1945-55: 61
3. Hugh Taylor, Washington, 1947-54: 58

**MOST POINTS SCORED, LIFETIME**
1. Lou Groza, Cleveland, 1950-62: 902
2. Robert Walston, Philadelphia, 1951-62: 881
3. Don Hutson: 825

**MOST TOUCHDOWNS SCORED, LIFETIME**
1. Don Hutson: 105
2. Jim Brown: 81
3. Steve Van Buren: 77

# AUTHOR'S NOTE

Obviously, in writing a book as comprehensive as a history of the National Football League, the author must acknowledge a debt to an army of people. All of the publicity directors of the fourteen NFL clubs offered unstinting help, as did the owners and coaches. To them, my most heartfelt thanks. Pete Rozelle, the commissioner of the NFL, was enthusiastic in his backing of this venture and in the assistance he made available to me; Jim Kensil, the very competent publicity director of the League, offered both technical and moral aid.

Without the indefatigable and conscientious assistance of George Bloodgood, who selected the pictures for this book, the book could not have been completed. George is the deputy editor for photographs of *Sports Illustrated;* Andre Laguerre, the managing editor, made available the files of the magazine for the selection of these pictures and graciously consented to their use.

Paul Lapolla, of Random House, performed the function of gadfly with all the courtesy and charm the office allows. To him, my deepest thanks.

A special thanks is due Richard McCann, who is the director of the Professional Football Hall of Fame, in Canton, Ohio. Mr. McCann not only made all of his files and old pictures available; he was actively interested in the compilation of the history for this book and gave of his time without thought of recompense. The Pro Football Hall of Fame has just completed a graceful and imposing building in Canton which will serve as the repository for the mementos of the sport; there could be no better custodian than Dick McCann.

This book does not purport to be a comprehensive, detailed history of pro football; that would require a multi-volume encyclopedia. All I have tried to do is to capture the sweep and excitement of the most exciting sport on the American scene today. By necessity, some great players are not mentioned. Ace Parker, who played with the Brooklyn Dodgers and certainly rates with the finest, is an example: unfortunately he played with a team which lived too briefly.

To all those not mentioned, my deepest apologies. You were overlooked not through ignorance, but only through lack of space. To everyone else, my deepest thanks.

*New York, May, 1962*                                                    TEX MAULE

# ILLUSTRATION CREDITS

Credits set in bold face refer to color illustrations.